How to Sell Anything on eBay®

How to Sell Anything on eBay® . . . and Make a Fortune!

Dennis L. Prince

McGraw-Hill

New York   Chicago   San Francisco
Lisbon   London   Madrid   Mexico City   Milan
New Delhi   San Juan   Seoul   Singapore
Sydney   Toronto

The McGraw·Hill Companies

6 7 8 9 0 2DOC/2DOC 0 9 87 6 5 4

ISBN 0-07-142548-9

How to Sell Anything on eBay® . . . *and Make a Fortune!* is in no way authorized by, endorsed, or affiliated with eBay or its subsidiaries. All references to eBay and other trademarked properties are used in accordance with the Fair Use Doctrine and are not meant to imply that this book is an eBay product for advertising or other commercial purposes.

Readers should know that online auctioning has risks. Readers who participate in online auctions do so at their own risk. The author and publisher of this book cannot guarantee financial success and therefore disclaim any liability, loss, or risk sustained, either directly or indirectly, as a result of using the information given in this book.

McGraw-Hill books are available at special quantity discounts to use as premiums and sales promotions, or for use in corporate training programs. For more information, please write to the Director of Special Sales, Professional Publishing, McGraw-Hill, Two Penn Plaza, New York, NY 10121-2298. Or contact your local bookstore.

Prince, Dennis L.
    How to sell anything on eBay . . . and make a fortune! / Dennis L. Prince.—1st ed.
        p. cm.
    ISBN 0-07-142548-9
    1. eBay (Firm) 2. Internet auctions. I. Title.
    HF5478.P753 2003
    658.8'7—dc22   2003013879

 This book is printed on recycled, acid-free paper containing a minimum of 50% recycled de-inked fiber.

For Dave and Deanna Prince—
my beloved brother and sister,
benefactors and creative cohorts
in our shared passion for fun and fortune.

Contents

Acknowledgments   xiii

Introduction   xv

    Fortune or Folly?

    Your Path to Success in Online Selling

    A Promise to You

    Our Roadmap, at a Glance

    This Book, at Your Service

    Embrace Change, Sound Off

Part 1: Getting Started   1

Chapter 1   A Brief History of Auctions, e-Commerce, and eBay   2

    Auctions 101

    Online Selling: The Early Years

    AuctionWeb at eBay

    A Fast Lesson on eBay Auction Formats

    Growing, Growing . . .

    Would You Like to Know More?

Chapter 2   Gearing Up: Hardware, Software, and 'Net Results   9

    Making Sure Your Computer Is Up to Speed

    Making Your Way Through the Software Jungle

    Your Internet Connection

Chapter 3   Welcome to eBay   14

    Home, Sweet Home

    Tapping into the Toolbars

    What About the Other Toolbar Selections?

Chapter 4   Getting Registered, Getting Ready,
                    and Getting to Know You   28
             eBay Registration Made Easy
             Getting Acclimated to the Marketplace
             Setting Up Your Seller's Account
             About Me Is All About You

Chapter 5   Find It, Bid It, Win It   42
             Browsing the Categories
             Searches Made Simple
             The ABCs of Bidding

Chapter 6   Fighting Fraud   60
             The Top 10 Auction Offenses
             Misdeeds or Just Misunderstandings?
             Additional Protections and Provisions from eBay
             Prepare Yourself with a Plan for Action
             Knowing When It's Time to Take a Loss

Part 2: The Basics of Selling on eBay   **71**

Chapter 7   Becoming an Online Auctioneer   72
             First Things First: What Will You List?
             Using eBay's Single-Item Listing Forms
             Before You List Again

Chapter 8   Understanding Online Payment   85
             The Fear Factor: Is Online Payment Safe?
             The How's and Why's of Online Payment
             Who's Who in Online Payment Services?
             The Fortune Factor: If You Offer It,
                    They Will Pay (More!)

Chapter 9   Developing a Successful Sales Policy   91
             The Rules to the Riches
             Summing It All Up
             Posting Your Policy
             What to Do if Your Policy Comes Under Fire

Chapter 10   Determining the Value of Your Goods   98
             The Popularity of eBay
             Finding the Right Stuff to Sell
             So What's It Worth?
             Where Else Can You Turn for Valuation Advice?
             What Is It Worth to You?

Chapter 11   Closing the Deal   104
             Prompt Action Prompts Buyers to Act
             The End-of-Auction e-Mail
             Collecting the Money
             Transactional Troubles?
             The Key Is Communication

Chapter 12   Packing and Shipping Like a Pro   111
             Setting Up Your Ship Shop
             Tools of the Trade
             Sources of Supplies
             Packing Protocol
             Getting Specific; What Are You Shipping?
             Additional Packing Considerations
             Little Extras Make a Big Difference
             Packing as Customer Service

Chapter 13   Dealing with Difficult Customers   119
             Fix the Problem, Not the Blame
             Personality Parade—Different Types
                of Challenging Customers
             Share the Ownership
             Defuse the Situation
             A Word About Leaving Negative Feedback
             Rising Above It All

Chapter 14   Satisfaction Guaranteed—Keeping Customers
                Happy and Coming Back for More   124
             Get to Know Your Newbie
             Keeping Your Buyers Informed

Dealing with Damaged Goods

Transforming Customers into Repeat Buyers

Customer Satisfaction—Their Words, Not Yours

Chapter 15 Building and Maintaining a Stellar Online Reputation   133

Understanding eBay's Feedback Forum

Buy First to Establish Your Good Reputation

More About You at About Me

Represent Your Merchandise, Represent Yourself

The Art of Feedback at eBay

Part 3: Techniques for Boosting Your Sales   141

Chapter 16 Keys to Better Auction Listings   142

Keys to Using Keywords

So How About an Example?

Writing Better Descriptions

Simple HTML for Spectacular Results

What About eBay's Listing Features?

Chapter 17 Boost Your Sales with Better Photos   152

Imaging Equipment

Setting Up a Simple Photo Studio

Touching Up Your Item Images

Picture Imperfect: Eight Common Imaging
    Mistakes to Avoid

Is All This Effort Really Worth It?

Chapter 18 Selling Strategies—Tried, True, and Groundbreaking   162

It All Starts with Timing

Using Counters to Chart Your Success

The Power of Persuasive Pricing

Reserve Bids

Salvaging Unsuccessful Auctions

Appealing to Buyers' Senses

Keys to Relisting

Chapter 19 Building and Managing Your Inventory   174

Setting Your Goals Before Stocking Your Shelves

Identifying Sources of Supply

Care and Storage of Your Inventory

Keeping Track of Your Inventory

Reinvesting Wisely

Chapter 20   Buying for Resale   180

The Reseller's Resolve

Casting a Critical Eye on Reinvestment

The Percentages Don't Lie

Finding Lots to Sell

More Insights into Buying on Speculation

Establishing the Proper Flow for Your Merchandise

Chapter 21   Identifying Trends: What's Hot and What's Not   187

Understanding Online Sales Mining

Learning to Anticipate the Next Wave

Follow the Fickle Market

Getting the Jump by Preselling

Chapter 22   The Forbidden Zone: What You Can't Sell at eBay   197

Items eBay Forbids

Who Says These Items Are Forbidden, and Why?

Deals, Steals, and "Gray Market" Goods

The ABCs of Copyright

Your Checklist to Avoid Posting Infringing Items

Doesn't Everyone Infringe Just a Little?

What Is eBay Doing About Copyright Infringement?

The Agencies Who Take Action

The Auction Vigilante

Part 4: Business Specifics   207

Chapter 23   Becoming a Business and Managing High Volume Sales   200

Pastime, Part-Time, or Full-Time?

Bulking Up Your Business with Bulk Listing

Downloading Turbo Lister

Chapter 24   Establishing an Auction Workplace   220

Establish Your Own Auction Office

Allowing for Necessary Office Amenities

Auction Office Tools

Staging Your Auction Items
            Establishing a Shipping Station
            Organizing Your Supply Room

Chapter 25 Record Keeping—The Best Methods and Tools   226
            Keeping Up with Keeping Records
            Identifying the Key Data
            Establishing a Record-Keeping Plan
            Adding Efficiency to the Task
            An Important Note About Security
            Records That Pay Rewards
            Declaring Income and Paying Taxes

Chapter 26 Cutting Costs, Controlling Expenses,
               and Improving Your Profitability   235
            Controlling eBay Fees
            Savings Through Simplicity
            Timesaving Strategies That Will Save You Money, Too

Chapter 27 Creating Your Own Online Storefront
               and Presenting Your Business as a Brand   241
            Creating an eBay Store
            Creating a Store Outside of eBay
            Developing Your Brand, Boosting Your Business
            Auctions Versus Stores—A New Price War?
            Ten Tips for Improving Your Fixed-Price Sales

Chapter 28 Keeping Up with Changes at Online Auctions   253
            Mining the eBay Community Boards
            Keeping Current with Other Online Sources
            The Power of Print

Glossary   257
Index   263

Acknowledgments

Though only my name is credited on the cover of this book, the truth is that any good book one person writes is made better by the team with which he works. Certainly my case is no exception, and it's my duty, no, my pleasure, to extend my deepest thanks to those with whom I've worked to bring this book to completion.

At McGraw-Hill, I must first recognize my editor, Donya Dickerson, whose perpetual upbeat attitude and unfailing attention to detail has made this writing experience one of my best yet. Also, I extend an equal gratitude to the rest of the terrific McGraw-Hill team with whom I've worked: Mary Glenn, Ruth Mannino, Brigid Brown, Anthony Sarchiaponi, Brian Boucher, Eileen Lamadore, and all the fine folks who serve as the creative and inspirational heart of the McGraw-Hill Sales and Marketing teams. Thanks to each of you.

Next, my thanks to Ed Holm, copyeditor par excellence, at North Market Street Graphics. Thanks for your insightful observations and keen eye that resulted in such a fine interior layout. Your enthusiasm for this particular project was much appreciated.

Special thanks to Gerry McIntyre of McIntyre Photography, Sacramento, CA, for the cover photo. It was a fun shoot, that's for sure.

And, last but not least, thanks to all the "eBaysians" I've worked with throughout the course of preparing this book. Whether buying, selling, or just sharing experiences, your presence has made this book all the more timely, relevant, and rewarding. Thanks to all with whom I've interacted along the way. Naturally, I look forward to interacting with even more of you in the months and years to come.

Introduction

During the dot-com boom of the late-1990s, seemingly everyone was realizing astonishing success and amassing previously unheard-of fortunes in the burgeoning expanse known as cyberspace. Among the myriad overnight successes that quickly dotted the dot-com landscape came a rather unpretentious web site named "eBay." In the spirit of experimentation and with the purest gleam of entrepreneurial vision, the little online trading site set off on a journey to bring people together, virtually, on the cusp of the Internet Revolution. But when conditions turned treacherous and many hopeful online companies struggled and fell in the maelstrom of the dot-com crash, eBay was among the few that thrived, becoming a firm fixture in the new realm of the e-commerce marketplace. Here's where you come into the picture.

Just as eBay has weathered the economic storm, so too has its vast community of merchants, an online population that fills eBay's virtual shops, storefronts, and bazaarlike booths. Every day, the hard-working population of industrious sellers has upheld the site with a limitless and ever-changing inventory of wares. From coveted collectibles to shabby chic; from high-end treasures to bottom-of-the-barrel baubles; from the practical to the whimsical; from the unimaginable to the unmentionable, eBay has been host to almost everything and anything, all on display, all for sale, and all brought forth by its legions of sellers, traders, and hagglers who have found it to be *the* place to test their entrepreneurial prowess and create a business outlet that suits their own unique needs. At over 50 million strong, both amateurs and professionals, these sellers have found their success—their *fortune*—on their own terms. Why not join them?

FORTUNE OR FOLLY?

Webster defines fortune as "a prosperity attained," "the turns and courses accompanying one's progress," "riches," and "wealth." Each of us adds our own flavor to those definitions, personalizing the concept and developing a unique meaning that fits our individual wants, needs, and beliefs. But, regardless how we slice, dice it, or quantify it, we tend to agree on this basic underlying precept: *fortune* means *success.* Irrespective, then, of how you define fortune for yourself, if fortune is your goal, eBay is your gateway.

Even though the online marketplace is maturing and the original luster of eBay's novelty has faded somewhat, it's no longer a quirky little Web hangout; it's a serious endeavor and a reliable enterprise where you can set your own stake in the ground and open up shop for yourself, sell anything and everything that suits your fancy, and earn a tidy profit or even an honest-to-goodness fortune. Of course, there is still a bit of quirkiness to eBay; it never runs short of those peculiar curiosities and odd artifacts that pique the interest and often tickle the funny bone; these are the real-world testimonies that you *can* sell anything at eBay and often for far more than you would ever have previously dared to imagine. And though eBay continues to host sellers who dabble in fun and sometimes frivolous goods that lend character and allure to the site, it's equally teeming with legions of sellers who recognize it as the best arena for breaking into the world of small business, for enabling a global reach to established brick-and-mortar proprietors, and for genuinely serving as a viable sales channel to major manufacturers and retailers. Rarely will you find a business model so adaptable to uniquely suit your needs—whoever you are, wherever you are, whatever your goals.

YOUR PATH TO SUCCESS IN ONLINE SELLING

Your goals at eBay, then, are likely to include establishing your business identity or broadening the visibility of an existing identity, attaining and perhaps surpassing your bottom line aspirations, increasing your ever-important customer base, and enabling yourself to function as a full-fledged enterprise regardless of whether you work alone or are one of a greater team. Accordingly, this book's goal is to help you hit your targets head-on by revealing the mindset and methodologies that can best support your personal view of success, your definition of fortune.

The good news for you is that I've already seen or done just about everything that either handsomely pays off or unceremoniously flops in the online marketplace. Whether you're curious about buying in bulk for resale, in listing sparingly for maximum sales price, in going offline to salvage missed opportunities, or in keeping ahead of the undesirable element that would rob you blind and waste your time, I've been there, sold that, and closed the deal—and I don't mind sharing with you what I've learned.

As one of the original members of the "eBay community," having first navigated the fledgling site back in December 1995, I was initially struck by the fun and fancy the online trading post offered, and I loaded up on the nostalgic knickknacks and doodads that greeted me at every click of the mouse. Quickly, I realized the potential for selling off my own stockpile of trinkets and memorabilia to the mere thousand-strong enclave of the day. And though

I culled a modest profit in my initial sales at the site, the earliest "fortune" I gained, I now realize, was to have been fortunate enough to grow in pace with eBay, evolving my business savvy and reinvesting what I had earned and learned back into my auctioning efforts—the same approach eBay itself was applying to its own growth. With my first fortune ("good fortune," I like to call it) in the bag, I saw my quantifiable fortunes clearly laid in front of me. In the years since, eBay has become the ready-when-I-need-it virtual storefront that has given me the freedom to earn as much or as little as I want; to work as often or infrequently as I choose; and to apply what I've learned however it best suits me as a recognized PowerSeller, shrewd buyer, and seasoned professional (not to mention this ongoing stint of writing about eBay and auctioning for the past five years).

A PROMISE TO YOU

Before you begin reading this book, know this: I firmly believe that time is money. My time is valuable; your time is valuable; our time equates to an opportunity to make money and otherwise amass fortune. As it is a most precious commodity, I won't waste your time just as I wouldn't have you waste my money. This book will move ahead quickly, covering the critical information you want and need to get your auctioning moving from the start. If you're new to eBay and online auctioning, don't worry that you might be left in the dust but, by the same token, recognize that I'll refrain from detouring heavily into cutesy little details and potential distractions you'll sometimes encounter at eBay. The site has much to offer, but quite frankly I'm most interested in *your* success and, therefore, steering you to the best features of eBay while perhaps passing by some of the less-effective attractions. With so many features to wrangle, if it's key to making you successful, you'll read about it here. If it's potentially beneficial and of possible interest, I'll direct you to where you can learn more about it on your own. But if it's potentially a time waster or not a great way to boost your income, you won't be seeing it in these pages. We've got a fortune to make, right, so why waste time? I assure you we won't.

OUR ROADMAP, AT A GLANCE

Over the years of guiding people in the best ways to use eBay, I've learned that most folks want specific direction and uncomplicated answers to their immediate questions about buying and selling in the online auction format. With so much to teach, though, I've also learned folks need to be able to quickly refer back to previously covered information without having to wade through a sea of text to find an elusive answer. To that end, I've arranged this book in a very natural flow and one that follows the eBay experience, start to finish. As a quick preview, here's how the information has been conveniently broken up into four sections for you:

Part 1: Getting Started at eBay

This first section provides a quick history of eBay and then wastes no time in taking you on a tour of the site and getting you registered and ready to go. From there, it's time to search the site, bid on an item or two, and *win*. Sure, *selling* is the focus of this book, but some of the best sellers, you'll learn, are likewise some of the best buyers—those who know a great deal when they see it, can skillfully ferret out a hidden treasure, and can equally assess the person they'll be dealing with to ensure the experience is beneficial in the end.

Part 2: The Basics of Selling on eBay

Now it's your turn to offer the goods, and this part of the book gets you off and running on the right foot. Besides learning the fundamentals of listing items for auction, you'll also learn the ins and outs of getting paid, getting items shipped, and managing any customer problems that might arise.

Part 3: Techniques for Boosting Your Sales

This is it, the fount of knowledge that is the product of years of mining the online auction space. Here is where you learn how to easily create professional-looking listings, how to use item images and other enhancements to boost your profits, and how to wisely reinvest into more inventory when your closet, attic, or basement runs dry.

Part 4: Business Specifics

By this point you have become an expert seller and accomplished auctioneer, but why stop there? This final section guides you into ways of improving your efficiency, increasing your output, and beefing up your bottom line. Here, you're ready to go beyond "just auctions" and will learn how to create a virtual store of your own to the point where you can venture outside the confines of eBay and become an online businessperson in your own right.

THIS BOOK, AT YOUR SERVICE

Whether you're new to eBay or consider yourself a seasoned vet, you'll find this book has plenty to offer. For better or worse, the Internet has made us an impatient people, demanding of immediate results. For those who bemoaned the lengthy learning curve that typically preceded first-time auctioning or those who sought out more efficient methods of boosting their net results, this book is ready to answer the call. The information in each of the parts and each of the chapters has been presented in a way that makes it easy to refer back to whenever you need to refresh yourself of the tools and techniques that you'll soon be using every day as you become a premier online seller.

Understand, too, that this book is an advocate to *you* the seller, not eBay the venue. With your best interests firmly in mind, the book reveals what works at eBay and what doesn't. It leads you to the best features the site has to offer and steers you away from the useless fluff. It identifies the services that are worth paying for and exposes the gimmicks that would needlessly eat away at your profits. I have enjoyed the fortunes to be had at eBay and see no reason why you shouldn't also attain the level of success available to you, thanks to (and sometimes in spite of) what the site has to offer.

EMBRACE CHANGE, SOUND OFF

Before getting started, expect that eBay will be a site in constant flux and perpetual change—just like the market it serves. With that in mind, don't be concerned if, eventually, some of the screen captures in this book no longer exactly depict what you might see at the site. Not to worry, since the changes you'll likely encounter will be minor and will not prevent you from applying the methods and strategies contained in this book.

Whatever you encounter, though, I welcome your thoughts, observations, and comments about your experiences at eBay. Therefore, feel free anytime to drop me a line at *dlprince@bigfoot.com*. After all, we're all friends here.

The bottom line is this: eBay is positioned to stay. It has become a staple in our lives and livelihoods, an immediately recognizable brand, and a firm fixture of our present pop culture. Its potential is being tapped every minute of every day by businesspersons from all professions, from all levels of experience, and from all over the globe. For fun or profit, eBay delivers. Like any other endeavor, you reap what you sow. So why not get at it right away?

There's a fortune waiting out there. Want some?

PART I

GETTING STARTED

1

A Brief History of Auctions, e-Commerce, and eBay

Although knowing just how we got where we are today with auctions, e-commerce, and eBay is not immediately critical to your success in the online auction industry it is nonetheless helpful. There was a time, you know, when ARPANET was the veritable Sputnik to what would become cyberspace, when the Commodore PET was a breakthrough in minicomputers, and when Atari's Super Pong was all the rage with home video gamers. We've come a long way.

Looking back on the evolution of technology is not only interesting but also fun. By doing so, we gain perspective, insight, and an appreciation for how much has changed in a very short time as well as how essential—perhaps vital—technology and the Internet have become in our everyday lives. From the perspective of online commerce and eBay in particular, a quick look back is useful in understanding how trading and haggling have emerged from the earliest days of recorded history and been transformed into the online realm of new opportunity for anyone who has goods to sell. So, in this chapter you'll get a high-speed tour of the tradition of auctioning, the creation of the Internet, and the ultimate birth of eBay.

AUCTIONS 101

To acquire a truly instinctive feel for what auctions are, how they came to be, and why they're a staple of our longstanding bartering system, it's worthwhile to understand the origins of the bid-and-sell technique. Fear not—you're not in danger of being tricked into a protracted historical lecture; this will be brief. Yet, if ever you've heard or wondered yourself, "How do auctions really work?" here's the quick answer you may find interesting.

Set the Way-Back Machine to about 500 B.C. and you'll encounter the earliest known auctions, those held in Babylon, employed for the distribution of eligible maidens. Skip ahead to ancient Rome and you'll find yourself at the *atrium auctionarium,* the designated gathering place for the toga-clad masses where triumphant returning soldiers would auction land and other spoils of their successful battles. Proven an efficient method to garner highest prices for wares offered (the "market value" of the day), auctions found their way to Great Britain around 1595 and are most notably documented during the seventeenth century with the emergence of the historic Sotheby's and Christie's auction houses. Within short order, the favored format crossed the big pond and was put to continual use within America as well. The point here is this: auctions have been an effective and time-proven method of distributing goods in the dynamic market of supply and demand, ages before eBay or the Internet were ever conceived. Who would have ever thought?

ONLINE SELLING: THE EARLY YEARS

While 1979 is of "Future Shock" status when compared to the dusty days of 500 B.C. Babylon, it's similarly ancient history when considering the overall life and growth of the Internet. Although the Internet began in the late 1960s (as the Department of Defense's ARPANET), the creation a few years later of the Unix User Network, or *Usenet,* was what got people connected and ready to do business. Termed a "store-and-forward" network where individuals could post news, views, and other communications to be read by others, the Usenet was quickly adapted as a high-tech classifieds circular. Usenet categories (known as *newsgroups*) were established to help Usenet visitors quickly hone in on those areas where items were being posted "for sale." While the Usenet is still heavily active in this fashion of person-to-person trading, it was in September of 1995 when a new sort of *for sale* listing began popping up, similar to this:

> For Sale: Rare Art Deco piece—now taking bids for this great vintage piece. See it at *www.ebay.com/aw.*

The rest, as they say, is history.

AUCTIONWEB AT eBAY

For many, eBay is a hobby. Fittingly, it started as precisely that—a hobby. Launching the site on Labor Day 1995, its founder, 27-year-old Pierre Omidyar, introduced a simple trading post called AuctionWeb to online enthusiasts. Omidyar's motivation: he sought what he called the emergence of a "perfect market" and a "level playing field" within which individuals, as buyers and sellers, could connect directly with one another as opposed to being relegated to more controlling and often manipulative centralized sources. Besides, his fiancee, Pam, an avid PEZ™ collector, wanted to meet and trade with other collectors of similar passion. In addition to bridging geographical boundaries (something that would help Pam fill in her family of PEZ), Omidyar's notion of an open trading space would truly enable buyers to make fully informed decisions since everyone would have the same access to prices and offerings, while sellers would all have an equal opportunity to present their wares to the masses. The result: the theoretical "perfect market" where price is determined at the precise (and dynamic) juncture where supply meets demand. Omidyar stepped up to the lofty challenge—and opportunity—that lay before him.

About as stylish as a simple Usenet listing, AuctionWeb was unveiled in its modest gray-screened, simple text design (see Figure 1-1). Omidyar had developed and now hosted his creation on a PC in his back bedroom. He poised his brainchild for success largely upon the reliance in his fundamental belief in the goodness of people (users or employees) and their limitless abilities to solve problems in a self-governing environment. AuctionWeb's "community" was founded on the tenet of "power to the people" in a genuinely free and open market.

While it's fun to snicker at the fact that the site's inaugural auction consisted of an awkward listing for a broken laser pointer, the useless gadget sold for $14 all the same, and AuctionWeb was off and running.

Auction **Web**

[Menu] [Listings] [Buyers] [Sellers] [Search] [Contact/Help] [Site Map]

Welcome to today's online marketplace...

Welcome to our community. I'm glad you found us. AuctionWeb is dedicated to bringing together buyers and sellers in an honest and open marketplace. Here, thanks to our auction format, merchandise will always fetch its market value. And there are plenty of great deals to be found!

...the market that brings buyers and sellers together in an honest and open environment...

Take a look at the listings. There are always several hundred auctions underway, so you're bound to find something interesting.

If you don't find what you like, take a look at our **Personal Shopper.** It can help you search all the listings. Or, it can keep an eye on new items as they are posted and let you know when something you want appears. If you want to let everyone know what you want, post something on our wanted page.

If you have something to **sell,** start your auction instantly.

Welcome to eBay's AuctionWeb.

Join our community. Become a registered user. Registered users receive additional benefits such as daily updates and the right to participate in our user feedback forum and the bulletin

Figure 1-1 These days, screen grabs of Pierre Omidyar's original AuctionWeb site are extremely scarce.

Ultimately, the site dropped the AuctionWeb moniker and became known simply as eBay (*www.ebay.com* used to be host to several home pages; AuctionWeb shared server space with a biotech start-up, a management consultancy, the San Francisco Tufts Alliance, and an Ebola virus site). Even though Omidyar had no formal training in auctions as a market mechanism, his instincts told him that people would naturally be drawn to a destination that offered fair market value for goods, benefiting buyers and sellers alike. If you've ever wondered why auctions are touted as the optimum form of barter, this concise discussion should have summarily answered that question.

A FAST LESSON ON eBAY AUCTION FORMATS

As auctions have evolved through the centuries, so have auction methods. Most folks envision the venerable, "I have twenty, who'll make it twenty-five? Twenty-five, who'll give me thirty? Going once, going twice, SOLD to the man in the brown tweed jacket!" auction dialog. Known as the *ascending-price* auction, this is the most common format for auctioning. There are a good many other formats that have been and still are being used in different auction venues. With an eye on efficiency and to expose you to just what you'll need to be aware of for auctioning at eBay, here are the formats you'll encounter:

The Ascending-Price Auction

Historically known as the *English* auction and the *Open-Outcry* auction, this is the most widely used format at eBay. Items are offered at an opening bid value and additional bids of incremental value are accepted, increasing the potential final sales price. Successive bids must satisfy at least the minimum *bid increment* but can also represent a bidder's *maximum bid* value.

The Dutch Auction

An auction format new to many users is eBay's *Dutch* auction. This likewise longstanding format of auction history enables sellers to quickly dispense of multiple, identical items. Here, bidders bid the price they're willing to pay while also specifying *how many* of the item they're contesting for. While Dutch auctions aren't as tricky as they might sound, the strategy for winning this breed of auction is a bit complex and thus will be explained later in this book rather than now. A version of this is the *Yankee* auction, where each winning bidder pays the exact amount of their winning bid.

Reserve Price Auctions

This is a slight variation of the ascending-price auction in which the seller establishes a minimum price at which the item will be sold and which bidders aren't able to see. That is, if the competitive bidding fails to reach or eclipse the seller's reserve price, the seller is not required by eBay's rules to sell the item. This variation is especially useful to sellers who are uncertain whether competitive bidding will return a price that either suits their needs or ensures recovery of their original investment. Greedy sellers like this format, especially (wink-wink).

Fixed-Price Auction

If you have a price in mind for which you'll sell an item outright, this format (which eBay terms "Buy-It-Now") allows the willing buyer to dispense of the competitive bidding and offer the seller's asking price, thus ending the auction immediately. There are several ways to manage this feature at eBay, and these will also be discussed later.

Private Auctions

Got some erotica or other adult-themed items to sell? Want to prevent other sellers from seeing who's bidding on your stuff? Whatever your motivation, *private* auctions allow bidders' identities (user IDs) to remain concealed from other nosey users.

Restricted-Access Auctions

A close cousin to the private auction, this format was designed to help users easily locate or summarily avoid adult items. Bidders searching for restricted access items must provide credit card information for age verification. Items of this sort, corralled in the "Mature Audiences" category, are not listed in general search results and require adult verification logon to access, thus shielding those of us who are easily embarrassed.

GROWING, GROWING . . .

With the formats established, the community values in place, and the lure of online bargaining ready to peak, eBay grew exponentially, practically overnight. Although Omidyar had intentions of providing AuctionWeb as a free-of-charge service site, his mounting server bills pushed him into levying fees. Upon initiating his *final-value fees,* he culled a meager $250 in his first month. Still, this was enough to pay his monthly service provider bill. Just two short months after that, he gathered $2,500 in fees, and each successive month thereafter earned still more as word of AuctionWeb quickly spread across the cybernetic landscape. Of course, eBay has since become a billion dollar venture. Along the way, Omidyar turned over the CEO reigns to former Hasbro leader Meg Whitman. The site now plays host to over 45 million registered users and its operators believe it can reach a profit goal of $3 billion by 2005. And, if its resilience in an otherwise downtrodden economy serves as any sort of testimony, that goal can hardly be mocked as far-fetched by any stretch of the mind. There is a fortune out there, remember? It's up to you to step forward to stake your personal claim on a piece of it.

WOULD YOU LIKE TO KNOW MORE?

Clearly, this was something of a short-and-sweet tour of how we got from ARPANET to making fortunes on eBay. For some, this is all we really need to know since those untapped riches await us at the turning of the page. Yet, I suspect this will merely whet the appetite of others who are eager to immerse themselves in the minutiae of *exactly* how we got here. Having been one of those curious folk myself, here are a few books I recommend for spare-time reading:

- *Auction: The Social Construction of Value* by Charles W. Smith; University of California Press, 1989.

  If you truly wish to be a student, and master, of the auction, Smith's book will fill your head with the intricacies of the dynamic pricing. Beware, this one is about as dry as a cold piece of toast, yet makes up for it in the good information within.
- *Fire in the Valley: The Making of the Personal Computer* by Paul Freiberger and Michael Swaine; McGraw-Hill, 1999.

  If thinking back to 1974 only conjures up painful memories of Nixon, Watergate, and the Energy Crisis, look deeper and see what geeks like Steve Jobs, Bill Gates, and Paul Allen were busying themselves with in their cluttered garages.
- *The Perfect Store: Inside eBay* by Adam Cohen; Back Bay Books, 2002.

  Time magazine journalist Cohen convinced the powers that be at eBay to grant him total access to the story behind the scenes of the Big Dog of auction sites. Though Cohen's style rarely breaks free of the magazine article mold, his is an interesting documenting of the activities both in front of and behind the home page we lovingly know as eBay.com.
- *Collectible Microcomputers* by Michael Nadeau; Schiffer Publishing, Ltd., 2002.

  Don't toss that old Commodore 64 or Apple Lisa before you've read Nadeau's book. As many of us expected, technology has become quite collectible (see Figure 1-2). Heavily illustrated and simply fun to leaf through, this is a great pictorial jaunt through the hallowed halls of computer history.

Figure 1-2   One last look back: anyone remember where they left their Super Pong? This sort of funky tech treasure is gold on eBay and often garners hundreds of dollars in bids (really!).

- *F'd Companies: Spectacular Dot-Com Flameouts* by Philip J. Kaplan; Simon & Schuster, 2002.

    If irreverence is your bag and you simply revel in listening in to the acidic attacks made on some of the biggest flops of the dot-com era, Kaplan has the tabloid tales sure to entertain. An extension of his wildly popular web site, F****dCompany.com, this book chronicles the stories that broke on his site as the bad news for web businesses were unfolded daily, often with those in the companies' employ learning of their imminent demise on Kaplan's site before the boss ever distributed pink slips. A fun read but not to be taken too seriously.

2

Gearing Up: Hardware, Software, and 'Net Results

If you're like most people, the task of updating your business tools—your PC, software, and so on—is likely low on your priority list. Further, the notion of being in continual "change mode" to keep up with the tech world makes many cringe, especially considering the time and effort that would be drained away from your bidding and selling activities. Yet, realistically speaking, there comes a time when running on inefficient tools is also detrimental to your well-deserved fortune. With that in mind, you can be well served if you look to upgrade your high-tech gear methodically and by piecemeal: a new PC every three years or so, new software applications as often as you deem useful, and upgraded Internet access when it becomes financially prudent (especially as fees continue to drop for high-speed services). Making upgrades one piece at a time will usually cause only minimal disruption to your activity and avoids the potentially overwhelming prospect of "gutting" the works.

While you don't have to be a hard-core gearhead to get the most from the Internet and your eBay business, you should make sure you've got the tools to run a respectable shop. Although you might already feel secure in your current hardware and software configurations, here's a quick look at the whiz-bang stuff that drives your online business efforts. This will be a brief checkup of your goods and won't hurt a bit, I promise. In fact, you'll probably be surprised to find that you are already in good shape.

MAKING SURE YOUR COMPUTER IS UP TO SPEED

If you are interested in online auctions, you probably already have a PC or two in your home. A 2002 survey conducted by *PC Magazine* concluded that one-

third of American households have a personal computer, another third of households have two or more, and the final third have yet to purchase their first magic box (and are likely still fiddling with the remote for their first-ever VCR). If you're in one of the two former groups and if you've upgraded your PC within the past 18 months, feel confident the hardware you now own is more than suitable for an eBay venture. But what if your tech toys are older than that? Should you be agonizing whether what you've got is good enough to cut the mustard in an online buying and selling marketplace? You'll be happy to know that a desktop or laptop system purchased within the last several years, even if it isn't cutting edge, will probably work perfectly and offer you plenty of power and features to make an eBay experience quite pleasant. Then again, if perhaps you've yet to purchase a PC or maybe you're still not sure the equipment you have is up to par, here are some simple specifications you might follow:

- *Processor/Speed:* In older PCs, if the "brains of the operation" is at least a 450MHz Pentium II, you'll be in decent, albeit slightly out-dated, shape. Intel's 800MHz P-III with a 256 L-2 cache (buffered memory) is better yet even though it, too, is considered a bit nostalgic when compared to Intel's new P-IV and Celeron processors. Also feel comfortable if your machine is running off the more cost-effective AMD Athlon (K7) chip. If you're working on an Apple iMac, the 500MHz PowerPC will provide you plenty of power for your online exploits. Granted, neither of these PC or Mac configurations are state of the art and you can easily surpass these speeds in a fiber-optic flicker.
- *Memory:* Simply enough, try to ensure you're working with at least 128MB of RAM, but, as with the processor, it's easy to surpass this lowest-point benchmark, too.
- *Storage:* How big is big enough when it comes to your computer's storage space? Well, considering the number of images you might be storing up for selling online wares, models of several years ago will deliver a serviceable 12GB but you're better off if your system is sitting atop around 20 to 30GB of open space.
- *Additional Drives:* You likely have a 3.5-inch floppy disk drive and an internal CD-ROM drive in your current box. Slightly newer systems will sport a CD-RW drive that's an excellent addition for cost- and space-effective external storage. Oh, and the DVD-ROM is cool—but if you're watching movies instead of working towards those riches, consider putting that drive out of commission.
- *Internal Modem:* If you'll go this route, make sure the modem card is at least 56-kilobit yet, in these days of cable modems and DSL connections, internal 56Kb modems are downright prehistoric by comparison.

- *Monitor:* A 15-inch CRT monitor is fine and a 17-inch model is better yet (more on-screen real estate to work with). The newer flat-panel LCD monitors are certainly spiffy but definitely not required spending to ensure your success.

Sure, the specs given here aren't likely to impress your technically predisposed friends and coworkers but they'll do just fine as you venture into online fortune finding. There's no need to run out and upgrade if your hardware measures up as just described. But, if you do find yourself needing a new PC or simply want to upgrade, expect that a decent system will cost about $1500 (that includes a CRT monitor or possibly a low-end flat panel). You can always spend more and you can certainly spend less, but that's up to you. The bottom line is this: if you're satisfied with your online activity today and don't find that your PC is dragging you down, you're probably in good shape and can spare the immediate expense of shopping for a PC. Besides, when it comes to making that fortune, money saved is as good as money earned.

MAKING YOUR WAY THROUGH THE SOFTWARE JUNGLE

The bundled PC solutions of the past several years have been rife with nifty applications, some of which suit your auctioning needs perfectly and others that are, well, generally expendable. The first step in determining whether you need any more applications is to decide first what it is you want to *do* with your PC. Here's a simple list of the basic applications that you'll certainly need as an online entrepreneur.

- *Word Processor:* Usually a bundled application that came along with the operating system on your system. Applications as old as 1995 will work just fine for you.
- *Web Browser:* Also embedded into bundled systems, these should provide you with a choice between Netscape or Internet Explorer. Keep your browser updated (free downloads are available at the Netscape or Microsoft home pages) to ensure you can display and access current design features at eBay and around the Internet.
- *E-Mail Application:* You can get by with the e-mail tool that accompanies web browsers but you might want to upgrade anyway to gain better features. I like both Eudora and MS Outlook.
- *Image Editor:* Fear not, because you don't need to master Photo-Shop to get the images of your items into tip-top shape. MS Picture-It, Paint Shop Pro, and even L-View are great little packages that will deliver enough features to help you easily manage images.

- *Spreadsheet Application:*   Don't risk your sales and customer records to scraps of paper that tend to hide when you need 'em most. Pick a spreadsheet program you like best and get that vital business information safely stored where it'll be easy to retrieve whenever you need it (see Chapter 25 for more details).

- *Antivirus Application:*   If you've been online for any length of time, you're likely all too familiar with the *Love Bug,* the *Klez worm,* or the *Slammer worm.* Virtual viruses are nasty little demons that come to you unexpectedly as you access the Net and communicate with your customers. Protect your business by protecting your PC.

There are additional auction-specific applications that you might also want to use in your eBay exploits. Those will be discussed in greater detail in Chapter 23. For now, however, those just listed are the basic software tools you'll want on board your computer.

YOUR INTERNET CONNECTION

A few years ago it took a concerted effort to catch a cyberwave, but today getting connected to the Internet is practically unavoidable. Go to a library, visit a cyber café, or just sit in the waiting room at your car dealer's service bay and you'll find the Net up and running, 24×7. For your home, the options are getting better and better every day. If you like choices, you got choices. Just look at how you can be connected:

- *DSL:*   It's fast, and how. Figure the monthly service bill to tally up to about $40, but if you want to prioritize your business costs, put this at the top of your list.

- *Cable:*   Playing piggyback on your home cable TV service, this connection uses the same COAX connection to provide high-speed, always-on Net access. Of course, if you don't have cable TV, see "DSL" above. The cost is similar to DSL.

- *Satellite:*   Broadband satellite is also quite quick but requires a dish to gain access and a clear view of the southern sky.

- *Dial-Up:*   The regular old phone line in your home will still do okay in a pinch, though you'll probably want two separate lines if you don't want to hamper incoming calls. These days, though, what you'll pay to an ISP—to the tune of around $15 to $20 per month—is better applied to a high-speed connection.

Whatever your choice, getting connected to the Internet is easier than ever. Better still, it's super simple to change up these days, so don't be afraid to upgrade to a different service; if you don't like it, change up again.

ADDITIONAL EQUIPMENT

Of course, there are plenty of additional gadgets and pieces of equipment that you'll need to be thoroughly efficient and successful in your auctioning. From printers to scanners, from digital cameras to copiers, from telephone headsets to office furniture, there's much more needed to establish an optimal auction headquarters. All of these and more will be covered fully in Chapter 23. The intent here is to ensure you have the basics at hand so that you can make your way into the wonderful world of online auctioning. Next stop: eBay!

3

Welcome to eBay

Even if you've never sold anything on eBay, you've probably at least checked out the site. You've heard all the buzz about eBay: the great finds you can buy there and the money to be made by regular folk like you and me. It's rare that I encounter a person who's *never* logged on to the site. If you're a complete newcomer, though, terrific! Welcome to the place that will likely alter your life from this point forward. Though it may sound a bit sappy, eBay truly is a life-changing phenomenon, just as was television and the Internet itself. eBay is a bustling shopping hub where you'll rub virtual elbows with millions (and I mean *millions*) of users from all cultures, from nearly every age category, from practically all points on the globe. Its attraction goes beyond global, though, in terms of "meeting the masses." The most remarkable element of eBay is its arguably *individual* appeal, that is, its ability to cater to and satisfy the unique wants, needs, and desires of just about anyone who cares to visit.

Although it's appealing to some, it can be daunting to others; how do people navigate through all this? Whether you're new to the site and feel understandably overwhelmed or you're a repeat visitor who wants to make sure you're hitting all the "hot spots," this chapter is your tour of the site, its key features, and its main points of interest that will help you quickly find your fortune.

HOME, SWEET HOME

Mention the URL, *www.ebay.com,* and some folks will bubble over with enthusiasm. For many, this Web destination is like a home—everything they need at their fingertips (literally) and all available any day, any hour, and from the comfort of their own . . . home. Take a look at Figure 3-1 and you'll immediately see that eBay is busy, busy, busy.

Where to begin? Well, before zipping off to hunt for great buys or find the place to list your own merchandise, take a careful look at the home page itself. Notice immediately the toolbar situated across the top of the page (as illustrated in Figure 3-2). The links from this toolbar are the main entryways to the site. In fact, you'll see this toolbar uniformly positioned on just about every eBay screen you visit. You'll also see it's actually two toolbars in one, with *Browse, Search, Sell, my eBay,* and *Community* links in the main bar and *home, register, sign out, services, site map,* and *help* in the smaller, topmost bar. I'll take you deeper into each link in just a moment. Right now, recognize the convenience of this ever-present toolbar and keep in mind that you'll be making regular use of it.

eBay TIP: Clicking on the eBay logo on any site page will also take you directly back to the home page.

Figure 3-1   eBay's busy home page puts you just a link or two away from finding your fortune.

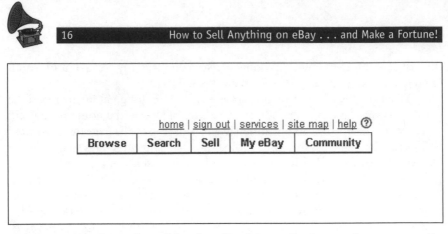

Figure 3-2 The eBay toolbar will be a best friend to you. Nearly everywhere you go on the site, you can count on it being there at the top of the page.

In Search of . . .

In addition to the toolbar, you'll see a white box just below the toolbar, preceded by the text, "What are you looking for?" This is the quick search box—one that you'll also see on most site pages (although it will appear on the left side in succeeding screens and is labeled simply, "Basic Search"). Use this box to immediately begin combing the site for whatever it is you want or need. Keep in mind, though, that this box only searches for matching words in item titles and not in the text of item descriptions (we'll cover other searches in detail later). Regardless, this is another key home page feature you'll probably use every time you visit the site.

Categorically Speaking

On the left side, running nearly the length of the home page display, are links to *Specialty Sites* and item *Categories.* The Specialty Sites are those additional branches of eBay that you might make use of (some more than others) and which comprise of either new spin-offs created by eBay (such as eBay Motors and Half.com) or acquired along the way (such as PayPal, an electronic payment site). The Categories links just below Specialty Sites are your paths into a browsing excursion that is practically unrivaled anywhere else on the Net. These are top-level links, each branching farther into more specific groupings of goods, ultimately taking you to the various individual listings of products for sale. The category under which each listing is found is determined by the sellers themselves; they choose the category placement that best represents their item and that they believe will be the most likely category to attract the buyers.

eBay TIP: Remember, the eBay Search function will also bring buyers directly to items from across categories. Although categories are great for casual browsing, they can be too time-consuming to navigate if a specific item is being sought, so most eBay users go directly to the Search function.

Eye Candy

The rest of what you see on the home page is really just "splash and filler." While there are plenty of useful links here, most of the pages can be accessed from elsewhere within the site. To give the site a feeling of "buzz," eBay has loaded up the home page with the expected offering of "eye candy." There is so much going on just inside, and the content changes every time you visit the site. In addition, eBay works on having a fresh marketing appeal (notice the main "billboard" in Figure 3-1 promoting jewelry auctions just in time for Valentine's Day). You'll also see various other groupings of item links as well as *thematic* links (such as the PGA items or Romantic Bear auctions) on the home page. These are just additional methods eBay employs to generate interest and to help users determine a starting point for their shopping adventure. As it's just marketing, there's nothing to be missed if you skip over these transient links.

The Bottom Line

The bottom links are what fill up the final quarter of the eBay home page. Here are the partner links and advertisements that eBay thinks might be of interest to you (or by which they have a contractual agreement to put on display). Finally, there are redundant text links that will take you to many of the same site destinations—such as my eBay, Browse, and so on—as the main tool bar does. In the world of effective Web design, it's a general rule of thumb that a single display page should provide visitors with multiple links to the same most-popular or most-used site features.

TAPPING INTO THE TOOLBARS

So what makes the home page toolbars so useful? Glad you asked because there's more than meets the eye in those simple little labels. In fact, each acts as a useful portal to some key site functions and features. To start, let's look again at the most useful features (see Figure 3-2).

The Browse Button

As its name implies, this button is for those eager to stroll the site's "virtual aisles." As with any brick-and-mortar store, shoppers are guided by signposts that identify the different departments or, in eBay terms, categories, such as music or clothing and accessories. Although the home page lists many category links, the Browse link on the toolbar will take you to the entire listing of category headers on eBay.

Regardless of What You Want to Sell, eBay Has a Category for You

ANTIQUES
Architectural and Garden
Asian Antiques
Books and Manuscripts
Decorative Arts
Ethnographic (pre-1900)
Furniture (pre-1900)
Maps and Atlases (pre-1900)
Maritime
Musical Instruments (pre-1900)
Primitives
Rugs and Carpets
Science and Medicine
Silver
Textiles and Linens
Antiques (post-1900)
Other Antiques

ART
Digital Art
Drawings
Folk Art
Mixed Media
Paintings
Photographic Images
Posters
Prints
Sculpture and Carvings
Self-Representing Artists
Other Art

BOOKS
Antiquarian and Collectible
Audio
Children
Fiction and Literature
Magazines and Catalogs

Nonfiction
Wholesale, Bulk Lots
Other

BUSINESS AND INDUSTRIAL
Agriculture
Businesses for Sale
Construction
Electronic Components
Healthcare
Industrial Supply, MRO
Laboratory Equipment
Metalworking Equipment
Printing Equipment
Restaurant and Foodservice
Retail
Test and Measurement Equipment
Other Industries

CLOTHING AND ACCESSORIES
Infants
Boys
Girls
Men
Uniforms
Wedding Apparel
Women
Vintage Clothing and Accessories
Wholesale Lots

COINS
Coins: U.S.
Coins: World
Exonumia
Paper Money: U.S.
Paper Money: World
Scripophily

COLLECTIBLES
Advertising
Animals
Animation Art and Characters
Autographs
Barware
Bottles and Insulators
Breweriana, Beer
Clocks
Coin-Op, Banks, Casino
Comics
Cultures and Ethnicities
Decorative Collectibles
Disneyana
Fantasy, Mythical, Magic
Furniture, Appliances, Fans
Historical Memorabilia
Holiday and Seasonal
Housewares and Kitchenware
Knives and Swords
Lamps and Lighting
Linens, Fabric, Textiles
Metalware
Militaria
Pens and Writing Instruments
Pez, Keychains, Promo Glasses
Photographic Images
Pinbacks, Nodders, Lunchboxes
Postcards and Paper
Radio, Phonograph, TV, Phone
Religions, Spirituality
Rocks, Fossils, Minerals
Science Fiction
Science, Medical
Tobacciana
Tools, Hardware, Locks
Trading Cards
Transportation
Vanity Perfume and Shaving Items
Vintage Sewing
Wholesale Lots

DOLLS & BEARS
Barbie
Bears
Doll Clothes and Furniture
Doll Making, Patterns, Repair

Dolls
Dollhouses and Miniatures
Paper Dolls
Wholesale Lots

ELECTRONICS AND COMPUTERS
Cameras and Photo
Car Audio and Electronics
Computers and Office Products
Gadgets and Other Electronics
Home Electronics
Networking and Telecom
PDAs/Handheld PCs
Phones and Wireless Devices
Portable Electronics
Professional Video Equipment
Radio Equipment
Software
Video Games
Wholesale Lots

HOME
Baby Gear and Furnishings
Bath
Bedding
Building and Repair Materials
Food and Wine
Furniture
Home Decor
Housekeeping and Organizing
Kitchen, Dining, Bar
Lamps, Lighting, Ceiling Fans
Lawn and Garden
Major Appliances
Outdoor Living
Pet Supplies
Tools
Windows and Floors
Wholesale Lots

JEWELRY AND WATCHES
Costume Jewelry
Designer and Artisan Jewelry
Ethnic and Tribal Jewelry
Fine Jewelry
Hair Jewelry
Jewelry Boxes
Jewelry Supplies

Loose Beads
Loose Gemstones
Men
Watches
Wholesale Lots

MOVIES AND TELEVISION
Memorabilia
Video and Film
Wholesale Lots

MUSIC
CDs, Records, Tapes
Music Memorabilia

MUSICAL INSTRUMENTS
Brass
Electronic
Equipment
Guitar
Harmonica
Keyboard, Piano
Percussion
Pro Audio
Sheet Music and Music Books
String
Woodwind
Wholesale Lots
Other Instruments

POTTERY AND GLASS
Glass
Pottery and China

REAL ESTATE
Commercial
Land
Residential
Timeshares for Sale
Other Real Estate

SPORTS
Sporting Goods
Sports Memorabilia

STAMPS
United States
Australia
Canada
Br. Comm. Other
U.K. (Great Britain)

Europe
Latin America
Other World
Philately
Topical

TICKETS
Event Tickets
Experiences
Other Items

TOYS AND HOBBIES
Action Figures
Baby Toys
Building Toys
Classic Toys
Crafting, Art Supplies
Diecast, Toy Vehicles
Educational
Electronic, Battery, Wind-Up
Fast Food and Advertising
Games
Model Railroads and Trains
Models
Outdoor Toys, Structures
Pretend Play, Preschool
Puzzles
Radio Control
Robots, Monsters, Space Toys
Slot Cars
Stuffed Animals, Beanbag
Toy Soldiers
TV and Character Toys
Vintage and Antique Toys
Wholesale Lots

TRAVEL
Airline
Cruises
Lodging
Luggage
Vacation Packages
Other Travel

EVERYTHING ELSE
eBay User Tools
Education and Learning
Genealogy
Gifts and Occasions
Health and Beauty

Memberships	Services
Metaphysical	Shipping and Packing Supplies
Personal Security	Show Supplies
Personalized, Customized	Test Auctions
Religious Products and Supplies	Weird Stuff
Reward Pts, Incentive Progs	Mature Audiences

While you're gawking at all the category headers, take note of the parenthetical numerals to the right of each header title. These figures reflect the number of individual listings to be found within each main category and are ultimately dispersed among the category's subheadings. It's an amazing amount of stuff, indeed, but there's still plenty of room for your great stuff, too.

The Sell Button

Since you're here to make a fortune, the sell button is your doorway to opportunity. Click this button for a direct path to the *Sell Your Item* forms where you'll enter information to list the items you'll be putting up on the auction block. Figure 3-3 shows the initial form page where you'll begin crafting your

Figure 3-3 The *Sell* toolbar button starts your selling adventure with this first form used in listing an item for auction.

listing, with numerous other pages to follow, all of which will be covered in Chapter 8.

eBay TIP: Don't be alarmed if eBay asks you to sign in before granting you access to the *Sell Your Item* forms. After all, sellers are required to have an account in good standing before an item can be listed. If you hadn't previously signed in to eBay before clicking the *Sell* button, eBay requires you to do so at this point.

The Services Button

If there's one thing eBay never runs short of, besides the millions of items constantly up for bid, it's user services. This toolbar selection will take you to an overview page (Figure 3-4) where you can quickly link to registration pages, buying and selling features, SafeHarbor (eBay's trouble-busting policies and user aids), *my eBay* features, and more. Generally, once you're up and running and have a flow to your regular eBay activities, you won't be visiting

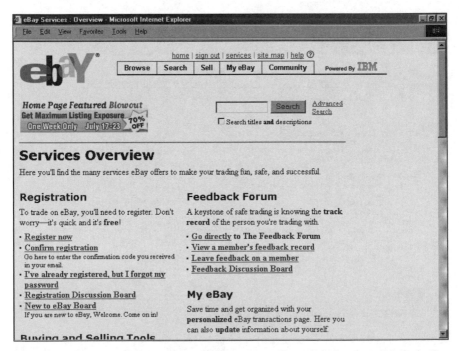

Figure 3-4 There are a number of eBay services at your fingertips when you click on the *Services* toolbar button.

this page very much. At the outset, though, this is a useful place to use as a springboard to your buying and selling adventures.

The Search Button

Although every eBay page is equipped with the search box we looked at earlier, this link takes you to eBay's full-featured search page (Figure 3-5) where you can hone in on what it is you're actively seeking. Whether you're searching for items in a particular geographic region, curious about items offered by a specific seller, need to see what a particular buyer has been bidding on, or want to browse only those goods offered in the eBay Stores, this is the place to begin your quest. I'll discuss detailed search methods and tactics in Chapter 5.

The Help Button

One of the biggest investments eBay has been undertaking is the addition of more useful on-site instruction pages. Click on the *Help* button and a small pop-up window will appear on your computer monitor (as shown in Figure 3-6), offering active links to eBay pages that will provide an explanation to any site usage questions you might have.

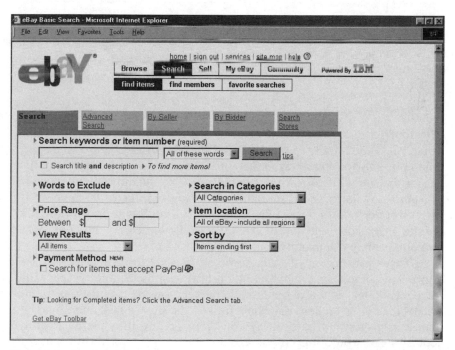

Figure 3-5 The *Search* button takes you to eBay's powerful and flexible search screen.

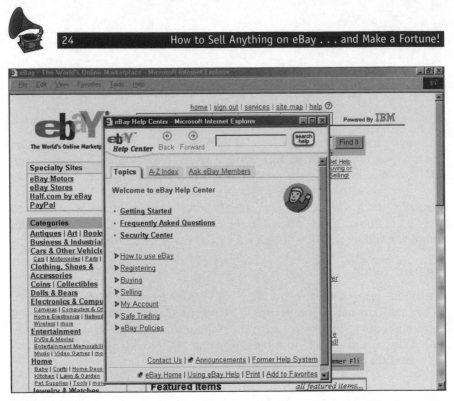

Figure 3-6 The *Help* button provides this pop-up window with links to online instruction and advice for eBay users.

The Community Button

eBay founder Pierre Omidyar envisioned that the underlying success of eBay would be its community of users. Beyond that, he also recognized the opportunity not only to offer a way for users to interact with and help one another but for the site itself to reach out in the spirit of philanthropy by providing assistance to charitable organizations. If you're curious to learn about the various opportunities in the eBay community—both within and outside of the site—set aside some time to explore the different community links you'll find on the eBay Community page (see Figure 3-7).

There you have it, the run-down on the key toolbar features. You'll notice how some main toolbar selections lead to subselections (visible within some screen images you've seen in this chapter). I won't take the time to fully discuss the follow-on links that you'll find on the site—a task that would take numerous pages and likely delay you from getting into the meat of the action—but I would suggest you explore the site on your own if you truly wish to see and experience all the site has to offer.

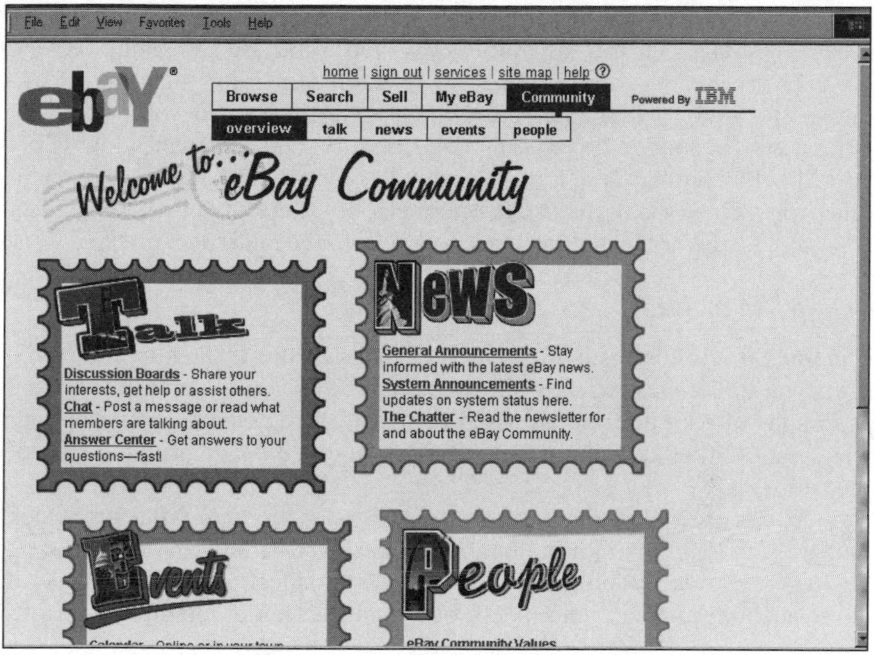

Figure 3-7 The *Community* button leads you to the site's veritable Welcome Wagon where you can learn about and interact with the legions of eBay enthusiasts as well as discover how eBay is working to provide assistance to people in need outside of the site.

WHAT ABOUT THE OTHER TOOLBAR SELECTIONS?

Yes, there are still a few more toolbar selections to consider. For starters, skip past the *home* link; it does just what it indicates and returns you to the home page. Then, the *sign out* link is likewise self-explanatory: it ends your active session on eBay, requiring you sign in again if you wish to list an item for sale or bid on some treasure you stumble across. The two remaining links, though, are more intriguing and require further discussion.

My eBay Is Your eBay

If you've surfed many Web sites of late, you're probably familiar with the "my site" feature, a method that allows regular users to assemble a personal portfolio of their favorite site features, settings, and what have you. The intention of "my site" is to provide each user with a self-configured, self-maintained personal version of the site. This feature makes viewing your favorite spots on the site faster and more straightforward, allowing you to avoid traversing the multiple standard pages upon each visit. eBay's version (see Figure 3-8) is called *My eBay.* Here is where you can set and monitor the site activity that best suits your needs. My eBay helps you easily watch your recent buying and selling activity, set up favorite search criteria to be easily re-entered, monitor your account status, follow your feedback rating (tracking comments about you entered by other users), and more. It's certainly not necessary to pour a tremendous effort into My eBay settings and, frankly, you can navigate the data just as easily in other ways. However, if you like the "at a glance" simplicity of My eBay, it's a great tool ready for use and easily accessible from the mini toolbar.

What a Site to See

The final link to discuss is *site map.* As it implies, this is the link that transports you to the massive eBay site map and allows you to survey the virtual geography of the site from an aerial perspective. Click on the *site map* link and see all that eBay encompasses. Look at Figure 3-9 for a small sample of the entire map.

This is probably the easiest page to navigate if you're looking for a quick link to functional or informational eBay pages. Whether you want tips on buying, need to review policies about selling at the site, want to stay abreast of latest site news and announcements, or are curious about joining the various

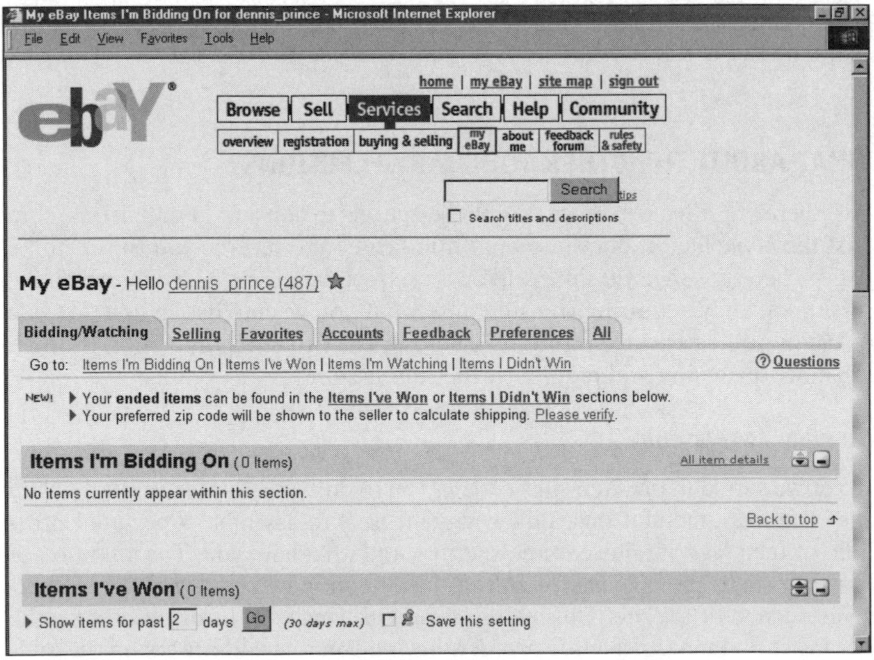

Figure 3-8 Ever ready to suit your unique wants and needs, *My eBay* allows users to configure their personal window into the goods and goings on of the site.

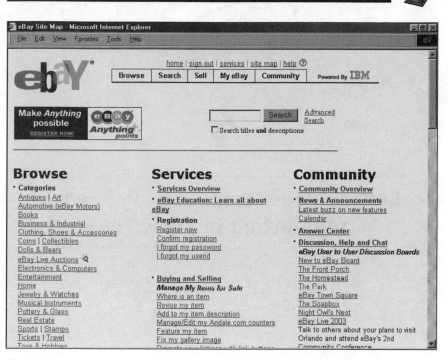

Figure 3-9   I told you it was a big site, evidenced by this lengthy list of links on the site map.

eBay forum discussions, the site map is the best launching pad to quickly get anywhere and everywhere at eBay.

> **e B a y   T I P :**   Most often, I turn to the site map when I'm managing the items I have up for sale. For example, should I need to end an auction early, the site map is the best place to connect to that otherwise elusive link. You'll likely discover some site functions that are difficult to find—perhaps intentionally—yet the site map will typically get you where you need to go, fast.

Perhaps you didn't think it possible, but you've just completed an introductory tour of eBay in less than 30 minutes. By understanding the most important features of the eBay home page up front, you can begin your buying and selling activities quickly and confidently without becoming overwhelmed by everything else the site offers. As you continue through this book, the details will be clarified and the skills and methods will be sharpened to develop your expertise. For now, either take a break and spend a bit of time exploring more of what I've shown to you, or move on to the next chapter and find out what's critical for getting registered and getting ready to harness the site.

4

Getting Registered, Getting Ready, and Getting to Know You

Before you can begin bidding or selling at eBay, you'll need to register. However, it's fast, it's simple, it's safe, and it's necessary if you want to do business. After registering, you can then consider how you'll use eBay. Do you want to browse awhile? Do you want to buy, buy, buy? Do you want to avoid shopping entirely and get right down to selling your goods? Whatever your approach, a bit of preplanning is advisable. You'll also want to consider sharing a bit of who you are with the other buyers and sellers. At eBay, introducing yourself is easy, and the small effort can pay some big dividends. This chapter will cover all of this to help you to get started on the right foot.

eBAY REGISTRATION MADE EASY

Starting at eBay's home page, look for the set of three blue buttons just below the *What are you looking for?* search window. Note that the third button is clearly labeled, "register now" (see Figure 4-1).

Click the *register now* button and jump to the initial registration screen, pictured in Figure 4-2. In the first part of this registration screen, enter your name, address, and phone number(s). This information will be stored by eBay and could be provided to other users to help contact you. Don't worry, eBay isn't in the practice of loosely distributing this information, but in an effort to promote and enable safe trading, and sort out any issues related to transactions it does make the information available upon legitimate request.

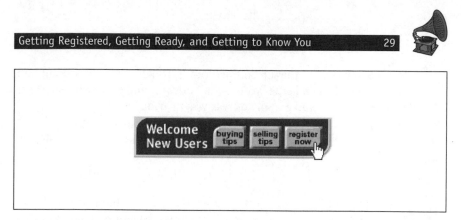

Figure 4-1 The link to registration can be found on the eBay home page.

e B a y T I P :   Notice in Figure 4-2 that logos for both eBay and eBay's Half.com sites appear at the top of the registration page. This process automatically qualifies you to operate at both the well-loved auction venue and the fixed-price site. You'll learn more about Half.com later in this book.

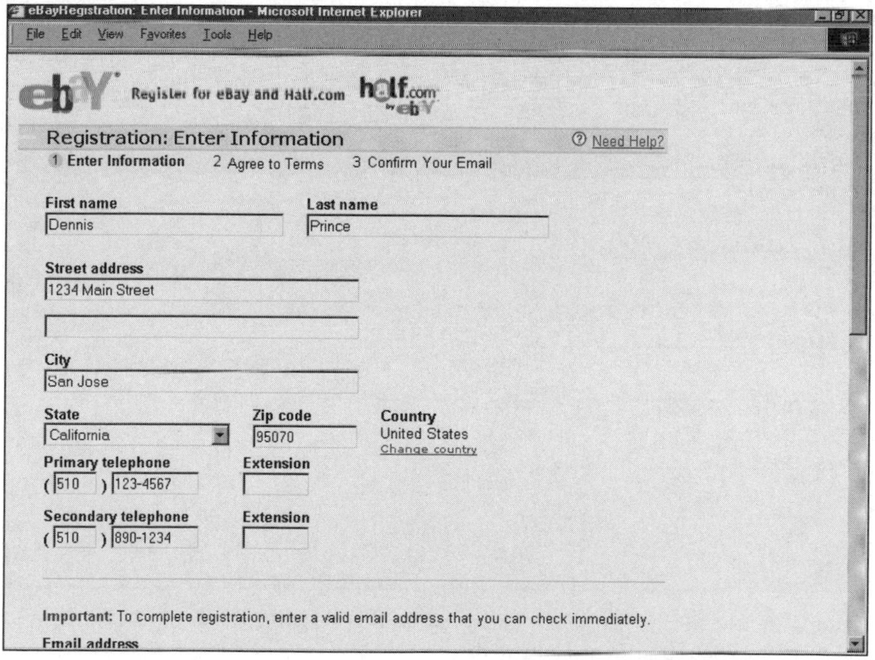

Figure 4-2 Begin the registration process by filling out your personal information.

With the first half of the screen filled out, scroll down to the second half (pictured in Figure 4-3) and enter your e-mail address and establish your User ID and password. The valid e-mail address you provide here is critical in completing the registration process as eBay will send a confirmation message to that address, providing critical information you'll need for the final step in registering.

eBay TIP: Your eBay User ID is more than just a catchy screen name, it's also a form of privacy protection. Time was that eBay would use your e-mail address as a user ID—then along came the "harvesters," individuals and customized "bots" (automated programs) that would collect all the e-mail addresses they could find, using them for addressing unsolicited e-mail messages, annoying sales pitches, and other forms of spam. eBay responded by implementing the User ID, which allows users to protect their e-mail addresses from prying eyes.

---

eBayRegistration: Enter Information - Microsoft Internet Explorer

File   Edit   View   Favorites   Tools   Help

Email address
dlprince@bigfoot.com

Re-enter email address
dlprince@bigfoot.com

Create your eBay User ID
dennis_prince
Example: rose789 (Don't use your email address)
Your User ID identifies you to other eBay users.

Create password
******
6 character minimum
Enter a password that's easy for you to remember, but hard for others to guess. See tips.

Re-enter password
******

Secret question   **Secret answer**
What street did you grow up on?   ▼   ****************
You will be asked for the answer to your secret question if you forget your password.

Date of birth
–Month– ▼   –Day– ▼   Year

Continue >

Figure 4-3 The second part of the initial registration screen requires your e-mail address and creation of your User ID and password.

Once you've filled out the rest of this information, click on the "Continue" button to move forward in the registration process. Be advised, eBay checks to ensure the User ID you've chosen hasn't already been used by someone else. If it has, you'll see a screen like that in Figure 4-4 indicating that you need to make another selection. You can elect to have eBay help you determine a different ID (as noted on the left-hand portion of the screen) or you can directly enter a new ID of your own (using the right-hand portion of the screen). Click the "Create Another User ID" button to validate your new selection.

The Agreement Policy

If the User ID you've selected is valid, your next step in the registration process is to confirm acceptance of the site User Agreement and Privacy Policy. I advise you to read the text in each of the scrollable windows carefully so you understand the terms under which you'll be expected to operate and to

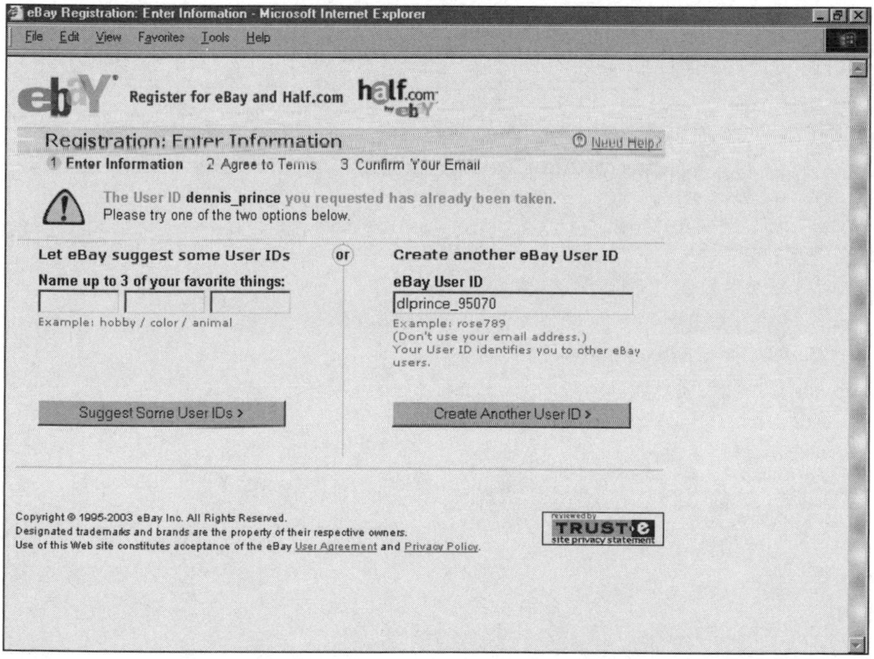

Figure 4-4 If the User ID you chose has already been taken, this screen will help you select another.

what degree eBay will bear any responsibility for your encounters. While there's nothing in the policy that will unjustly ensnare you, understand that eBay stands by its assertion that it is a venue only and cannot be held liable for your actions or the actions of others on the site. For many years, there's been a bone of contention for many users who assert that eBay should bear some of the burden for deals that have gone significantly awry. Nevertheless, the text you'll read here is the latest legalese that extricates the venue from liability. Again, nothing here is dangerous and, by applying the safe trading methods presented later in this book, you'll find trading on eBay is quite safe. So, if you agree to the terms, indicate as much by clicking the "I Agree To These Terms" button at the bottom of the page. Oh, and don't forget to click on the checkboxes indicating you're of legal age (no one under 18 allowed) and that you understand you can change your notification preferences at a later time. If you disagree with all of this, click the "I decline" text link. Keep in mind, though, that by choosing this option you'll be unable to use the site.

If you've agreed to the terms and processed the User Agreement screen, you'll see another screen (as shown in Figure 4-5) instructing you to check your e-mail for a special message that holds the final key to eBay registration.

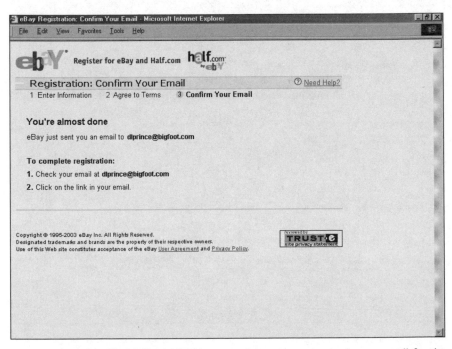

Figure 4-5   You're almost finished! This screen instructs you to check your e-mail for the final steps of registration.

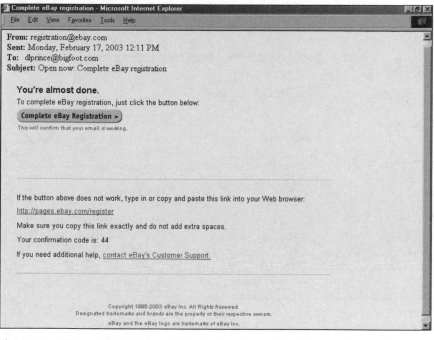

Figure 4-6   Click on the button you'll find in the eBay confirmation e-mail to complete your registration.

The message you'll receive (as pictured in Figure 4-6) provides an active link, labeled "Confirm eBay Registration," that confirms communication with the e-mail address you've provided. Click on the link, and you'll be taken to the eBay site where you'll be greeted by the screen pictured in Figure 4-7.

Armed with your active User ID, you're ready to set out on your quest for great finds and even greater fortunes at eBay. By the way, you might have also seen the pop-up window, also pictured in Figure 4-7 where eBay is curious to learn a bit more about you. Answer only if you want; this information isn't required to proceed into the site. For the moment, though, congratulations; you're a bona fide eBay community member.

GETTING ACCLIMATED TO THE MARKETPLACE

Before you jump headlong into the fray, I suggest that you take a bit of time to survey the site, sample the wares, and look at what the other buyers and sellers are doing. Many new users, once their User ID is activated, dive into the listings and embark on a veritable feeding frenzy; they are lured to bid on and buy so many items they never knew were available. Unfortunately, their

Figure 4-7　Congratulations and welcome to eBay. Your registration is complete!

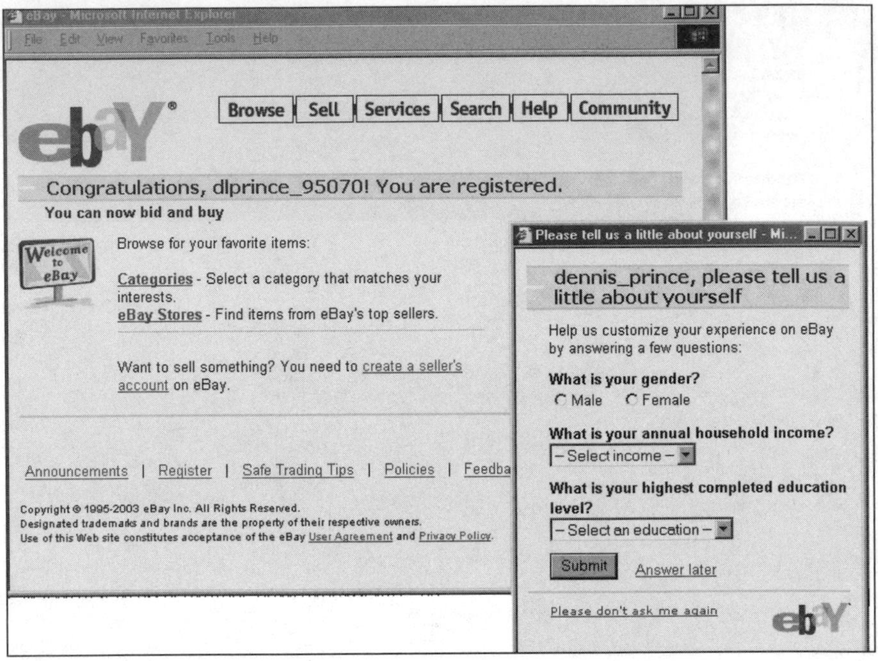

excitement and ambition are often met with a hefty bill to be paid when all is said and done. When the dust settles, many first-time bidders/buyers discover they've paid too much for an item or have purchased an item of lesser quality than they would have wished, only to see a better example become available shortly thereafter. The excitement is understandable, yet, at this early stage of eBay use, try to temper your enthusiasm with a sage bit of knowledge: the items you see on eBay tend to pop up time and time again. Even the rarest of pieces generally show up multiple times, maybe within a week, a month, or a year's time, but rarely if ever does a piece surface only once. Armed with that insight, take time to shop, compare the wares, compare the prices, compare the sellers' sales policies, and get a feel for how the whole business works. If you see an item that truly commands your bid, move ahead to Chapter 5 where you'll learn the best methods for finding and bidding on the items you'll encounter.

SETTING UP YOUR SELLER'S ACCOUNT

Presuming you're here to sell, now is the time to establish your seller's account. Look back at Figure 4-7, and you'll see the text link labeled, "create

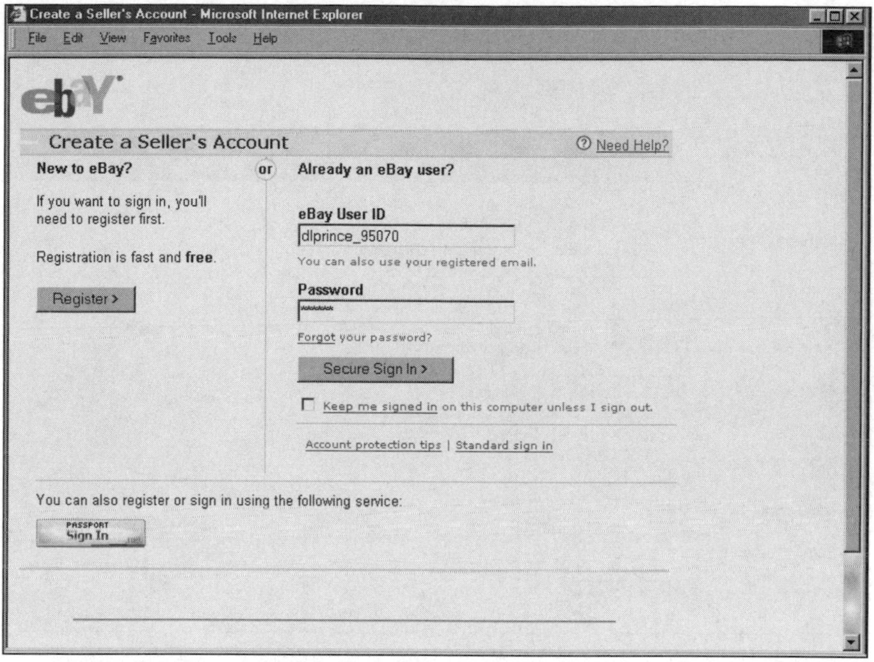

Create a Seller's Account - Microsoft Internet Explorer

File Edit View Favorites Tools Help

ebY°

Create a Seller's Account   ⑦ Need Help?

New to eBay?   or   **Already an eBay user?**

If you want to sign in, you'll
need to register first.   **eBay User ID**
                                    dlprince_95070
Registration is fast and **free**.   You can also use your registered email.

[Register >]   **Password**

                                    Forgot your password?

                                    [Secure Sign In >]

                                    ☐ Keep me signed in on this computer unless I sign out.

                                    Account protection tips | Standard sign in

You can also register or sign in using the following service:

[PASSPORT Sign In]

Figure 4-8   eBay will ask you to verify your identity as you create your seller's account.

a seller's account." Click it, and you'll find your way to the sign-in page where you'll validate your User ID and password, as shown in Figure 4-8. When you are ready to sell, click on the sign-in button and proceed to the first step in creating your seller's account. Figures 4-9, 4-10, and 4-11 illustrate the screens you'll encounter.

To become an active seller on the site, you'll need to provide a valid credit card and checking account information for eBay to keep on file. Here is another sensitive area that has been a topic of controversy in years past—users uncomfortable with having to surrender their sensitive financial information to a Web site. However, to avoid fraud and prevent general tomfoolery, eBay instituted the verification of credit card and bank account information to ensure that users are of legal age to use the site, are identifiable via their chosen financial institutions, and are serious about selling on the site. All of the information you'll enter in this form is protected by the SSL (Secure Sockets Layer) protocol, a secure method whereby sensitive information is transmitted in encrypted format, being unreadable unless a specific *decrypting* key is available. Practically all online transfers of this sort of data are handled via SSL transmission.

Figure 4-9   Begin creating your seller's account by providing credit card information.

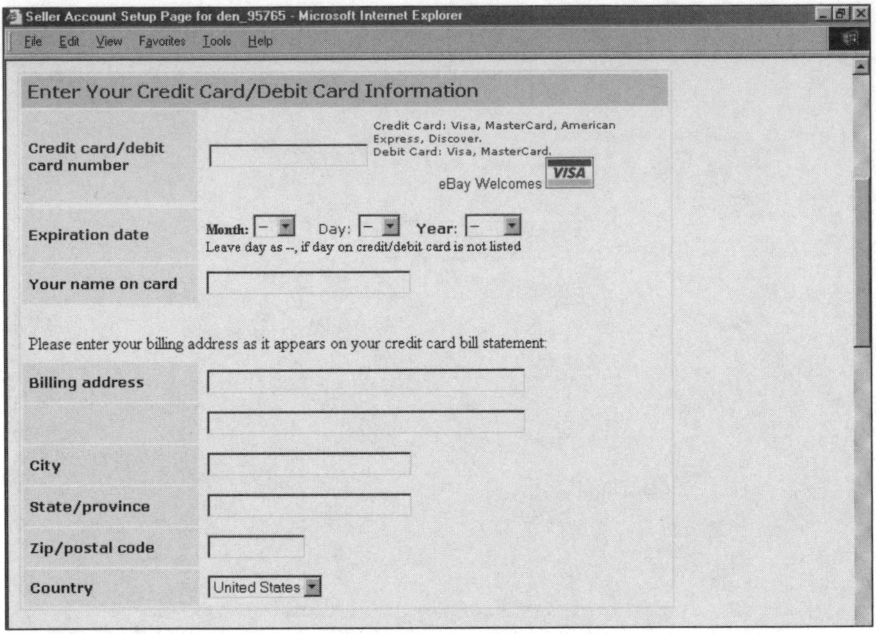

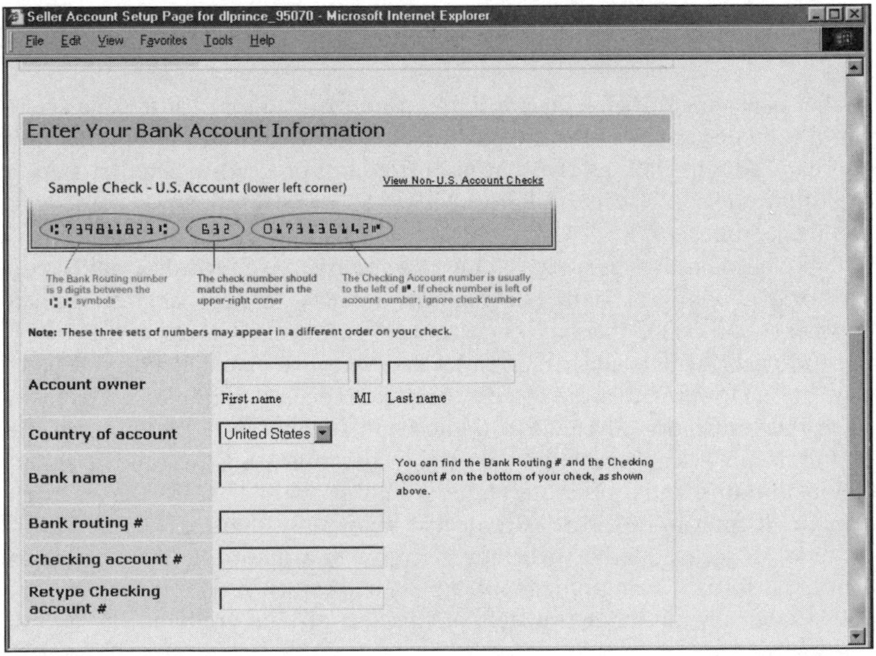

Figure 4-10   Next, enter your bank account information.

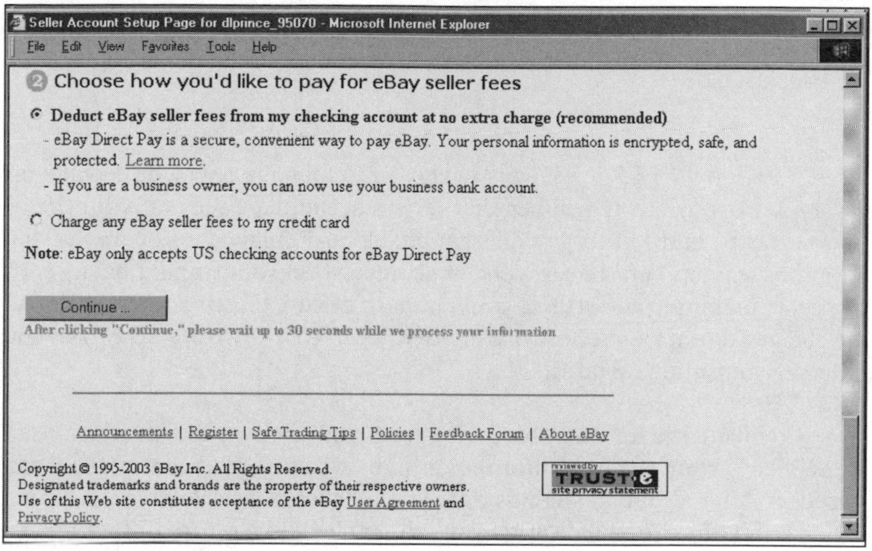

Seller Account Setup Page for dlprince_95070 - Microsoft Internet Explorer

File   Edit   View   Favorites   Tools   Help

② Choose how you'd like to pay for eBay seller fees

⊙ **Deduct eBay seller fees from my checking account at no extra charge (recommended)**

- eBay Direct Pay is a secure, convenient way to pay eBay. Your personal information is encrypted, safe, and protected. Learn more.

- If you are a business owner, you can now use your business bank account.

○ Charge any eBay seller fees to my credit card

Note: eBay only accepts US checking accounts for eBay Direct Pay

Continue ...

After clicking "Continue," please wait up to 30 seconds while we process your information

Announcements | Register | Safe Trading Tips | Policies | Feedback Forum | About eBay

Copyright © 1995-2003 eBay Inc. All Rights Reserved.
Designated trademarks and brands are the property of their respective owners.
Use of this Web site constitutes acceptance of the eBay User Agreement and
Privacy Policy.

TRUST
site privacy statement

Figure 4-11   Last, select how you would like to pay your eBay fees.

eBay TIP: Despite all the online security and privacy steps that have been taken over the years, providing sensitive account information such as this can be an uncomfortable proposition for many computer users. For maximum peace of mind, don't rely simply on what sites promise but check with your credit card issuer and financial institution to determine what sort of privacy and fraud protection they offer. Seek out the sort of protection that provides for assisted dispute of charges and blocking of account activity, which are both necessary if ever you believe your information has been compromised. With these extra protections in place, you can feel safe about proceeding through this step of setting up your seller's account.

Figure 4-11 illustrates the last part of the registration form. Here, you'll decide how you wish to pay your eBay fees. Whenever you list an item for sale, a fee will be assessed. When you select special selling features, additional fees may be assessed. When you sell an item, a sales commission (known as the *final value fee*) will be assessed (incidentally, all of these fees will be discussed in detail in Chapter 7). The fees aren't exorbitant by any means, but you will be charged to list and sell your items in this worldwide marketplace. At the end of each month, you'll need to pay your outstanding balance for the month's accumulated fees, and this last part of the seller's account form is where you indicate whether you wish eBay to automatically deduct the fees from your checking account or if you'd prefer to have your credit card charged instead.

eBay TIP: How you choose to manage payment is really up to you, but remember that if you accumulate fees on your credit card and fail to pay off that credit card balance at the end of the billing cycle, your card issuer will charge interest on your unpaid balance. In respect to making your fortune, you'll want to be sure the assessment of interest charges doesn't unnecessarily increase your cost of using eBay, thereby reducing your ultimate profit.

Complete the information on the form and click on the button labeled "Continue." Your account information is being encrypted and verified via VeriSign. After about 30 seconds or less, if all checks out, you'll see a screen like that in Figure 4-12 indicating you've completed the setup of your seller's account. Good work!

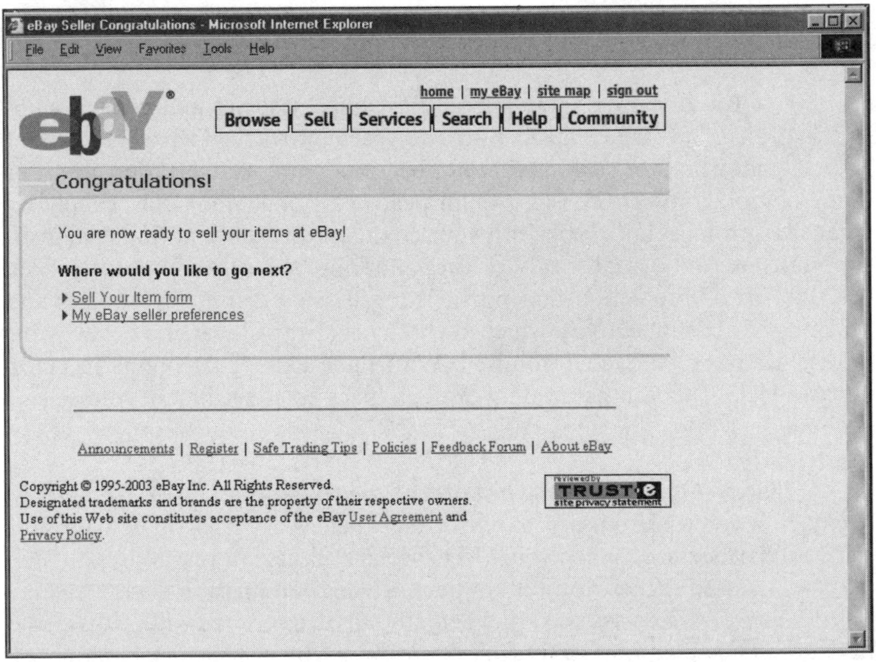

Figure 4-12 The simple yet effective confirmation screen indicates that your seller's account has been successfully set up.

ABOUT ME IS ALL ABOUT YOU

Your setup steps are nearly complete. At this point, you have a valid User ID and you've established your seller's account, so what could be left to do? Though it's not a requirement, consider creating an on-site home page of your own where other users can learn more about you as they prepare to buy from the newest seller to set up shop—*you*. To make this easy, eBay offers a simple-to-use personal page creation tool called *About Me*. About Me is an opportunity for you to tell other community members about you, your likes, dislikes, and so on. As part of furthering the concept of online community, the About Me page is where you can provide that personal touch and give others a feeling of who they're dealing with (a definite bonus if you're a seller eager to instill confidence and ease in the minds of your potential customers). Don't feel you have to create the ultimate About Me page immediately. For starters, you can simply enter some basic information just to lay the foundation. Upon more thought, you can go back and re-edit your page as you like.

To begin creating your About Me page, visit the eBay Site Map, scroll down about a third of the way and locate the *About Me* link under the Buying and Selling heading. Clicking the link will take you to a preliminary page

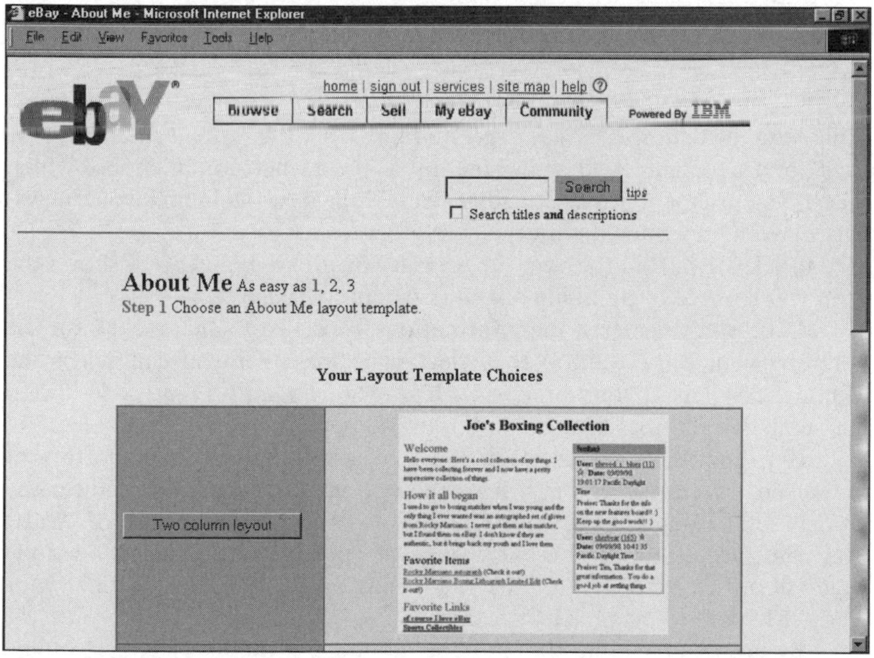

Figure 4-13   eBay makes it easy to create your own *About Me* page by offering three easy-to-use layout templates.

eBay - Select Template Elements - Microsoft Internet Explorer

File   Edit   View   Favorites   Tools   Help

Personalize Your Page

Page Title
Create a title for your page.

Title: Dennis' eBay Back Office

Welcome Message
Create a short paragraph to welcome visitors to your page.

Heading: Work was never this much fun!

Text: It's easy to "whistle while you work" at eBay, knowing my efforts to trade here have paid off more than handsomely.

Another Paragraph
What else do you want to share with others?

Heading: Who am I?

Text: AuctionWatch.com), and a steady demand for my commentary on all things auction for various radio, television, and print outlets.

Picture
Link to a picture that you've posted on the Web.

Caption: Me on the cover of Access Magazine, Jan. 2000

URL: http://

Show Your eBay Activity

Feedback
Display your feedback comments.

Show 10 most recent comments

Items for Sale

Caption:

Figure 4-14   Fill in the form to establish your personal page.

explaining the feature. On that page, find and click the "Create and edit your page" button. Figure 4-13 shows the initial page where you'll choose which format you use for your page (readily available as a two-column layout, newspaper layout, or centered layout).

Click the button to select the format you'd like. Figure 4-14 shows the form you'll use to begin filling out your About Me page.

Once you've entered the information you'd like to share, click on the "Preview your page" button to review your work (or you can select the "Choose new layout" button if you'd like to start again). Figure 4-15 shows the humble beginnings of my new About Me page.

If you are satisfied, click the "Save my page" button at the bottom of the screen. Of course, you also have the option of utilizing the "Edit some more," "Edit using HTML" (for you serious Web programmers), or "Start over" buttons. Again, at this early stage of your eBay experience, a simple page will suffice. Later in this book you'll learn additional ways to utilize your About Me page to maximize your sales.

By now, you're a member in good standing at the 'Net's largest online trading post. Along the way, you likely saw several links that would lead you to different areas of the eBay site or likewise directed you to pages that con-

eBay View About Me for dlprince_95070 - Microsoft Internet Explorer

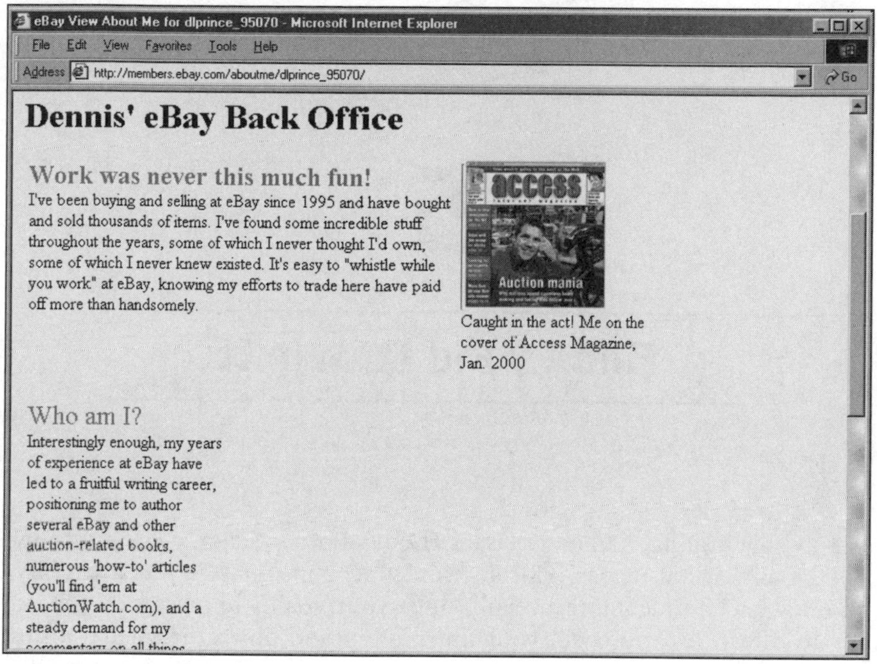

File Edit View Favorites Tools Help

Address http://members.ebay.com/aboutme/dlprince_95070/   Go

Dennis' eBay Back Office

Work was never this much fun!

I've been buying and selling at eBay since 1995 and have bought and sold thousands of items. I've found some incredible stuff throughout the years, some of which I never thought I'd own, some of which I never knew existed. It's easy to "whistle while you work" at eBay, knowing my efforts to trade here have paid off more than handsomely.

Caught in the act! Me on the cover of Access Magazine, Jan. 2000

Who am I?

Interestingly enough, my years of experience at eBay have led to a fruitful writing career, positioning me to author several eBay and other auction-related books, numerous 'how-to' articles (you'll find 'em at AuctionWatch.com), and a steady demand for my commentary on all things

Figure 4-15   A simple About Me page like this can be created in just a few minutes.

tained more information. Feel free to explore those links at your leisure, remembering the Site Map can always lead you to the same destinations whenever you choose. But, if your goal is to start selling, what's been covered here has established your eBay presence and you can now move forward quickly.

5

Find It, Bid It, Win It

Now that you have an active User ID, it's time to begin culling through the millions of items up for auction. Recognize that finding great buys on eBay isn't accidental (especially since your goal is to master all the site has to offer). As you begin your journey up and down the virtual aisles, make use of some searching methods and approaches discussed in this chapter that will help you find exactly what you want and help you uncover some hidden treasures that perhaps have gone unnoticed. By using these methods you will be able to place your bid with complete confidence, certain that your decision is the most sound and likely to yield the best result (both in terms of quality and price). Then employ these best bidding strategies to increase your chances of winning while still paying the best possible price. The tools and techniques for such success await you in this chapter.

BROWSING THE CATEGORIES

Since it hosts millions of items every day, eBay survives by organizing everything in a logical and intuitive manner. You've already seen how eBay utilizes main categories and subcategories to collate the myriad goods being offered by the legions of sellers. But if you worry that finding a specific item on the site is analogous to finding the proverbial needle in a haystack, rest assured the task can be as simple as finding a number in the Yellow Pages (even simpler). Searching through the categories is a useful activity if you're inclined to simply browse a particular type of item. In fact, browsing rarely goes unrewarded: you're likely to stumble across

Ten Reasons to Buy Before You Sell

1. Gain familiarity with eBay functions and features
2. Understand market trends, bidding tendencies, and potential prices
3. Recognize different sales strategies in use
4. Learn how postauction payments work
5. Recognize shipping costs and lead-times
6. Learn how to interact effectively with others
7. Determine which seller policies seem to be best
8. Uncover potential sources of goods for resale
9. Identify elements of exceptional customer service
10. Build a reputable feedback rating before selling

something you weren't aware would be of interest to you or that you had completely forgotten about but, now that your memory's been jarred, cannot live without.

eBay TIP: I try to make time to browse the categories for two reasons: I, too, stumble across items I had forgotten about and am glad to find them, but more important, as a collector I often find items I was previously unaware existed and which serve as valuable information to my areas of expertise. I recommend that category browsing be added to your regular online regimen.

Browsing the categories is also a useful way to find misplaced gems. Since sellers choose the category under which their items will be listed, it's not uncommon to find items that seem out of place. Of course, to browse the entire site for such mislaid treasures would be an overwhelming task, but it's a useful exercise to do for those who wish to specialize in certain types of goods. You should be able to quickly understand what might get accidentally filed in a category of specialty.

SEARCHES MADE SIMPLE

When you're ready to look for a specific item, eBay has numerous search tools available to help you in your quest. Some of the essentially same tools are found at various places within eBay as a convenience. Other search tools are highly customizable to help you narrow your focus and hone in on *exactly* what you're looking for. Expect to make regular use of each tool to help you slice and dice the millions of listings to find just what you want.

The Basic Search

The first way to search is quite basic, as the name implies. Look to the eBay home page and recall the search window labeled, "What are you looking for?" (see Figure 5-1). This search allows you to type in specific words that will be compared to item titles, returning a list of matches for you to further explore.

When search results are returned, that is the listing of items that match your query, you'll encounter another basic search window at the upper left-hand corner of the search results page (see Figure 5-2).

The difference between the home page search and the listings page search is the latter provides a small check box labeled "in titles and descriptions." Checking this box allows you to perform your next search by seeking matches not only in item titles but within the text of item descriptions as well. Of course, searching through item descriptions is likely to result in a larger number of inappropriate matches since the keywords you've specified could randomly appear within an item description without actually being associated with the sort of item you're seeking. There's still one more basic version of the search tool, this one being found on most every eBay page you'll see. As you navigate the site, you'll frequently see the basic search window in the upper right-hand corner of an eBay page. This third type of basic search is functionally identical to the listing page search tool, offering the ability to search item titles and descriptions. Many users find it convenient since it's at hand whenever an urge strikes to search for something that's just come to mind.

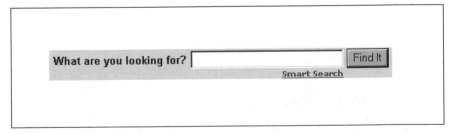

Figure 5-1   The quickest and most basic search tool is found right on eBay's home page.

Figure 5-2 Another basic search window is found on a search results listing page.

eBay TIP: Be ready to use these handy basic search tools at a moment's notice. Often, search ideas will suddenly come to mind, only to vanish as quickly as they came. The moment you consider, "Hey, I ought to see if I can find . . ." you're best served if you run that search immediately rather than later being unable to recall just what it was you thought you might hunt. Such a lapse isn't a sign of old age; it's the effect of millions of items vying for your attention.

The Refined Search

Notice that beneath each of the basic search tools is a subtle colink that reads "Smart Search," "Refine Search," or "Advanced Search." These links, as well as the more prevalent "Search" button on the main toolbar all lead to the same place: eBay's search screen. The main eBay search page (curiously titled "eBay Basic Search") is your window to a more narrowly defined search criteria. Here, you can better define how your search keywords will be used by specifying which additional words to exclude (to restrict close but unwanted title matches), which specific categories to search, which geographic locations to consider, and what price range is of interest to you. Additionally, you can sort the results of your search. With the objective of zeroing in on a certain item or type of item, these additional search delimiters help you perform more efficient searches and avoid needlessly wading through "close but no cigar" search hits.

The Advanced Search

In the eBay main search window, notice the second tab labeled, "Advanced Search;" click on the tab and you'll see a slightly different screen as pictured in Figure 5-3.

Plainly speaking, the Advanced Search isn't *all that*. A quick comparison between this tab and the first search tab display reveals only a few additional checkboxes and sort and display options. Much of what you see on the

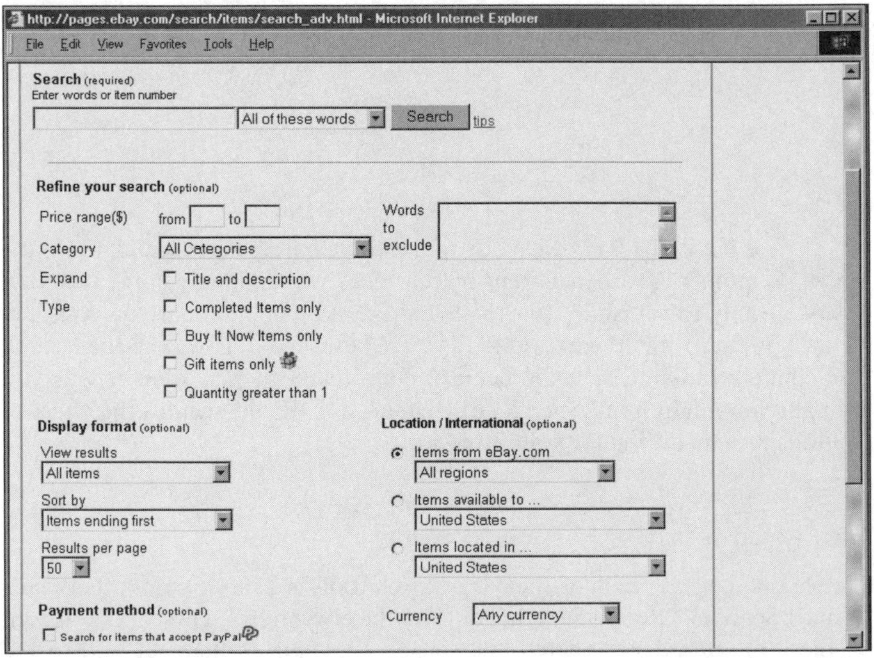

Figure 5-3 The Advanced Search tab offers a few more criteria to help you in your quest for a specific item.

Advanced Search can be accomplished from the previous search tab. Despite its promising name, the Advanced Search doesn't offer significantly more than the previous search screen and whether you use it becomes a matter of personal choice.

The Keys Are in the Keywords

Before moving ahead to the additional search tabs, take a moment to consider the importance of the keywords you use when you perform an item search. Keywords are just that: *keys* to unlocking the vault of treasures within eBay. They help you uncover exactly what it is you want so you don't have to laboriously sift through thousands of category pages. Your success here comes from knowing the best keywords to use in searching for items, which you can learn to do by observing how sellers seem to be crafting their item descriptions for these goods. Here are some quick tips for utilizing keywords in your searches:

- Use specific names and brands
- Use common terms associated with the item you're seeking
- Use associative terms (i.e., genre, era, and so on)
- Use proper spelling

As you sort through the listings that match your keyword search, take special note of any additional terms that seem to be commonly used with these goods and consider including those (or excluding them if they're not *exactly* what you're looking for) in future searches. Remember the commonly used words later when you are selling your own goods.

Harnessing Search Commands

Besides utilizing good keywords in your searches, recognize that there are several character commands you can incorporate to further refine your search results. This is an aspect of eBay searching that many users overlook but which can have a significant impact on your search results. The most successful character commands you can include in your keyword searches are:

- Use quotation marks (" ") around your keywords to return only items containing the words in a grouping in the order you specified (example: "my mother the car").
- Use the minus sign (–) to exclude words that might commonly accompany items that contain your keywords but in which you aren't interested (example: spider man – movie).
- To exclude multiple words, place the minus sign before a parenthetical listing of words to exclude, separated by commas but no spaces [example: harry potter – (movie,toy)].

- Use the asterisk (∗) as a wild card to match items that contain a partial keyword string you'll enter (example: sac* kings to find "sac," "sacto," or "sacramento").
- Use the plus sign (+) to specify a particular word that appears along with multiple other words [example: (Wedgwood,Lennox) + cup].

These search commands can be utilized in any Basic or Advanced item search window.

Searching by Seller, Bidder, and Within Stores

The next option in the eBay main search window is the tab labeled "By Seller." Clicking this tab will provide a new window of search conditions as shown in Figure 5-4.

Searching by seller is the quickest way to see what your favorite seller is selling. When you find a seller that seems to offer the sorts of items that most interest you, this is the easy way to keep up with what the person is offering. A look at past auctions from the seller also provides an indication of the volume of sales the seller has been managing, what prices the seller has been getting for goods, and how many of the seller's auctions have been successful. As

Figure 5-4 Search by seller to find only those goods offered by a single user.

Figure 5-4 shows, it's easy to enter the seller's ID, select whether completed items (closed auctions) should be queried, and how the results should be sorted. Also note that a hybrid search exists in the lower half of the screen: a keyword search box coupled with a field to list multiple seller IDs for which items should be searched or, conversely, from which results should be excluded (by selecting the radio button below the "Multiple Sellers" field).

The fourth tab, "By Bidder," allows a similar search, this time by specifying goods associated with a particular bidder ID (see Figure 5-5).

eBay TIP: It's often revealing to perform a bidder search using a seller's ID. To get a better feel for whom you're dealing with and what sorts of items these folks are buying as well as selling, take a look at their activity on both sides of the virtual sales counter.

Often, searching by bidder is a fast and simple way to monitor *your own* bidding activity. This option is equally useful in determining what others might be bidding on, especially those who have a propensity to outbid you on certain items (more about that and bidding strategies later). Finally, the last

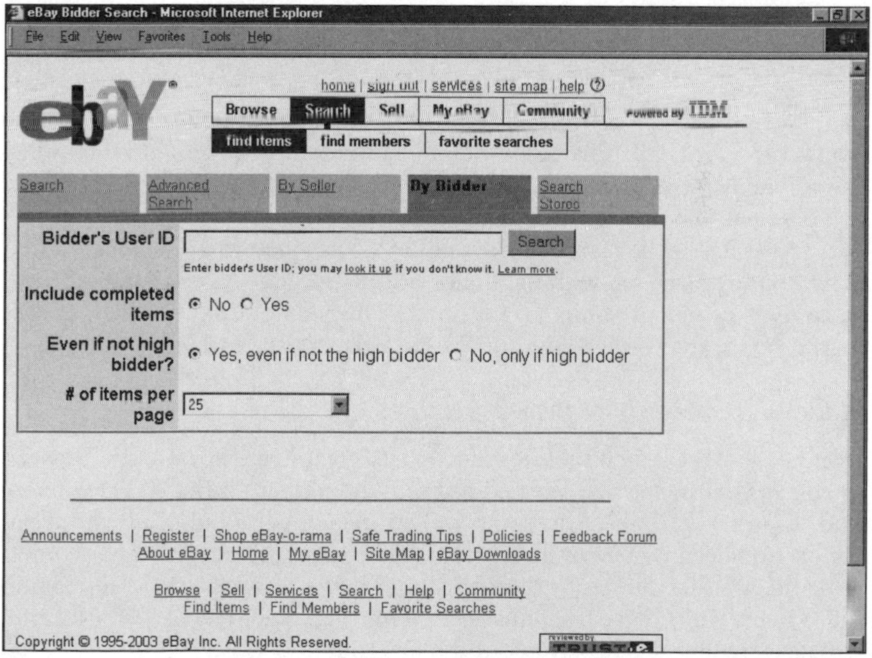

Figure 5-5 Searching by bidder allows you to investigate what a particular user might be bidding on.

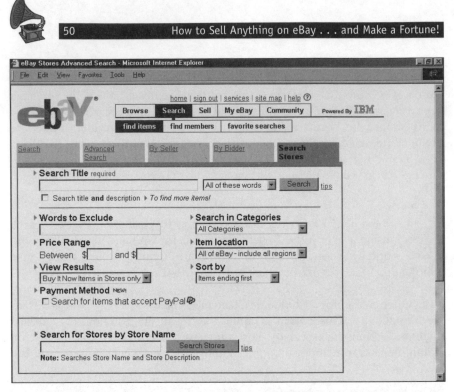

Figure 5-6   Search eBay Stores to find only those goods offered in the fixed-price sales format.

tab, "Search Stores," provides a way to restrict your search results to those items listed for fixed-price sale in eBay Stores (shown in Figure 5-6). eBay Stores are direct-sale outlets where sellers can offer items for immediate sale, at a designated price, outside of the usual auction method.

Notice how the search fields for eBay Stores are nearly identical to that of the basic search tab with the minor addition of the "View Results" field. Naturally, the search results for this smaller division of eBay will be far fewer than if you searched the entire site for both fixed-price and auction items.

Other Ways to Search for Hidden Treasures

Even with all the search tools just described, great items can still slip between the cracks. Although you've tried mightily to extract all the goods you can find using the various tools, some will still elude you (and other shoppers) and, if found, can often result in great finds at great prices. You can become a bona fide treasure hunter by turning over the virtual stones on the site to find those items which have been mislabeled, misfiled, and, if you're not careful, will be incredible deals on which you'll miss out.

To begin, review the results of your usual searches carefully. Identify the categories where these items seem to be referenced and take a bit of time to search through all listings in that category to determine if there any other terms you've yet to consider. Look to see what other goods appear in the category of listings and whether they're the sorts of things you're seeking and have been titled or described in a way you hadn't considered or expected. More important to the treasure hunt, this is also how you'll determine if there are any common misspellings used in association with these items (as in "Beanie" versus "Beenie" versus "Beany") which you'll likewise want to make note of in order to ferret out the mistitled, and thereby passed over, treasures.

Another hunting method to employ frequently is to review the eBay listings that have moved into the "ending today" and "going, going, gone" links found at the top of every category page. Although it isn't feasible to review these listings in all categories, it is worthwhile to scan these listings in the categories you would typically review. Whether you missed an item in your various search efforts or there was yet another variation or "oops" on the seller's part in titling or listing the item, this is another proven method to unearth potentially lost goods.

Finally, keep an eye open for completed auctions (in your various searching and browsing activities) where the item perhaps didn't sell. If the item never received a bid and essentially slipped by you during its run, it's still possible to query the seller about the item to see if a sale is still possible. Oftentimes, sellers will elect to relist their item and give it another go—yet many are highly motivated to make the quick sale upon receiving your inquiry.

Save Time by Saving Searches

You may have noticed that each search results page has a text link labeled "Save this search," located at the upper right-hand and lower left-hand corners of the screen. Upon clicking the link, you'll capture the search criteria in your My eBay settings under the "Favorite Searches" heading (see Figure 5-7), and your searches will be much more efficient.

Rather than try to recall what you've been searching for, the searches you save are readily available for another query just by clicking the "Search Now" link in the My eBay screen. Better yet is the checkbox labeled "Email me" where, when enabled, an e-mail message will be sent to you whenever a new item is listed at eBay that fits your search criteria. Essentially, eBay is now doing the searching for you.

THE ABCs OF BIDDING

Sometimes, bidding at eBay is as much about gamesmanship as it is about commerce. There are several auction formats in use at eBay, and there are certain tactics and strategies in each format that will yield the best results. Before you can become an expert seller, striving to make your fortune, you'll need to

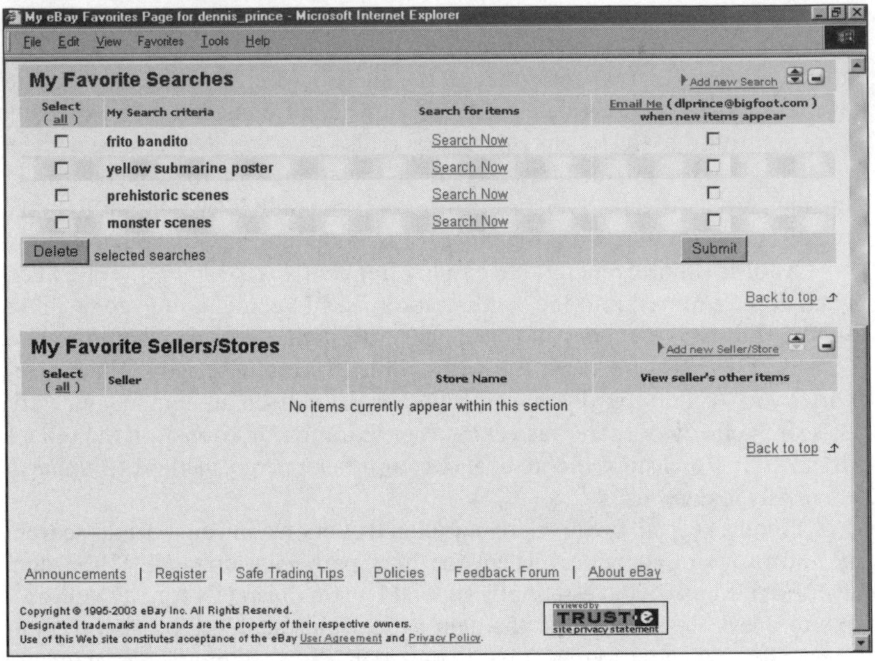

Figure 5-7 Save your searches for easy reuse in the My eBay Favorite Searches area.

become an expert bidder, understanding the methods used to win auctions and applying that knowledge to your eventual sales strategy. Moreover, there are some great items available on eBay that perhaps you'd simply like to own for yourself. The following section shows you how to approach the exciting world of eBay bidding.

Things to Do Before Bidding

We've all been counseled to "comparison shop" before buying anything, and the same advice is just as applicable—perhaps doubly so—at eBay. Unlike the brick-and-mortar world of commerce where you can hold the item, stroke the finish, or kick the tires, the wares at eBay exist in the ether (during the bidding process, at least), requiring that you take some extra measures to ensure that you won't get cheated. To guarantee that what you bid on is what you really want and is coming to you from a reliable source, you'll need to do a bit of homework up front. *Before* you bid on anything, do the following:

- Carefully review the item description to be certain you know what you may be buying.
- Closely examine the illustration(s) of the item and make sure that what you see matches what is being described.

- Determine the costs of shipping, handling, or other "adders" to your final price.
- If you're unclear about anything, use the link to "Ask the seller a question." A good seller will respond via e-mail to answer all of your questions clearly and completely.
- Using eBay's "search by seller" function, research other items the seller is currently offering as well as what has been offered in the recent past.
- Review the seller's feedback rating and read the comments others have left regarding their experiences with this seller.
- Compare and contrast the item you're interested in with the same or similar item(s) being offered by other sellers. Look for description consistency, condition, and price.
- Be certain that you understand and agree with the seller's terms including postage and handling costs and options, insurance, accepted payment methods, and refund and return privileges.
- If anything you discover causes you uncertainty or anxiety, best skip this item (or seller) and look for another.

eBay considers all bids as "binding contracts to purchase." Should yours be the winning bid, it's critical you are certain about what you'll bid on *before* you bid.

Placing a Bid

It's simple, really, to get into the action. When you find an item you like and which you believe is what it's advertised to be, simply click on the "Place Bid" button you see on the item page (see Figure 5-8 for an example).

Immediately, you're whisked to another area of the screen where you'll enter your maximum bid amount (which must equal at least the current high bid plus the minimum bid increment but can be as high as you'd be willing to ultimately pay), then click the "Continue" button to complete the process and see how your bid fares against the previous bidder (see Figure 5-9).

It's as simple as that. If your bid surpasses the current high bidder's maximum bid amount, you'll be declared the new high bidder. Of course, the job now is to withstand any subsequent bids from others who might come along to try to take the item. A dose of good bidding strategy will help you win more auctions; that conversation coming up next.

Bidding Strategies

Here's where the real fun begins and the point at which the experts distance themselves from the novices. It's perfectly acceptable to place incremental bids on an item, hoping to ultimately get in the last winning bid before the auction ends. Nevertheless, the good news is that winning can be much easier

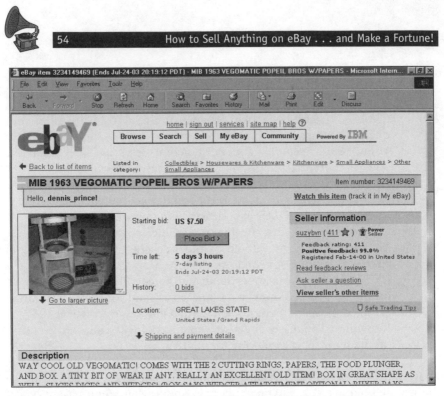

Figure 5-8   Ready to bid? Just click on the bidder's paddle and place your bet.

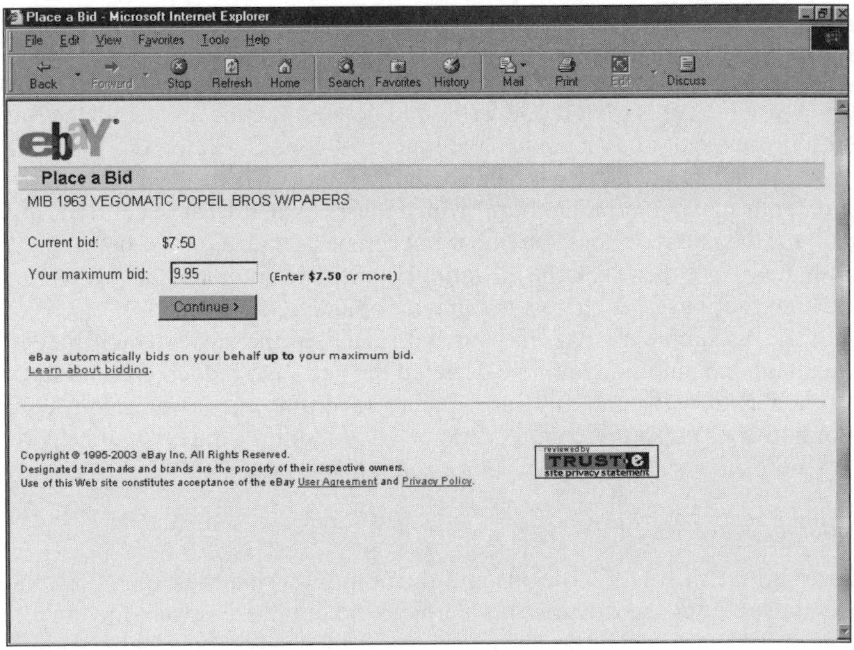

Figure 5-9   Enter your maximum bid amount and launch your bid.

and less time intensive than maintaining an active presence in the virtual auction parlor. To begin, it's helpful to understand how eBay's *proxy bidding system* works. As previously mentioned, when bidding on an item you're prompted to enter your *maximum bid amount;* this is the most you'd ever be willing to pay for a particular item, your ultimate "drop out" price. eBay's proxy system will only consume as much of your maximum as is needed to maintain your high bidder status, incrementing the current bid value for you (bidding on your behalf) when other bidders come along and up the price. You'll retain your high-bidder standing so long as your maximum bid value isn't eclipsed by another bidder. Once that happens, you will be outbid and another user will be proclaimed the high bidder. There's no trick to the proxy bidding system; it all comes down to who puts more money on the table. There are few things you can do, though, to increase your odds of winning.

THE PENNY PRINCIPLE   Would you laugh if I said that you could win an auction with a mere penny? Here's how it's done. First, understand that whenever two bidders submit the exact same maximum bid value (say, $100), eBay will recognize the first to have submitted that maximum as the winner of the tie. At this point of incremental bidding, you'd need to enter another bid that satisfies the minimum bid increment in order to become the new high bidder (in this case, an additional $2.50). However, if the current bid is $50, the high bidder having previously stated a maximum of $100, you can win this auction with a penny by bidding a maximum of $100.01. Your maximum will meet the minimum bid increment (that required while the current value is at $50) and, as eBay's proxy bidding system takes over to bid on behalf of you and the current high bidder, your bid will ultimately win out because you succeeded in bidding more than the previous bidder—*just a single penny.* Since you laid more money on the table, you walk away victorious. This principle works in reverse as well. In other words, your maximum bid of $100.01 will thwart other bidders who might come along long after you originally submitted your bid, they submitting a maximum value of $100. Your single penny will retain your high bidder status. To this end, it's good to be in the habit of bidding odd values such as $100.01, $25.37, and so on. Those few extra pennies might be all it takes to gain you the win without sending you significantly beyond your intended spending budget.

SNIPE BIDDING   Perhaps the most maligned bid practice of all is snipe bidding or "sniping." Essentially, you lie in wait for an auction to approach its conclusion, then, just seconds before the time expires, you launch a stealth bid in hopes of supplanting the current high bidder while leaving no time for a rebutting bid. It sounds sneaky but it's a perfectly allowable and widely used practice by many veteran bidders; only those who are "sniped" are squawking about it. In essence, it's no different than traditional ascending-price bidding, only the timing is different. In step-by-step fashion, here's how snipe bids are executed:

- Snipe bidding is most effective when using two browser windows, one to load and hold the bid to be placed, another to count down the auction clock (see Figure 5-10).
- If you haven't already signed in at eBay, be sure to do so before proceeding. This saves you the time and inconvenience of signing in as you're preparing to place your snipe bid.
- Refresh the item window to monitor the count down of the clock. *Pay special attention to how responsive eBay and your Internet connection are, noting the number of seconds before the refresh completes.*
- Open a second screen to the same item (CTRL-N on your keyboard will do the trick) and click the "Place Bid" button. Enter your maximum bid amount *and wait.*
- About two minutes before the auction ends, click on the "Place Bid" button in the second window. eBay will display a "Submit Your Bid" screen with a button labeled "Submit" (see Figure 5-11). *Don't bid yet!*
- Toggle back to the other item page (using your keyboard's ALT-TAB key sequence) to continue refreshing to count down the auction clock. Position the two windows in a staggered arrangement so that you have clear access to the "Submit" button on the bidding window.

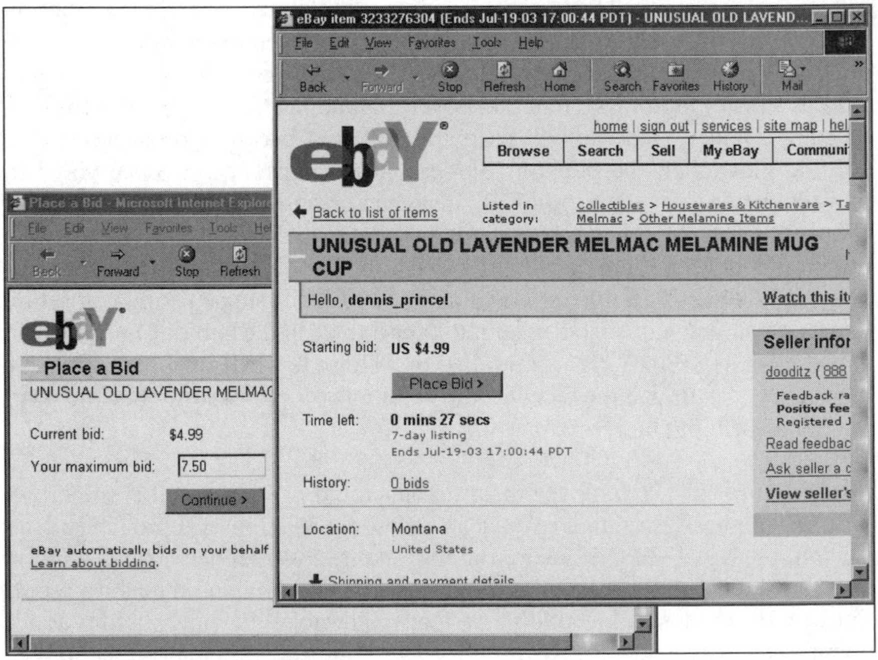

Figure 5-10   Use two item screens when preparing to execute a snipe bid.

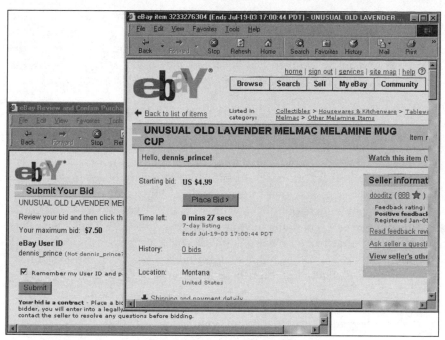

Figure 5-11   At the two-minute mark, the snipe bid lies ready in wait.

- Refresh the main item window until the clock counts down to the point where you feel you can just place the bid before the auction closes. Quickly click the "Confirm bid" button in the second window.
- If you were successful in placing your snipe bid, eBay will report the results of your bid, either naming you the winner or revealing that you were outbid by the previous high bidder's proxy.
- Recognize that a last-minute bid will *not* ensure a win; the *maximum bid amount* in effect when the auction ends is what determines who will win. However, a successful snipe bid that does supplant a previous high bid is usually successful in that there is scant time left for another bidder to place a follow-on bid.

Again, there's nothing unfair about snipe bidding (if there was, eBay would prevent its use) since, in the end, no matter how late you wait to place a bid, if another bidder has offered more by way of a maximum bid amount, that amount will still win out.

As exciting as sitting at attention to launch a snipe bid can be, sometimes you can't be present to monitor the end of an auction; you can still snipe, however. There are several automated snipe programs you can use to place your snipe bids for you. My personal favorite happens to be located at *www.esnipe.com.* This server-based sniping assistant allows you to enter your snipe bid information long before the auction ends and will then log on to eBay and place the snipe bid on your behalf. Though you'll pay a fee to use eSnipe, it costs only pennies on the dollar and often delivers big results. Again, no manipulation going on here, just well-timed last-second bids.

DUTCH AUCTION AND YANKEE AUCTION BIDDING   Recall the Dutch auction format discussed in Chapter 1? These are auctions where multiple units of the same item are offered in a single listing. Each bidder will specify how much he or she wishes to bid, maximum, and *how many* units are desired. The current price remains at the opening bid value set by the seller until all units have been bid upon, and then incremental bidding takes over to push the lower-maximum bidders out of the winner's circle. If you bid low on a Dutch auction and are barely clinging to your winning status once all units have been bid for, you're said to be "on the bubble;" you're primed to be bumped off should another bidder come along and outbid you. To increase your chances of winning a Dutch auction, take these steps:

- Unique to Dutch auctions is the ability to review the current bank of bidders and their bid amounts (see Figure 5-12).

---

eBayItem Bid History - Microsoft Internet Explorer

File   Edit   View   Favorites   Tools   Help

View page with email addresses and locations (Accessible by Seller only)   Learn more.

Dutch Auction High Bidders (View Bid History)

User ID	Item Price	Quantity	Date of Bid	Payment
smith10_3 (6)	$2.40	5	Feb-22-03 09:03:46 PST	Payment options available when auction ends.
rkpoppy (217) ☆	$2.30	10	Feb-22-03 06:50:38 PST	Payment options available when auction ends.
nowisthetyme (191) ☆	$2.25	10	Feb-16-03 09:44:38 PST	Payment options available when auction ends.
mdiman (6)	$2.25	20	Feb-17-03 08:09:48 PST	Payment options available when auction ends.
sea4ever@aol.com (30) ☆	$2.25	30	Feb-18-03 20:17:21 PST	Payment options available when auction ends.
638522 (51) ★	$2.25	10	Feb-22-03 08:35:43 PST	Payment options available when auction ends.

Quantity still available. Lowest successful bid is minimum bid amount.

Announcements | Register | Safe Trading Tips | Policies | Feedback Forum | About eBay

Copyright © 1995-2003 eBay Inc. All Rights Reserved.
Designated trademarks and brands are the property of their respective owners.
Use of this Web site constitutes acceptance of the eBay User Agreement and Privacy Policy.

TRUST☰
reviewed by
site privacy statement

Figure 5-12   In Dutch auctions, you can monitor who has bid and how much they've offered.

- Monitor whether the entire quantity of units has been bid upon and track how much time is left in the auction.
- To better ensure a win without needlessly driving up the final price, place a bid that falls in the mid-range between the high and low bid amounts.

The key to Dutch auctions is that, in the end, each winning bidder will pay only *the price he or she offered;* the auction will entail that the group of bidders will likely be paying different prices for the number of units they've won. True "winning" of a Dutch auction, then, is achieved when you successfully win a quantity of units but do so at the lowest possible price among the winning bidders. The Yankee Auction is a variation of the Dutch auction where each winning bidder pays the exact amount of their winning bid.

THE STRATEGY OF NOT BIDDING   Sounds crazy but it's true—sometimes it's more advantageous *not* to win an auction. Simply put, it's easy to get caught up in the excitement and competition of an auction, losing sight of the price being paid, and winning the item but at an undesirable final cost. Always consider the following when you're tempted to get caught up with "winning" an auction:

- If the item offered has reached a price equal or higher than what you could pay for it elsewhere, there's no reason to bid.
- If an item isn't in the condition you'd prefer, wait for another, better one, to show up.
- If the seller's feedback rating is low or sales policy is suspect, consider skipping this one.
- Consider avoiding an item where the bid history reveals two bidders have been active in back-and-forth bidding through the course of the auction. This might be a *bidding war* in the works, and you'll likely not fare well between the two impassioned bidders.

Searching, bidding, and winning at eBay is great fun and can result in some wonderful acquisitions along the way. As you constantly consider your "fortune," utilize the various search and bid strategies noted here to gain the greatest (yet fair) advantage in your find-and-bid-and-win exploits.

6

Fighting Fraud

Although eBay has been effective in implementing new safety programs and local and national government agencies have been prosecuting auction criminals, auction fraud still tops the National Consumer League's list of online scams. From fake paintings to undelivered goods, auction goers have encountered the sorts of illicit acts that threaten to taint the auction giant's good name. This is not to suggest that your experiences at eBay are destined for trouble, though; the site still accurately reports that 99.9 percent of all transactions are completed successfully by honest eBay users. Still, part of being successful in a business venture is to understand how the resident "undesirables" operate and what manner of sly shenanigans they busy themselves in. Recognize, also, that many of the common aggravating acts that eBay users encounter are just that—aggravating; few are blatantly criminal, and most are simply petty antics. Still, you need to be aware of the sort of bad business, prolific or paltry, that sometimes goes down at eBay; how you can detect it; and what steps you can take to protect yourself.

THE TOP 10 ONLINE AUCTION OFFENSES

This section describes the most common auction offenses attempted in the auction space, lists their warning signs, and offers some tips for responding to and avoiding them.

Offense No. 1: Bid Shilling

A dishonest seller will make use of multiple user IDs or will enlist associates to place bogus bids so as to unfairly and falsely raise the number of bids received and the price of an item. This scam is perpetrated by sellers who are looking to artificially increase the bidding activity and increase their final sales price.

DETECTING THE SCAM
- Watch for recurring user IDs that are used to place bids on several of a particular seller's auctions.
- Watch for a recurring pattern where the same bidder or bidders place last-minute bids on a particular seller's auctions.
- Watch for bidders and sellers who regularly bid on one another's auctions (especially if they never appear to actually win).

PROTECTING YOURSELF   If you think you've been target of a shill bidding operation, report the incident to eBay immediately via SafeHarbor (provide any supporting evidence such as other auctions where you believe the seller employed shilling). Your best bet for prevention is to block the user ID from your auctions by utilizing eBay's *Blocked Bidder/Buyer List;* the link can be found within the site map under the Buying and Selling heading.

Offense No. 2: Bid Shielding

This is a bidder's scam in which a ring of dishonest bidders (or a bidder using multiple user IDs) can target an item and inflate the high bid value to scare off other potential bidders. At the last moment, the high bidder or bidders will retract their bids, thus allowing the lower-bidding ring partner to win the item at the once again low—and dishonest—price. The innocent seller has been cheated out of a higher price and other bidders have been falsely steered away from a potential win.

DETECTING THE SCAM
- Watch for a bidder who seems to have a pattern of bidding and then retracting near the end of the auction.
- As with shilling, watch for patterns of apparent partnerships or use of multiple user IDs that tend to bid on the same items or one another's items.

PROTECTING YOURSELF   As with shilling, report a suspected shield to eBay immediately. Make note of bidders who appear to be involved in repeated shielding and block their user IDs.

Offense No. 3: Fake Photos and Misleading Descriptions

In this sellers' scam, auctioneers falsely embellish or distort the presentation of the items they're auctioning. Borrowed images, ambiguous descriptions, and falsified facts are some of the tactics a seller will employ when lacking confidence, knowledge, or good judgment. The eventual buyer will typically receive an inferior item that doesn't match what was promised nor be worth the bid price.

DETECTING THE SCAM
- Watch for item descriptions that seem too good to be true.
- Watch for disparities between a written description and an embedded image of the item.
- Watch for ambiguous or incomplete descriptions.
- Watch for seemingly "borrowed" images (something that appeared in a previous auction or concurrently, or something that looks as if it was lifted from a commercial advertisement).
- Watch for heavily touched-up photos.

PROTECTING YOURSELF   Be informed about the items you'll bid on. Carefully scrutinize all descriptive information including images. If you have any questions or hesitations, contact the seller to inquire. If the seller seems evasive, avoid the auction and the seller.

Offense No. 4: Final Price Manipulation

Another seller's scam. Here, the final price is not what it should be—perhaps you're asked to pay your *exact* bid for a Dutch auction purchase, instead of the lowest winning bid amount, or asked to pay your maximum bid if a previous high bidder retracted, even though your winning bid was registered at the site as just enough to beat the bidder below you. Alternatively, there may be superfluous "additional charges" tacked on—charges that were never previously disclosed and that don't make much sense, such as a "transportation fee," a "base fee," and any other creative fee a shifty seller might attempt to levy.

DETECTING THE SCAM   Really, price manipulation doesn't give you much advance warning since the costs requested by the seller come after the auction is over. However, be on the lookout for sales policies that ambiguously refer to odd or potentially excessive costs and end-of-auction prices.

PROTECTING YOURSELF   Your best protection is to quote the seller's policy back by return e-mail. If the seller seems confused as to the calculation of a final high bid (as in the case of Dutch auctions), refer the seller to the host site's rules. Do not pay if you believe price manipulation is occurring, and report the seller to eBay immediately. Avoid the seller in the future.

Offense No. 5: Inflated Shipping and Handling Costs

This one is akin to some aspects of final price manipulation, though it can be somewhat more subtle. Perhaps a seller requests $6 for postage, but the item is something small and light that wouldn't cost more than $3.85 (if that) to ship. Sellers sometimes inflate postage and handling costs to garner a few extra dollars for themselves.

DETECTING THE SCAM
- Watch for sellers who charge a "handling" or "supplies" fee, especially when they use free packing supplies from the major carriers.
- Watch for sellers who charge flat rates for shipping and handling that seem beyond the acceptable norm (say, more than $6).
- Watch for sellers who charge high flat rates for small items, regardless of the item's size and weight.
- Watch for sellers who are evasive or unwilling to clarify their shipping and handling fees.

PROTECTING YOURSELF   Start by being sure you understand all fees you'll be asked to pay, and question any fees that seem excessive. Politely ask the seller to clarify fees and how those fees were derived. Request specific carriers (such as USPS) and quote *to the seller* what the cost should be for shipping and any other services (politely, of course). Avoid the seller in the future.

Offense No. 6: Failure to Ship Merchandise

This is probably the most feared and most enraging of all scams: the seller simply never sends the goods. The buyer pays up front in good faith for an item that never arrives. A dishonest seller might claim the item was shipped and has since been lost—but most often the seller fails to respond or communicate at all after having received the buyer's payment.

DETECTING THE SCAM   You typically aren't aware that you're about to be scammed until after you've sent your payment. But, here's the modus operandi of most nonshipping sellers (also known as *deadbeat sellers*):

- They are quick to make contact and request payment.
- They don't send confirmation that payment has been received.
- They don't reply, even after repeated attempts to contact them.
- They leave bogus contact information (phone, street address) with the hosting site, so irate buyers can't get through to them by other means.
- They try to auction the same item again at the auction site, at a different auction site, or under a different User ID.

PROTECTING YOURSELF   The bottom line is that this is classic mail fraud and is high on the list at investigative agencies as well as at eBay.

- Keep complete records of all correspondence, including any messages received from the seller when payment was requested.

- Be sure all correspondence you send to the seller is professional and nonthreatening.
- Make a final request to the seller and advise him or her that you will turn the matter over to eBay and/or other agencies.
- When paying for items, try to use a credit card whenever possible: you will be able to dispute the charge and the card issuer will help you sort the matter out. But let justice take its course and be on the look-out for this seller in the future.

Offense No. 7: Selling Knock-Offs, Fakes, and Reproductions

It looks like the real thing, it sounds like the real thing, and it might even smell like the real thing, but it's *not* the real thing. Knock-off, reproduced, and copycat goods make their way into the online auction marketplace every day. Sellers might claim it's real or might hedge a bit about authenticity, but these scammers know they're selling a cheap imitation and are hoping to catch a high-paying buyer who doesn't know how to spot a fake.

DETECTING THE SCAM

- Watch out for truly rare and hard-to-find items suddenly appearing in unbelievably pristine condition.
- Watch out for scarce items that are suddenly plentiful and "like new."
- Watch out for roundabout descriptions where sellers say they *think* it's the real thing or got it from another source who *said* it has to be authentic—no it doesn't and it probably isn't.
- Watch out for sellers who can't seem to provide satisfactory information about the origin of an item.

PROTECTING YOURSELF   It's the old rule of *caveat emptor* ("let the buyer beware") at online auctions, so buyers need to know their stuff. Study up on the items you'll consider bidding on, especially if they have the potential to become quite expensive.

- Ask as many questions as you need in order to clearly identify the item—and beware of the seller who cops an attitude of, "It's real, OK? Just bid on it."
- If you receive an item that is not authentic, contact the seller immediately for a return and refund. If the seller "skips town," report the incident immediately.

Offense No. 8: Improper Grading Techniques

The seller states the item is "definitely in excellent condition. A real '10' here." The item the buyer receives is less than perfect, might be flawed or damaged, and could even be incomplete. The seller has painted a rosy picture to bring in the bids, even though the goods aren't of the top quality needed to command a high-end price.

DETECTING THE SCAM

- The seller claims the item is in "100 percent mint condition." Even newly manufactured items usually bear some sort of imperfection.
- The description fails to offer full disclosure of the item's condition or completeness, especially when it's a well-known item and highly desirable.
- The seller has omitted critical details that are key to accurate grading of the particular item.
- Embedded images seem to show signs of being altered, selectively photographed (only one side is displayed), or unnecessarily cropped where damage might be concealed.

PROTECTING YOURSELF   Your best protection in cases of gratuitous grading is to understand the item well, to be able to spot potentially problem areas quickly, and to ask specific questions about an item's condition. Grading can be very subjective depending on the grader's experience, expectations, and methods of comparison.

- If an item is less than stellar when it was billed as exquisite, send it back.
- In fact, if you're concerned about purchasing an item based on its grading, ask if the seller offers return privileges. If not, then it's *caveat emptor* all over again.

Offense No. 9: Phony Loss and Damage Claims

A buyer contacts a seller to state that an item never arrived or was seriously damaged. The buyer requests a refund and asks the seller to work out the details afterward. The item may have arrived just fine, but the buyer's hoping to ice the cake by getting the bid price back to boot.

DETECTING THE SCAM

- A buyer contacts you weeks or months after the item was shipped to claim loss or damage.
- A buyer demands a refund immediately, before you've had sufficient time to assess the situation or involve the carrier for resolution.
- A buyer offers to throw a damaged item away for you since it won't be worth anything in such "bad" condition.
- A buyer is on record of having signed for or otherwise received an item that is now claimed to be lost in the mail.

PROTECTING YOURSELF Again, this is a classic case of mail fraud. The best protection from phony claims is to insure your outgoing goods or to use tracking methods for all your packages.

- Be sure the buyer is aware of his or her responsibility for loss and damage if insurance or tracking is declined (remember, the buyer should pay for these services).
- Keep all receipts and tracking numbers until you have confirmed with the buyer that the package arrived safely and the contents are in the same condition as when shipped.

Offense No. 10: Switch and Return

Some buyers will purchase an item, receive it, claim they're dissatisfied, and return it for a refund. The scam: the item they return is *not* the same item originally sent. This is a method where unscrupulous buyers attempt to upgrade their items for free, sending back an item of lesser quality or condition.

DETECTING THE SCAM
- A buyer might seem overly interested in your return policy before they've bid or won.
- A buyer is vague about the reason for wanting to return an item.
- A buyer wishes to return an item after a significant lapse of time (weeks or months).

PROTECTING YOURSELF Unfortunately, this scam is the key reason why many sellers do not offer return privileges.
- You can still accept returns, but indicate that all items must be inspected prior to issuing a refund. Your clear description and good images will serve as proof of intrinsic details of your item, which helps identify a swapped item that was dishonestly returned.
- If the return is an attempt at a switch, notify the buyer that the item is not the same one shipped and return the bogus item to the buyer (accompanied with clarification of points of dissimilarity).
- Bar the buyer from bidding in any of your future auctions.

Bonus Scam No. 11: Bid Siphoning

While not a true scam, the unwanted practice known as *bid siphoning* can be quite active at eBay and bears some explanation. Essentially, this is a situation in which you're actively engaged in bidding on an auction item and unexpectedly receive e-mail notification from someone who's offering to sell you the same item elsewhere, either in another listing or offline. By this practice, some sellers are attempting to lure bidders away from an auction, thus potentially devaluing the item in the process. By eBay's rules, this is a prohibited practice.

Further, this could be a roundabout attempt for a scammer to entice bidders where they might be stung by any one or more of the other scams already described. Of course, if you're contacted in this manner, use your own discretion regarding whether you'll entertain the bid siphoning seller. Otherwise, feel comfortable in expressing your disinterest to the seller and possibly notifying eBay's SafeHarbor if you feel compelled to do so.

MISDEEDS OR JUST MISUNDERSTANDINGS?

With the exception of the infrequent but heinous frauds described here, recognize that some situations that appear to be scams are not scams at all—they may simply be missteps by inexperienced buyers or sellers. Before jumping to a conclusion, take time to inquire and clarify, and you may end up helping another auction user get a grip on the ways and means of auctioning.

eBay TIP: Here's an example where the seller might be confused rather than dishonest. Recall the rules of the Dutch auction where winning bidders are only required to pay their exact winning bid price (plus the seller's shipping fees). Some newer sellers believe that all winning bidders are to pay the *highest* winning bid price, a rule that applies to the auction format known as the "Yankee auction." Your knowledge that Dutch auctions require only the winning bid price, not the Yankee pricing format, can be helpful in explaining the difference to the new seller who, again, might just misunderstand the format rules.

You should become cautious, though, if the other person becomes evasive, erratic, or irascible—signs that their original intentions were never designed to be honorable. This could be a scam in the works.

ADDITIONAL PROTECTIONS AND PROVISIONS FROM eBAY

Though it's useful to know how to spot, respond to, and avoid the top ten auction frauds, you're not altogether on your own. eBay is also very interested in keeping everyone happy. In cases where fraud has reared its ugly head, eBay steps forward with specialized policies and programs to help you recover from your loss and get you back in business. Here are the programs eBay provides to offer comfort and recovery in case a deal goes awry:

Auction Insurance

For buyers, eBay has acknowledged the risk involved with prepaying for an item and facing the possibility it may never be received. Therefore, the site offers a buyer's insurance program that will refund up to $200 (minus a $25 deductible) in reimbursement. eBay does require buyers to first exhaust all avenues in seeking a successful completion of the deal, as detailed in these steps:

- The buyer should request the seller's contact information (address and phone number) to attempt direct communication to resolve the problem.
- If such overtures go unanswered for more than 14 days, eBay encourages buyers to enlist assistance from an outside service. SquareTrade, a free dispute resolution provider, can attempt to mediate the impasse and is accessible from eBay. Buyers should also contact credit card issuers (many offering 100 percent protection and charge dispute assistance) as well as package carriers to assist with wayward package claims.
- After 30 days, eBay encourages buyers to file a *Fraud Alert* with the site to track the problem and attempt, collectively, to resolve the problem.
- If there is no resolution within 30 to 90 days, buyers are then instructed to file a *Protection Claim* to gain reimbursement (again, up to $200 minus $25).
- And, if this is a truly heinous fraud, eBay encourages buyers to seek assistance from the National Fraud Information Center, the Internet Fraud Complaint Center, local law enforcement agencies, and the U.S. Postal Inspection Service (when applicable).

Final Value Fee Refunds

For sellers who are scammed or otherwise subjected to unreliable bidders, eBay will offer to refund the *Final Value Fee* (the end-of-auction commission) if the winning bidder fails to pay; he or she has become a *deadbeat,* by eBay's own definition. Of course, eBay requires you take the prescribed steps to try to complete the sale successfully first:

- If payment hasn't been received within seven days of the auction's close (and you had previously notified the bidder of the amount due), file a *Nonpaying Bidder Alert* as a first form of escalation. eBay records these alerts and will suspend users who consistently ignore their commitments to pay.
- If payment still hasn't been received after 10 days of filing the Nonpaying Bidder Alert, request a *Final Value Fee Credit* from eBay; eBay promises to credit your account within 48 hours.

Unfortunately, you cannot recover your insertion and special listing feature fees, but the recovery of the Final Value Fee is a reasonable form of compensation when you encounter a deadbeat bidder.

PREPARE YOURSELF WITH A PLAN FOR ACTION

Being prepared ahead of time will be your best tack for detecting and responding to problems, be they simple miscommunications or premeditated con-jobs. Here are the steps to take as you manage auction encounters, seek mutual resolution, and guard yourself from online trickery:

- *Be informed.* Make sure you understand eBay's auction rules and methods, especially with the particular auction format you're participating in.
- *Investigate.* Research sellers and buyers by investigating their feedback ratings (the community grading system covered in depth in Chapter 15) and comments at the site; those numbers and notes will immediately reveal if you're engaged with a known troublemaker.
- *Know your rights.* Be sure you understand eBay's rules and recommendations for combating fraud and how to invoke the protections provided.
- *Communicate.* Keep your communication flowing with the other person and be professional at all times, *especially* if you believe a scam is in the works; never resort to threats or other such affronts.
- *Be direct.* If you suspect a scam (or at least a significant disregard for the site rules), indicate that to the other person and state how you intend to complete (or terminate) the transaction, including reporting misdeeds to eBay.
- *Follow through.* If it's a scam, take action by reporting the incident to eBay's SafeHarbor administrators, then consider going the next step to report particularly flagrant scams to the proper authorities and organizations.
- *Document and file.* Keep all correspondence of the incident as well as a record of how the events transpired. This is the sort of information that will be needed in the case of any investigation.
- *Keep a positive outlook.* Don't fall into the trap of becoming paranoid or otherwise suspicious about every person you deal with. Recognize that 99.9 percent of the time you'll enjoy simple and straightforward transactions with honest eBay users.

KNOWING WHEN IT'S TIME TO TAKE A LOSS

It's a bitter pill to swallow, but sometimes resolution and recovery just aren't in the cards. Though this should clearly be the exception to the rule, there is a time when it's best to accept a loss and move on. Sometimes a scam can get the better of you and you'll be best served by chalking it up to experience. Here are the indicators of when it might be best to cut your losses:

- The item you were buying was of low (practically negligible) value.
- The feedback rating of the user indicated potential trouble and you chose to ignore it (never again, though).
- The cost (in time, effort, and money) to pursue the situation is far more than the item is worth, or more than it's worth to you.
- The organizations you've gone to for assistance indicate that your loss will be unrecoverable.

While it's never pleasant to admit that someone has gotten away with an illicit deed, convince yourself to move on and let the situation go if it seems no restitution is in sight. Auction fraud is a rare occurrence, and it's highly unlikely that you'll ever endure such a hardship again. Apply the methods described in this chapter and you'll stand the greatest chance of avoiding and averting those nasty little deeds that someone might be trying to carry out.

Part 2

THE BASICS OF
SELLING ON eBAY

7

Becoming an Online Auctioneer

Now that you have a solid understanding of how eBay works, how bidding strategies help you become a better buyer, and how to determine if a deal is on the up-and-up, it's time to take the next step and become an auctioneer yourself. Listing items at eBay is quite easy and the site does a good job providing guidance along the way. Still, if you're new to listing at eBay, having someone alongside to guide you through the process can be a great help. This chapter will quickly walk you through the simple listing process and help you recognize all the features eBay makes available as you present your item for bid.

FIRST THINGS FIRST: WHAT WILL YOU LIST?

The listing process begins with the question "What will you offer for bid?" Surely there are plenty of items at your feet (figuratively or possibly literally) that you'd like to rid yourself of or cash in on. The best news here is that you can sell practically *anything* at eBay. Provided you've priced the item reasonably, there's generally a buyer out there for everything. Surely, while searching the site you have encountered pieces that likely caused you to muse, "Someone's really trying to sell *that?*" Moreover, you also might have been shocked that those quirky goods actually received bids. It's true—practically everything is worth something to somebody. Therefore, I work by this motto: *Don't throw it away, throw it on eBay!* I can practically guarantee you'll find a bidder for nearly anything you might offer up. To that end, start your listing adventure with some simple items. The best items are things you might have seen up for bid that you also have laying around the house. You don't need to necessarily strike it rich on your first sale; your goal is to get accustomed with the listing process. Of course, don't be surprised if you do fare better than you might have originally expected. Look at Figure 7-1; it's a picture of the first item I offered at eBay back in January 1996.

Figure 7-1 A Del Monte California Raisins premium helped me *earn it* through the grapevine.

The California Raisins premium consisted of three PVC figures that stood atop a musical sandwich stage that played, "Heard It Through the Grapevine." I originally offered this for sale within the Usenet (under rec. collecting) and was offered $49. It seemed a great price but I also considered this potentially collectible item could garner a higher price at the auction venue. At the close of the auction, those singing raisins sold for $79! Not bad for something that had been packed away in a box in my garage. The point is there's certainly something of interest that you're sure to sell and which likely isn't near and dear to your heart at this time. Do some quick rooting around, find an item, and get it listed.

USING eBAY'S SINGLE-ITEM LISTING FORMS

Start by Choosing a Format

Now that you have your item in hand, here's a quick review of eBay's single-item listing process. Assuming you had created your Seller's Account at the time you registered with eBay (refer to the discussion in Chapter 4), click on the "Sell" button from the main toolbar to access the *Sell Your Item* pages. The process begins with a first screen that asks you to choose your listing format (see Figure 7-2).

Your format options begin with the traditional auction format but also include the ability to list an item for a fixed-price sale within the auction space, similar as listing items at Half.com and eBay Store (eliminating bidding in deference to offering at a fixed sales price). Since we want to learn about traditional online auction listings, select the first radio button. Click the "Continue" button to proceed.

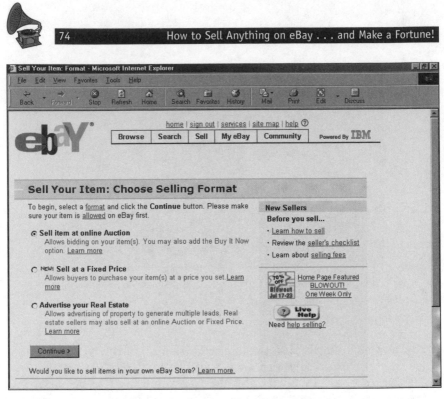

Figure 7-2 Listing an item begins with choosing a listing format.

The Perfect Category

Next, select a category header by clicking the appropriate radio button and then selecting the "Continue" button at the bottom of the screen (see Figure 7-3).

In the screen that follows, refine the category for your item as shown in Figure 7-4. Clicking on the subcategory title in each of the successive windows will allow you to zero in on the final subcategory for your item. Click the "Continue" button at the bottom of the screen to move along.

Your Title

Now it's time to create the title and enter the full description for your item. The two windows to do so are clearly labeled (see Figure 7-5). Remember, you have only 45 characters for the item title, including spaces, yet the description field is virtually limitless.

e B a y T I P : If you're handy with HTML (Hypertext Markup Language), you're free to enter your custom code within the item description window. Look in Chapter 16 for a full discussion on the best ways to utilize HTML in your listings.

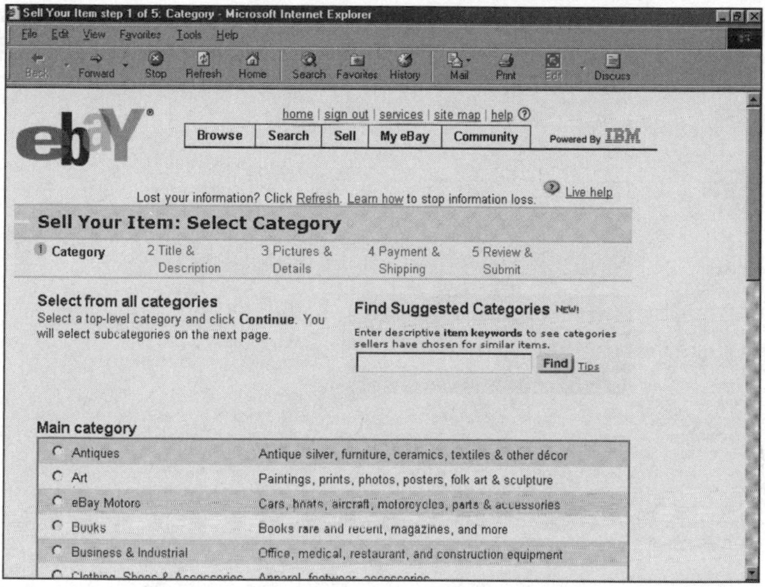

Figure 7-3   Carefully select a main category header that will best represent your item.

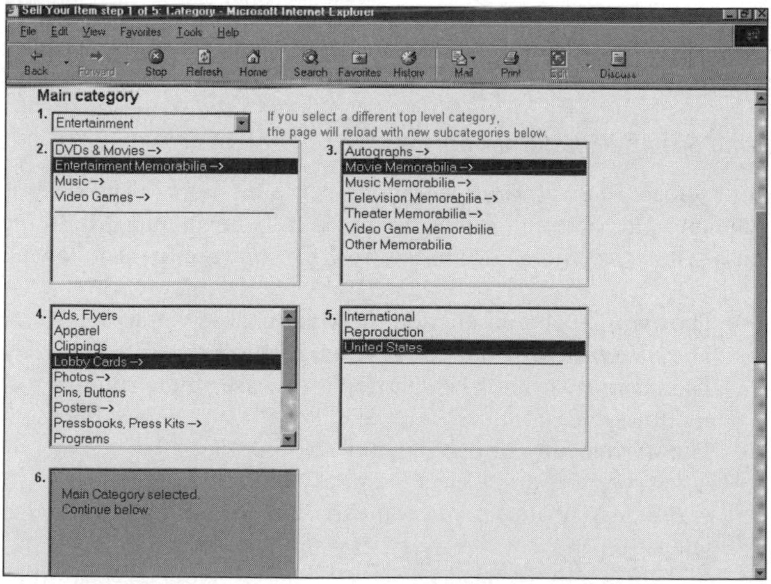

Figure 7-4   As you click in the subcategory titles in the successive windows, you'll complete the categorization process for your item.

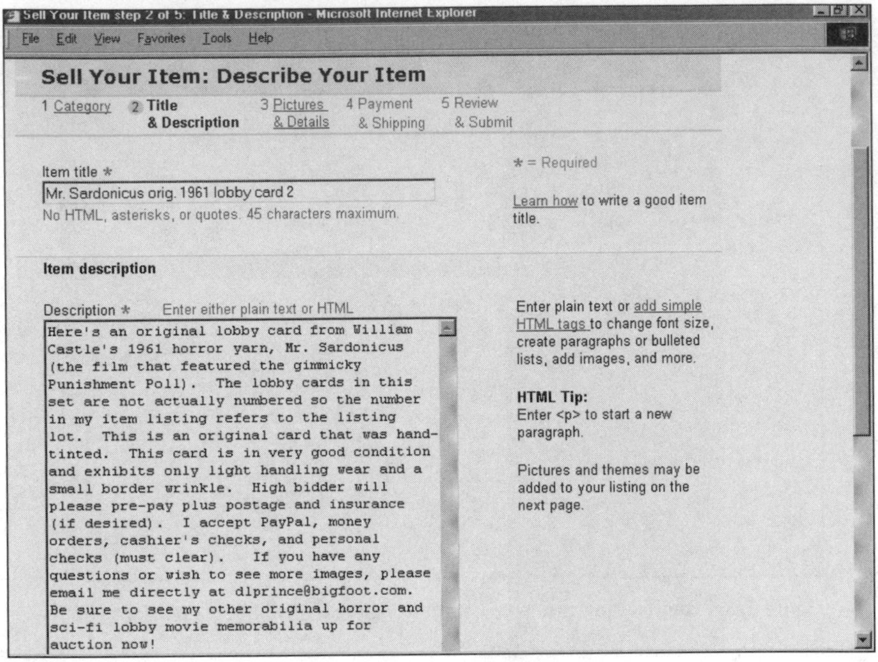

Sell Your Item step 2 of 5: Title & Description - Microsoft Internet Explorer
File Edit View Favorites Tools Help
Sell Your Item: Describe Your Item
1 Category 2 Title & Description 3 Pictures & Details 4 Payment & Shipping 5 Review & Submit
Item title *
* = Required
Mr. Sardonicus orig. 1961 lobby card 2
No HTML, asterisks, or quotes. 45 characters maximum.
Learn how to write a good item title.
Item description
Description * Enter either plain text or HTML
Here's an original lobby card from William Castle's 1961 horror yarn, Mr. Sardonicus (the film that featured the gimmicky Punishment Poll). The lobby cards in this set are not actually numbered so the number in my item listing refers to the listing lot. This is an original card that was hand-tinted. This card is in very good condition and exhibits only light handling wear and a small border wrinkle. High bidder will please pre-pay plus postage and insurance (if desired). I accept PayPal, money orders, cashier's checks, and personal checks (must clear). If you have any questions or wish to see more images, please email me directly at dlprince@bigfoot.com. Be sure to see my other original horror and sci-fi lobby movie memorabilia up for auction now!
Enter plain text or add simple HTML tags to change font size, create paragraphs or bulleted lists, add images, and more.
HTML Tip:
Enter <p> to start a new paragraph.
Pictures and themes may be added to your listing on the next page.

Figure 7-5 In the third listing screen, enter your item title and description.

Fill in the information and click the "Continue" button at the bottom of the screen.

Inserting Specific Details and Images

The next screen, *Pictures and Item Details,* gets a bit more involved (strategies do come into play here and will be discussed fully in Chapter 18). In the first section of this screen (as shown in Figure 7-6), you specify the following:

- The *duration* of your auction (how many days you wish it to run)
- The *start time* of your auction (immediate upon saving or delayed)
- The *quantity* or units being offered (in case you're running a Dutch auction)
- The *starting price* or opening bid amount
- A *reserve price,* if you elect to specify one
- A *Buy It Now* price if you want to offer the option of an immediate sale
- A checkbox to list this as a *private auction* (bidders' IDs will be visible to the seller only)

Breakdown of eBay Listing Costs

Insertion Fees: eBay charges a fee for initially listing (inserting) an item. The fee is based upon the opening bid price you designate for your item or the reserve price you might elect to specify. The general item insertion fees are as follows:

STARTING PRICE, OPENING VALUE, OR RESERVE PRICE	INSERTION FEE
$0.01–$9.99	$0.30
$10.00–$24.99	$0.55
$25.00–$49.99	$1.10
$50.00–$199.99	$2.20
$200.00 and up	$3.30

Reserve Price Fees: While the reserve price is accounted for when determining the insertion fee, there is an additional charge incurred when utilizing the reserve price feature. Unlike the insertion fee, the reserve price fee is fully refundable *if* the item successfully sells.

RESERVE PRICE	RESERVE PRICE AUCTION FEE
$0.01–$24.99	$0.50
$25.00–$199.99	$1.00
$200 and up	$2.00

Final Value Fees: This fee is levied in relation to the final selling price (high bid) of the item (this would also apply to the sales price of a Buy It Now item). The assessment of this commission is as follows:

CLOSING VALUE	FINAL VALUE FEE
$0–$25	5.25% of the closing value
$25–$1,000	5.25% of the initial $25 ($1.31), plus 2.75% of the remaining closing value balance ($25.01 to $1,000)
Over $1,000	5.25% of the initial $25 ($1.31), plus 2.75% of the initial $25 to $1000 ($26.81), plus 1.50% of the remaining closing value balance ($1000.01–closing value)

Additional Feature Fees: eBay also offers additional features during the listing process where you can "enhance" your item's appearance and placement. These upgrades are purely optional yet do incur additional fees as follows:

Listing Upgrade	Listing Upgrade Fee
Home Page Featured	$99.95
Featured Plus	$19.95
Highlight	$5.00
Bold	$2.00
Gallery	$0.25
Gallery Featured	$19.95

List in Two Categories	Double the insertion and listing upgrades fees (excluding Scheduled Listings and Home Page Featured).
10-Day Duration	$0.10
The longest listing duration available	
Scheduled Listings	$0.10
Buy It Now	$0.05
Gift Services	$0.25

Scroll down a bit to enter the details of the physical location (city, state, country) where you and your item are, then continue scrolling to specify images to accompany your item (as shown in Figure 7-7).

INSERTING PICTURES FROM YOUR COMPUTER   If you wonder whether it will be difficult to add images to your listing, fear not. When using eBay's iPIX uploading system, all you really need to do is specify the location of the image within your PC's file manager. Click on the "Browse" button to the right of the field labeled "Picture 1" to generate the pop-up window that lets you search through your computer's files until you find and choose the image you want (see Figure 7-8).

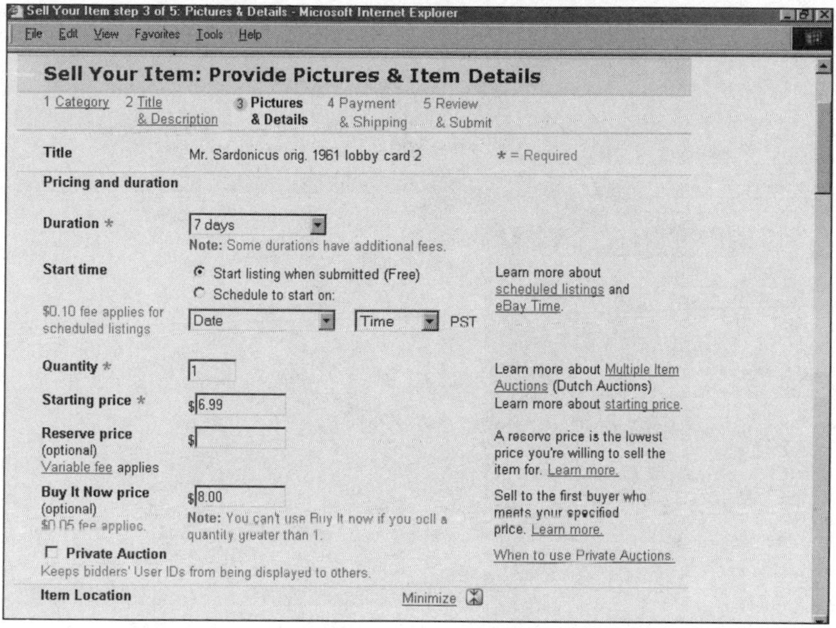

Figure 7-6 The first part of the item details screen allows you to specify time and price parameters for your auction.

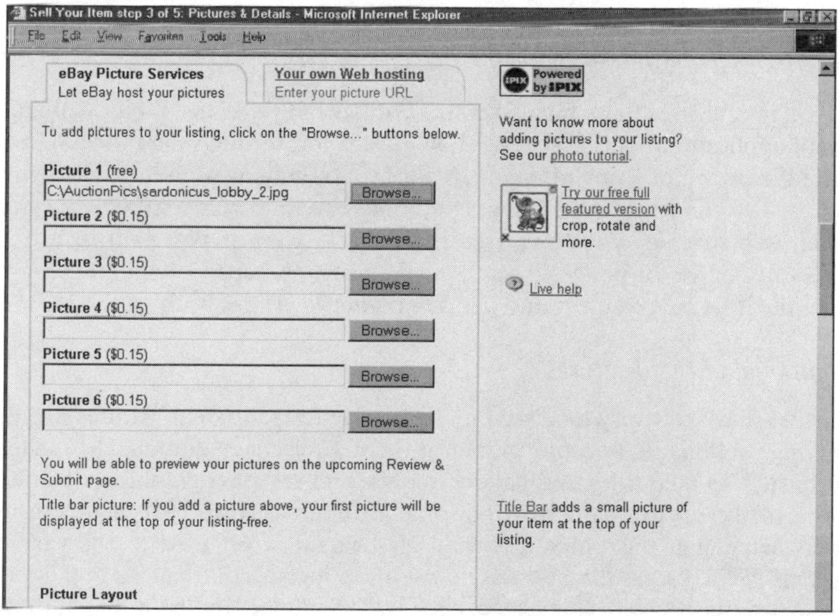

Figure 7-7 Images are critical to sales success; specify them in this portion of the listing screen.

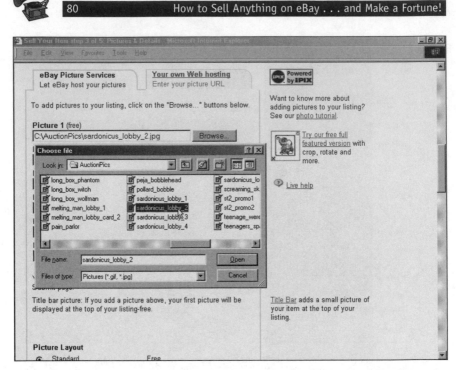

Figure 7-8   The iPIX browse function allows you to easily search your PC for the image you want to use.

Inserting Pictures from the Web

If you're utilizing eBay's image hosting tool, iPIX, you'll need to download a small application upon first use (eBay guides you through the process). You have the option of using eBay's iPIX tool to select images directly from your PC, or you can elect to use images you may have previously stored on a personal web space of your own (see Figure 7-9). Even if you plan to use an alternate source for images (your own Web site, perhaps), it's a good idea to have the iPIX tool resident and handy on your PC (I use both methods).

Additional Listing Features

Farther down this very long screen, you can select additional features for displaying your images, selecting graphical themes, selecting additional listing features such as bold titles and gallery images, and selecting graphical counters. Some of these features are free and some are not. Don't worry if all this seems overwhelming at this point. For your first sale, just get used to the various screens. We'll discuss the best way to use these item accoutrements in Chapter 16. When finished with this screen, click the "Continue" button at the bottom.

    The next screen is where you select the payment methods you'll accept, designate who'll be responsible for shipping costs, and insert any additional

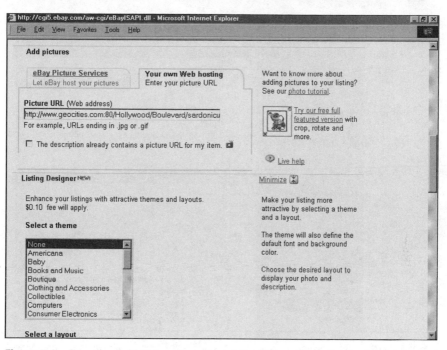

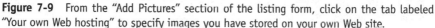

Figure 7-9 From the "Add Pictures" section of the listing form, click on the tab labeled "Your own Web hosting" to specify images you have stored on your own Web site.

shipping instructions you'd like displayed with your listing (see Figure 7-10). For more information on these different methods, see Chapter 9. Click "Continue" to proceed.

At last, it's time to preview your listing. Carefully reread your item title and description; be sure your image(s) display properly; and review the various other listing conditions and features you have specified.

Be sure to scroll down to the bottom of the screen and review the insertion fees that will be charged when you list the item. This is where individual listing fees for your selections of starting price, reserve or Buy It Now prices, additional iPIX images, and special features are tallied (Chapter 26 will help you sift through these fees to control your final costs). If you're not satisfied with what you see, use the active links across the top of the listing page to navigate back to the previous screens to make necessary adjustments. If all looks well, click the "Submit Listing" button at the bottom of the screen to launch your auction. Upon doing so, eBay will provide you a new screen that contains an active link to your item page (see Figure 7-11).

With your listing submitted, the auction clock is now ticking. Upon selecting the link shown in Figure 7-11, you can jump to the page that bidders will soon be reviewing (see Figure 7-12).

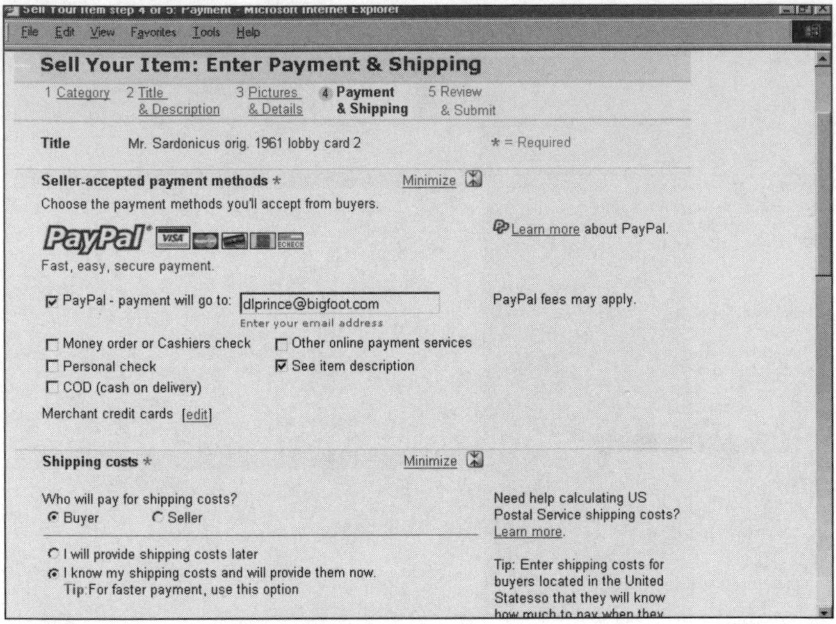

Figure 7-10   Using the various radio buttons and text boxes, establish your preferences for payment method and shipping instructions.

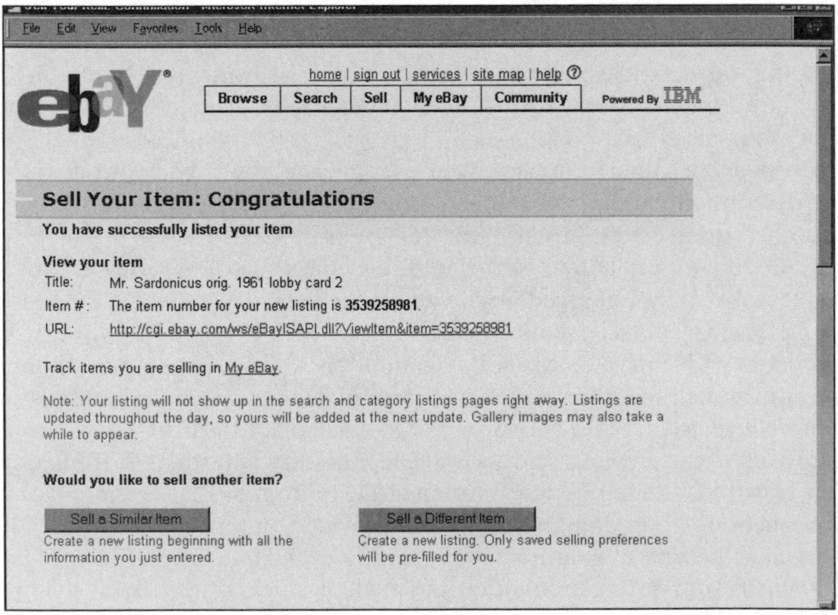

Figure 7-11   Your listing is live! Follow the text link to view the actual listing page.

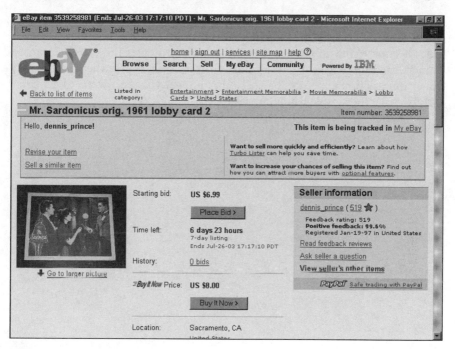

Figure 7-12   Your official item listing page.

eBay TIP: Although your auction is immediately active, it won't appear on search results right away. Results pages are updated about once every hour at eBay but soon you'll be able to search on a keyword and your item will show up in the search results. However, you will be able to find your item immediately if you (or your customers) search for items by your User ID; that always lists every item you have available the moment the listings are submitted.

eBay will send a confirmation e-mail message to notify you of your successful listing. As simple as that, you're off and selling.

BEFORE YOU LIST AGAIN

Chances are, seeing your item listed on eBay will motivate you to run off and find another of your treasures to offer up; that's the spirit! Before you grab some more goods to offer, take time to read through the next several chapters so you'll have a greater understanding for presenting yourself as a seller in the eBay realm. With matters of online payment, sales policies, and pricing considerations understood, you can successfully tinker with listing more items for bid. Of course, the subtle nuances and selling strategies the pros use can be found within the pages of Parts 3 and 4 of this book; that's where you'll truly hone your auction expertise. For now, though, get your feet wet and get comfortable with the simple listing process.

8

Understanding Online Payment

When talking about fortunes, you're talking about money. The great prices you earn in your auction exploits are only as good as your ability to actually *collect* the cash in the end. Although you've likely considered the venerable payment vehicles—money orders, cashier's checks, personal checks, and cash—dealing in the online realm practically requires you to become adept in these ways of online payment. In this chapter you'll learn what online payment is, where and how it's managed, and how it can gain you even higher prices to help you amass your fortune.

THE FEAR FACTOR: IS ONLINE PAYMENT SAFE?

If registering at eBay gave you reason to pause, leaving you uncertain whether it would be safe to provide sensitive credit card and bank account information online, the consideration of sending and receiving actual funds through cyberspace, not to mention having to again surrender personal finance account information, likely causes you great concern. However, take comfort in the fact that online payment services, a budding and sometimes bumbling cottage industry of a few years ago, have quickly evolved into a secure and increasingly preferred method for managing payment transactions. The payment sites have implemented additional customer safeguards and protections against unauthorized or otherwise illicit account tampering. And each site provides different levels of protection to put your mind at ease.

Likewise, your financial institution probably has also evolved in matters of online payment and has responded to your needs (and anxieties) for managing account-funded cyber-purchases. Most credit card issuers and personal bank account managers offer protections to their customers should something go amiss in an online transaction. Here again, check with your issuer and other financial institutions to be clear about their safeguards and your responsibilities as an account owner. The bottom line, though, is that millions of online transactions are carried out every day, the vast majority being completed as easily as those at your local department store.

THE HOW'S AND WHY'S OF ONLINE PAYMENT

Experienced bidders and other online buyers have found online payment is the fastest and arguably the easiest method to quickly pay for a variety of goods, at eBay and other venues. As easy as sending an e-mail message, online payments can be made in a few simple steps:

1. The buyer establishes an account with an online payment provider.
2. The seller, also with an active online payment account, indicates the User ID to which payment is to be forwarded (separate from an eBay User ID).
3. The buyer posts the agreed-upon payment amount and is provided verification of the seller's account that will receive funds.
4. Payment is posted to the seller's account, deducted from the buyer's account, and a notification of the transaction is provided via e-mail to both parties.

Thanks to online payment services, an auction transaction can be completed in a matter of minutes, with many buyers and sellers indicating they've been able to close the postauction deal in less than 30 minutes.

But is time of such importance in completing an online transaction? Can't the sending of a traditional *snail-mail* payment still suffice? Actually, traditional payment methods, as previously mentioned, are just as viable today as ever. Nevertheless, going hand in hand with the speed of the Internet and the access to vast goods and services at the click of a mouse, fast online payment simply makes sense and offers a truly integrated approach to selecting, purchasing, and paying for goods, all from the same computer.

eBay TIP: When dealing online, a speedy transaction is usually the best transaction. The seller is able to quickly receive payment, thus developing trust in the buyer, via online payment. The buyer is likewise able to receive goods quicker, thereby gaining confidence in the seller and in the entire online bidding and buying experience. And both parties are able to complete the transaction quickly, which spells success for all involved.

The most compelling advantage of online payment services, though, is that most enable buyers and sellers to transact via credit card. Without the cost and complexity of establishing a traditional merchant account, sellers can advertise acceptance of credit card purchase via an online payment venue. Likewise, buyers, no longer limited to funds in their checking or saving accounts alone, can manage their purchases via use of a credit card. For both parties, online payment serves as another convenient option in managing online business transactions.

WHO'S WHO IN ONLINE PAYMENT SERVICES?

Where do you go when you want to sign up to utilize online payment? Actually, there are numerous sites and services available online today, but to free you from hours of analysis and cross-comparison, here are the major players you'll encounter.

PayPal (www.paypal.com)

By and large, PayPal.com (Figure 8-1) is the biggest player in the online payment arena. Like eBay itself, PayPal arrived on the scene early (in October 1999) and gained fast brand and service recognition. Many other sites have come and gone but PayPal has stood fast. The site, boasting a registered user base of more than 16 million, was so successful it even supplanted eBay's former Billpoint payment site. In an about-face, eBay acquired PayPal for $1.5 billion in October 2002, making it a truly integrated tool in the eBay experience. PayPal is free for buyers and charges a sales commission to sellers (30 cents plus 2.2 to 2.9 percent of the total value per payment received), deducted from the amount of payment received. Account activation can be accomplished in a matter of minutes. Business and Premiere accounts are available to sellers, at a monthly fee, that give access to automated e-mail tools, an invoicing system, inventory management, and more. PayPal also enables transactions to 39 different countries and allows payment for both auction goods and nonauction-related goods and services.

Yahoo PayDirect (paydirect.yahoo.com)

Another of the suite of business and consumer tools offered by the online portal giant Yahoo, PayDirect (Figure 8-2) supports online payment activities. Unfortunately, the services fall dreadfully short of those offered by PayPal. PayDirect only supports transactions within the United States, charges a use fee to both buyers and sellers, and delays account activation until a snail-mail confirmation is received by the registrar.

BidPay (www.bidpay.com)

In a new twist on an old transaction, BidPay came along several years ago and allows buyers to purchase and forward actual money orders to sellers. Backed by Western Union, the long-recognized name in fund transfers, BidPay allows buyers to purchase money orders online using a credit or debit card (brick-and-mortar institutions typically accept only debit cards or cash). Sellers (recipients) need not be registered with BidPay to receive payment as

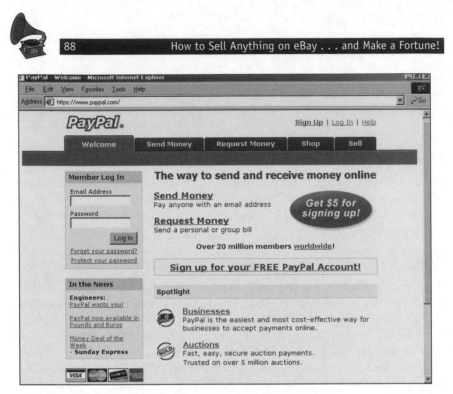

Figure 8-1   PayPal is the front-runner in the online payment race.

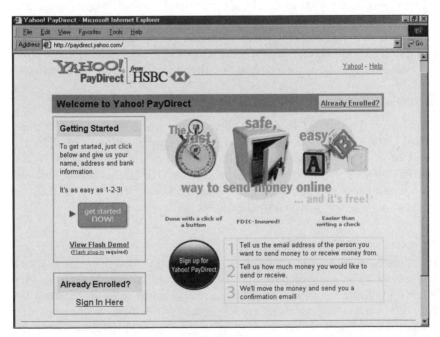

Figure 8-2   Yahoo's PayDirect is second in the running for preferred online payment services.

the money order is printed and forwarded to the seller's snail-mail address. The delay of awaiting receipt of the money order has also been eradicated; sellers are notified via official e-mail when a money order purchase has been approved and is in transit, instilling confidence so the item can be safely shipped prior to the actual money order being in-hand.

eBay TIP: Notice that using BidPay serves as a suitable compromise between the fast payment available via online payment methods without the need to offer credit card or bank account information to a relative newcomer like PayPal. While PayPal is genuinely secure for transactions, some buyers feel even more at ease dealing with long-time financial enabler Western Union.

International sales are also easily managed as BidPay delivers to countries outside of the United States. As with traditional money orders, the buyer pays a fee for the service and can also elect to pay additional fees for quicker delivery to the seller.

Escrow Services (www.escrow.com)

Another new service to spring forth from the evolution of online auctions and other forms of e-commerce is online escrow. Like a traditional escrow account, online escrow accounts serve to confirm and hold a buyer's payment, prompting a seller to send the item purchased. The buyer, upon receipt of the item, confirms delivery and satisfaction, thus prompting release of funds to the seller. If the buyer is dissatisfied, the funds in escrow are held until the seller confirms receipt of the returned item. If the buyer fails to even confirm item receipt, funds will be released to the seller within three days of the tracked delivery confirmation (per the package carrier's records). Escrow is typically expensive as it's generally used for high-value purchases (greater than $500). Buyers and sellers can negotiate who will pay the escrow fees or can agree to split the cost. Escrow.com (*www.escrow.com*) is recommended for use with eBay. The site also lists several other escrow sites for use outside of the United States.

Online Merchant Accounts

Although you may have your sights set initially on eBay activities alone, there may come the time when you endeavor to go beyond the auction space to further bolster your fortune-making opportunities. If you decide to create an online store or other such commercial Web site, you'll be glad to know that traditional merchant accounts are available online as well. If you keep your business restricted to the virtual storefront, you needn't bother with a credit card terminal or clunky charge plate. Instead, online merchant accounts are usually accompanied with online "shopping cart" solutions, enabling shoppers to select items from your inventory, carry them in a virtual cart, and check out by paying via a credit or debit card. Again, this is probably a consideration you'll want to defer until a bit farther down the road. For now, just be aware the option is available if and when you decide to expand your online horizons.

THE FORTUNE FACTOR: IF YOU OFFER IT, THEY WILL PAY (MORE!)

The original question still persists: if checks and money orders are still suitable and acceptable, why bother with online payment? It's a good question that evokes several good answers. Consider these reasons why online payment is something you should embrace, especially when you're the seller.

- It fits the bill. In the early days of online auctions and cyber-shopping, it seemed clumsy to utilize the speed and convenience of online buying, only to be relegated to the comparatively ancient process of actually *mailing* payment and waiting for checks to clear. Integration is what it's all about, and online payment fits seamlessly into this new way of doing business.
- More options draw more customers. As you will learn in Chapter 9, when it comes time to create a sales policy, bidders and buyers crave options and alternatives. Specifically, the more choices you offer customers regarding terms of payment (especially the cutting edge of online payment), the better your ability to encourage more business to your online offerings. Buyers love choices.
- Buyer profiling has concluded that consumers tend to spend more money when they can shop on credit. Since online payment services enable you to accept credit card payment, you stand a greater chance of earning higher prices for your goods. The best part of all: online payment services make the whole transaction transparent to you, ridding you of the cost and coordination of maintaining an actual merchant account of your own.
- Online payment services are adaptable to your business. As they service all manner of transactions, auction or otherwise, online payment can support all of your business transactions no matter where or when you sell goods or services.

9

Developing a Successful Sales Policy

At eBay, a seller's policies serve as the roadmap to the transaction to come. The sales terms and conditions you establish drive your customers' expectations and enable a smooth and successful transaction. Bidders and buyers typically look for clear and comprehensive sales policies when they consider bidding on items, and they seek out sellers who demonstrate their good business sense through sound and satisfactory transaction guidelines. Before jumping too deep into selling, ensure that you have a comprehensive and well-represented sales policy to help guide you and your customers through the actual exchanges to come.

THE RULES TO THE RICHES

Start by understanding what terms and conditions you want to have stated up front, keeping in mind that these are the guidelines buyers use to decide whether they'll bid on or buy your goods. Your listing should have clear and complete coverage of the different aspects of a sales policy to encourage more business at your virtual doorstep. This chapter discusses which policies will bring you the most success and make your transactions easy for both you and the buyer.

Defining Payment Methods

It all starts with the money, and your buyers will be looking for the most secure yet convenient ways to settle up (as are you). Remember, the more options you can provide, the more likely you are to attract buyers of all dispositions. At a minimum, consider offering the following payment methods:

- *Online Payment.*   Based on the discussion in Chapter 8, this should be first and foremost in your policy. You not only enable buyers to pay with their credit cards, you also offer the ability to pay quickly, they get their goods faster, and you get your cash quicker.
- *Money Orders and Cashier's Checks.*   A close second to online payment, these allow buyers quicker receipt of their goods since, once received, the seller knows this is as good as cash. If you accept money orders and cashier's checks, offer to ship immediately upon receipt of payment. And, don't forget about BidPay; you can ship within minutes of the buyer purchasing the online money order thanks to Bid-Pay's confirmation e-mail notification.
- *Personal Checks.*   Some buyers still prefer to whip out their checkbook and scribble out the payment. Cheerfully accept personal checks but make it obvious that the check will need to clear your bank before goods will be shipped. If you have a repeat customer who has successfully paid via personal check in the past, consider waiving the waiting period (a nice little touch that promotes trust and entices follow-up transactions).
- *Escrow.*   Again, this is one of the costliest methods and should typically be reserved for high-value transactions (at least greater than $500) and the buyer and seller need to agree upon who will pay the fees. It's a good idea to be open to utilizing online escrow if the buyer seems especially intent on it; the seller has the option to require the buyer to pay the entire escrow fee if, in the seller's estimation, the exchange could be managed simply and securely via a lower-cost alternative.

Don't expect to utilize COD (Cash On Delivery) much if at all, and try to steer your customers away from cash transactions as the money cannot be tracked or otherwise accounted for.

Payment Remittance Policies

You've been good to offer a variety of payment methods but don't forget to likewise establish *when* you expect to receive the funds. Some buyers will dally a bit or outright forget to pay unless they're prodded up front. There's nothing clever or mysterious about this condition: state that payment must be received within seven days from the close of the auction. Unless you intend to offer some sort of layaway service, you have every right to expect payment quickly. Typically, this isn't an issue as the majority of buyers are eager to collect their winnings. As pre-payment is the norm in online auctioning, the sooner they pay, the sooner you can ship their item. Just provide the boundary for when you expect to be compensated and explain that their high-bidder status could rightfully be revoked and the item offered to the next-highest bidder or relisted for another go-around.

Shipping and Handling Costs

Knowing that shipping and handling fees are sometimes the source of price-hiking attempts, buyers can be a bit skittish about what they'll be expected to pay to get their item from your hands into their own. Be clear and *honest* in quoting these charges, making absolutely sure you've stated your shipping and handling policy before bids are placed. You actually have a few choices to make:

- *Charge the exact shipping fee.*   This is generally the most desirable method from the buyer's perspective, yet it can be a bit cumbersome to the seller, who might not know what the fee is until the package is sent on its way. By that time, the buyer has either charged too little or too much for shipping costs. Of course, if you're selling similar items on a consistent basis, you'll likely be able to anticipate the exact postage amount or you can employ the use of a postal scale to help you in times of doubt.
- *Charge a flat fee.*   Many volume sellers are turning to this method. The key to being successful in levying a flat fee is to charge a cost that's within 50 cents (high or low) of the actual shipping costs. Remember, it's considered a scam if the seller charges $6.00 for an item that cost $3 or less to actually ship.
- *Offer various shipping methods.*   Options entice, and your buyers should be given a couple of alternatives when it comes to shipping, too. It's fine to state that your default method is USPS Priority Mail or UPS Ground—but also offer faster shipping to anxious buyers or those who need their item fast. Both of the carriers just mentioned have express delivery services available, and if overnight delivery is critical, consider providing FedEx or DHL delivery. Of course, you'll want to pass these added costs on to the buyer.

There is a sensitive area in the realm of shipping costs: *handling* fees. There's an ongoing debate over whether sellers should charge for their time to prepare, pack, and ship items. This is purely a personal choice, yet if you decide you will charge handling fees, be sure to clearly state those costs in your sales policy. If not, you risk being accused of the infamous Scam No. 5 (see Chapter 6).

eBay TIP: To avoid controversy when starting out, I suggest that you forego the "handling fees" and equate that time and effort as part of the cost of doing business. Instead of charging for this time spent, look for ways to make your end-of-auction routine faster and more efficient.

Insurance and Tracking

If you're shipping by UPS or USPS Express Mail, tracking and insurance are usually covered in the cost of delivery. However, for basic delivery, insurance and package tracking involve additional costs. Always offer the option for your buyer to purchase these services—yet be clear that if such insurance and tracking is declined, the *buyer* will bear the risk if something goes awry in transit. Most packages arrive at their final destinations just fine, but in that odd instance where something does go wrong, be sure you and your buyer are clear about who absorbs the unfortunate fallout.

Delivery Expectations

Buyers need to be shown that not all the onus is on them in terms of package delivery. A good policy will include information regarding when items will be shipped. If you can ship immediately upon payment confirmation, say so in your policy. If you can only ship on Mondays and Thursdays, be clear about that. Understand that buyers are taking the initial risk of prepaying for their winnings; ease their concerns by including shipment and delivery expectations within the body of your sales policy.

Refunds and Guarantees

There's not much debate here: you either support a "100 percent satisfaction guarantee with no questions asked" or you don't. Actually, there is some middle ground to be found when it comes to refunds and guarantees, but your first challenge is to decide whether you're willing to take back an item after it's been sold. If you're completely confident in your items and feel it best to offer total satisfaction (which includes absorbing the cost of buyer flubs and fibs), then proudly state you'll honor all returns. However, you can be just as successful if you provide *conditional* refunds. You can state that if the item received is not as advertised, you'll gladly accept a return. It's OK to stipulate that all returns are subject to inspection and verification (recalling Scam No. 10 from Chapter 6). It's likewise your prerogative to state that all sales are final (which is especially applicable for the sale of items easily duplicated such as music and video). You may need to experiment a bit with this portion of your policy but it's most prudent to begin with the conditional return at the outset.

SUMMING IT ALL UP

To wrap it all up, consider whether you might include either of these examples of a sales policy in your item descriptions (see the second paragraph of the item descriptions in Figures 9-1 and 9-2).

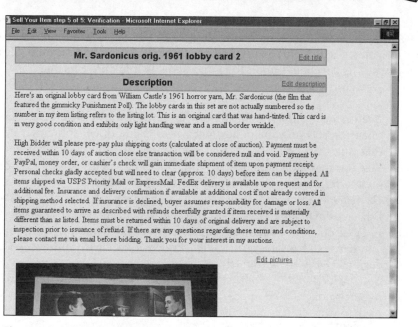

Figure 9-1   The policy spelled out here specifies full details, including an explanation of how returns will be handled.

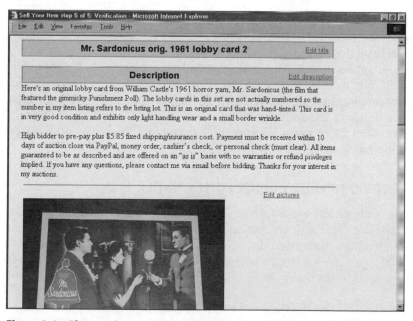

Figure 9-2   If your sales are to be made on an "as is" basis, this policy states that clearly, yet remains friendly as well as forthcoming.

Of course, you're free to adjust the terms shown in these examples to best suit your needs; these are merely templates (though actively in use) to help get you started. Note the intangibles, though: the success of your sales policy is just as dependent upon tone and style as it is on terms and conditions. As you craft your own policy, take these considerations to heart:

- *Be exhaustive but not exhausting.* Be certain you've covered all pertinent aspects of your policy, but avoid laying down so many rules that your sales policy winds up feeling more like an ironclad contract than a transaction guideline. If your policy comes off as too rigid or dictatorial, you might unwittingly drive away bidders.
- *Be customer-oriented.* The goal of your policy is not only to establish a roadmap for your transactions but also to encourage customers to buy from you. Therefore, remember to offer as many options and alternatives as is practical. Offer services that clearly protect your customers as well as yourself.
- *Say it with a smile.* Some sellers become "tone deaf" when presenting their policies, and appear stolid or overbearing. Read your policy back to yourself (or read it to a friend) and determine if it sounds relatively friendly in its delivery.

POSTING YOUR POLICY

With your policy ready to go, make sure to post it plainly for all bidders and future buyers to see. The easiest method of posting your policy is to include it in the body of your item descriptions. If you later decide you want to improve the visual appearance of your policy, consider utilizing HTML code in your item descriptions (see Chapter 16) to offset the text; present it in a different (slightly smaller) font; or enable an offsite link to your own Web page. However you decide to present it, be sure it's always available and easy to find. Go the extra step by encouraging potential customers to contact you directly *before* bidding if they have any questions, concerns, or doubts.

WHAT TO DO IF YOUR POLICY COMES UNDER FIRE

Whether truly sincere or sometimes sincerely belligerent, occasionally bidders and buyers will question your sales policy and may seek to coerce you into bending the rules. Being flexible is always a good idea, but if you simply cannot alter your methods or you take offense to a customer's *extreme* requests, here are some of the best ways to respond:

- Refer to and restate your sales policy as it appeared in your item listing; the bidder essentially agreed to these terms upon placing a bid, provided no other agreements were made with you in advance.

- Explain that your volume of business doesn't lend itself to making special arrangements of the sort requested and that your policy is constructed to offer a reasonable range of terms. Be comfortable in standing by your policy as stated.
- Ask the customer *why* special arrangements outside of your stated policy are necessary.
- If the customer remains insistent or proclaims dissatisfaction, offer to cancel the high bid and offer the item to the next bidder, or relist it. The customer will be faced with deciding if their need for special treatment is more important than acquiring the item won.
- *Give the special request thoughtful consideration.* This might be a legitimate and reasonable request and could well be an area where your policy could stand refining.

This final point is key in determining the effectiveness of your policy and its ability to encourage business. Always look for ways to improve how your business will operate and how you can best serve your customers. Remember that your sales policy exists to *enable* easy transactions, not hinder them. Keep an open mind to refinement and you'll be on track to continually improve your potential to acquire your fortunes faster.

10

Determining the Value of Your Goods

One of your greatest challenges as a seller is determining with confidence the value of the items you wish to offer. These days, everyone is looking for a deal, a steal, and items with unparalleled appeal. Sure, you've been told to "buy low, sell high," but is it really possible to sustain an existence in such a merchandising Nirvana? It's true that once or twice you can haul in a mint on a well-timed (or downright fortuitous) listing, but the fact is you won't find your auction fortune overnight, and not everything of yours that glitters will become gold. The task, then, is to determine how to run the marathon—not the short-lived sprint—on the track to your auction fortune. The method by which you determine the value of the items you hope to sell will position you for a glorious finish or a quick exit. It's all in how you price your goods.

THE POPULARITY OF eBAY

If you knew anyone who was vigorously selling at eBay between 1996 and 1998, you saw an individual gleeful and giddy, inebriated by his or her good fortune to be realizing astounding prices for the strangest of goods. The emerging opportunity of selling online, largely fueled by the astronomical success of eBay, created enough buzz to coax people to get online for the first time for the sole intention of bidding and winning. The novelty of online auctioning, coupled with the fact that previously elusive items were springing out of closets, attics, and local shops and onto the global online market fed the overnight success of online merchandising. As if intoxicated by the allure of the online treasure trove, buyers feverishly and often capriciously paid above-market prices for the goods they found. Whether relieved to simply find a long-sought-after artifact or entranced by the bid-and-win experience, buyers were happily *overpaying* for items in the fresh new auction place. Sellers savvy enough to jump onto this gravy train early were delighted to see their profits soar like never before. Of course, once word gets out about such an oasis, it's only a matter of time before it becomes an overcrowded tourist trap that sees its once-lofty status reduced to that of a commonplace attraction. That's what happened at eBay; once the novelty wore off a bit, and as soon as the die-hard buyers and collectors had scooped up their cherished acquisitions, the market cooled and so did the prices. The reality check, then, is to come to eBay with a level head and a well-founded education of the prices this "perfect market" will now bear.

eBay TIP: Don't misunderstand me—there are plenty of opportunities to strike it rich quickly, yet the staying power of such an income influx is difficult to predict or prolong. When the national and global economies sputter, prices fall; expect that. Interestingly, though, prices have never truly bottomed out at eBay, especially in the realm of collectibles and pop-culture curiosities; the "boomer" and "tweener" generations hold such items in high regard and are willing to continue paying well for those items that rekindle memories of simpler days gone by. There's plenty of water yet in this well.

FINDING THE RIGHT STUFF TO SELL

Before you can consider the value of the goods you'll sell, you need to determine which goods will bear the sort of value that propels your profit potential. For starters, you'll need to identify those sorts of goods that will sell at the profit margins that will support your income goals. As this book's title promises, you *can* sell practically anything at eBay these days (and, of course, make a fortune doing it). So what sells? Here's a high-level list of the sorts of items that consistently sell well in the virtual auction space:

- *Antiques.* The most venerable goods around are those that have been around for some time. These trade hands daily—furniture, artwork, tools, simple appliances, statuary, and more. While the official definition of an antique is "something that's at least 100 years old," there are plenty of "vintage" goods that are as young as 20 to 30 years old and which command good prices day in and day out. If you have this sort of stock—plenty of it—or have access to such goods, you're on the fast path to fortune.
- *China, Silverware, and Glassware.* Check your buffet, china cabinet, and anywhere that dishes, glass, and serving utensils may be stored up. Perhaps you aren't particularly thrilled with the looks of this out-

dated serving ware, but the auction market would likely break down your door if they knew you had it.

- *Advertising, Premiums, and Promotional Items.* Whether you saved up trading stamps or clipped box tops, those items you sent away for or were given as courtesy samples are real gold in today's nostalgic culture. Gas station giveaways, fast-food toys, and more continue to stay high on buyers' lists of most-wanted items.

- *Old Product Packaging.* It's no longer Prince Albert in a can that draws the attention of collectors worldwide. Collectors and speculators are paying handsomely for just about anything we once called garbage. Vintage milk cartons, cereal boxes, even TV dinner trays are hot commodities if they've been around 30 years or more. The trick to the big dollars here is to have the stuff in stellar condition.

- *Anything in Grandma's Attic or the Kid's Room.* That stuff that's been sitting in boxes since the late '60s and early '70s is pure treasure in today's retro market. While Grandma's stuff that dates back 50 years or more could be worth significantly more, it's now those of the Nixon and Ford generation who are eagerly seeking out the reminders of *their* old days.

Don't limit yourself to just these sorts of items, though. It's true that practically everything and anything is desirable to someone, somewhere. If you're not certain about that whatever-it-is that you're ready to throw away, run a quick search on eBay's current and recently closed auctions to see if people are bidding for this stuff. More often than not, you'll find your goods are in demand and you'll quickly discover which items you'll want to focus your attention upon as you discover their value.

SO WHAT'S IT WORTH?

The old adage applies: nothing is worth anything until two people want it. Your task is to determine what price will cause at least two bidders to tussle for ownership of your item. After having reviewed current and past auctions, you're likely developing an idea of what sort of price an item commands, but here are some other considerations to ponder to help you decide on a value that will be shared by your potential customers:

- *Supply and Demand.* Always, the value of your goods is determined at the time they sell by these two inescapable economic drivers. If supply is high, the value may be lower than you'd like unless demand is likewise high. If supply is low, the value can quickly climb unless there's simply little demand for what you're offering. Remember, supply and demand are the two factions that enable an accurate "current market value" for any item.

- *Condition and Completeness.* No matter how rare an item, no matter how many folks are clamoring for it, the condition of your goods will play a key role in determining its value. Your job here is to assess your item as compared to others like it that have recently sold. If your item is in lesser condition or is incomplete when compared to another similar item, expect the value to be lesser as well. However, if your item is in better condition than those that have been sold before it, expect the value to increase, sometimes markedly, especially if yours is in a condition rarely found in the marketplace.

- *Time Sensitivity and Seasonal Appeal.* This will be an aspect you'll consider later in your selling strategies. For now, just know that certain items that have strong appeal during specific times of the year will likely not gain maximum price potential if you attempt to sell them off-season.

- *Presentation and Positioning.* Again, this is an aspect to be discussed more fully when we examine applying a sales strategy, but understand at this point that *when* and *how* you present an item can directly influence its money-making potential. As you research other similar items that have sold (and those that didn't), look for differentiators that may have affected the item's value and see how those factors could play in your item's favor or against it as you assess its price potential.

WHERE ELSE CAN YOU TURN FOR VALUATION ADVICE?

If you're still somewhat stumped about the potential value of an item you have, here are some other resources you can tap to better determine whether what you have is trash or treasure:

- *Talk with other sellers.* Most merchants you'll encounter at eBay are generally quite friendly and forthcoming. The days of closely guarded sales secrets are pretty much gone, so many of the 14 million eBay users have summarily "seen that, done that, sold that item." Politely inquire of other sellers regarding their opinions about what you might offer, especially if it seems particularly obscure. I've yet to meet a seller who *didn't* have an opinion of the value of some item.

- *Consult price guides.* Most items, especially collectible fare, have been well catalogued and documented in one sort of price guide or another. Take heed, though, that price guides are just that: guides. Carefully read the author's grading policy (his assessment of an item's condition and how that is factored into the suggested value) to make sure you're clear how the value was derived. Make value adjustments as appropriate based on, again, the condition and completeness of the item you have to sell. Also take note of the date of publication of the guide; the market has likely changed and the value of the items described could have changed since the guide was written or printed.

- *Investigate the value of related items.* If you're having trouble finding another item just like yours, look for a close cousin to that obscure artifact in front of you. Search for items of the same time period, of the same manufacturer, and of the same or similar style. Much the way anthropologists assess the origin of their latest diggings, you might similarly need to do a bit of digging to identify what you have and what it might be worth.

WHAT IS IT WORTH TO YOU?

In the end, the ultimate value of any item is always determined by its current owner. Some sellers will hold out for months and years, insistent their goods are worth far more than any of the uneducated would-be buyers have yet to offer. Others turn treasures over for a pittance, happy to simply rid themselves of the burden of ownership. At this point, you'll need to do a bit of soul searching for yourself to decide what *you* feel the item is worth and what *you* consider a reasonable minimum selling price. To help you with this effort of personal valuation, think about the following:

- *Are you in distress or disillusionment?* If you simply need to get rid of an item or items quickly (emptying a storage unit, emerging from a divorce, or whatever), you'll probably be glad to get a few bucks and get the items out of your sight. You'll probably be satisfied with less in price and should consider this as you determine what it's worth to be rid of the stuff.
- *How much do you have invested in the item?* If you paid through the nose in hopes the value of an item would appreciate, you'll need to consider whether you can recover on your investment and how much opportunity you have to garner a profit in the current market. If prices are down, you might need to hold on to the item until the market rebounds. If, however, you need to cut your losses and recoup something, you'll want to take that into consideration as you look to get what you can.
- *How badly do you need the income today?* If you need quick cash, you'll be better served to make a fast nickel than wait for a slow dime. Often, this is the key reason some sellers "blow out" their merchandise. Whether they're getting out of the business or need quick cash to invest elsewhere, the need for funds has direct impact on how an item is valued by the seller.

- *How realistic are your expectations?*   This goes back to the reality check and requires you make an honest and well informed assessment on what your item is truly worth and not what you *wish* it was worth. Yesterday's gone and tomorrow's promise hasn't yet come to pass; don't dream about the prices that once were or those that you're sure are just around the corner. If you can afford to wait, by all means do so but make sure you're reasonable in your aspirations.

Take heart in the fact that even lesser valued items can pay off quite handsomely. Think of it this way: if ever you've seen those seemingly insignificant ATM purchases—a mere $14, $22, and such—add up to a bundle before you realized it, recognize that income can add up just as quickly. Suddenly, the comparative nickels and dimes you could earn in volume sales can accumulate quite quickly and deliver some tidy sums. Sure, you'll hit a home run from time to time, but few make their fortunes overnight. It's an endurance race and if you'll value your items accurately and reasonably, you'll be in perfect position to bring in a steady stream of sales. Add a bit of sales strategy to the mix (covered in depth in Chapter 18), and you'll see that you don't necessarily need gold to cash in at eBay.

11

Closing the Deal

When the auction ends, it's time for you to leap into action. Some new sellers harbor a certain anxiety over making contact with and collecting payment from virtual strangers, while others jump in too forcefully to exact their due. In reality, collecting payment and closing an auction deal need not be worrisome nor require a brash affront to ensure the transaction comes to fruition. A well-thought-out and skillfully executed end-of-auction routine is all that's needed to bring the sale to a close professionally, peacefully, and pleasantly.

PROMPT ACTION PROMPTS BUYERS TO ACT

Your first task is to set the stage for a fast, efficient, and satisfactory transaction. Your buyer, whether a seasoned user or a newbie to eBay, will look to you for guidance and direction. When you snap to attention as your auction closes, you'll establish the mood for the deal and can instill immediate confidence and responsiveness in the winning bidder. Most important, your fast action will encourage receipt of a prompt payment.

At the close of your auction, eBay will send an automated e-mail message to both you and your winning bidder (see Figure 11-1). The message serves not only as notification that the auction has ended but that now it's time for the buyer and seller to make arrangements for the exchange.

While it's perfectly acceptable to await eBay's official notification of the auction's close, it's likewise just as acceptable to initiate contact with the high bidder before eBay's automated message arrives (sometimes taking several hours to a day to be received). Again, a fast transaction is the best course for a smooth exchange. Here's why:

- Your quick action shows your buyer that you're well-organized and ready to complete the deal.

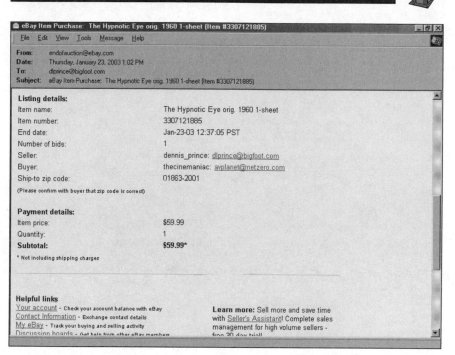

Figure 11-1 At the auction's close, eBay will forward an end-of-auction notification like this one.

- You catch the high bidder while he or she is still "high" on the win and motivated to receive the item they've just won.
- You'll typically be paid quicker.
- Your fast and customer-oriented action will likely gain you praise in the form of positive feedback in eBay's Feedback Forum.

THE END-OF-AUCTION E-MAIL

Another way to smooth the transaction is to develop your own end-of-auction (EOA) notification that you send directly to every high bidder/buyer. A fast notification is good but is only as effective as the manner in which you communicate. Look at Figure 11-2 for an example of how you can craft your end-of-auction message.

Notice the tone of the EOA message in Figure 11-2: it's simple, direct, and friendly. The pertinent information is present—the item number, the item title, the total price due. See how the payment methods and expectations from your sales policy are also reiterated. While it is clear in laying out the buyer's responsibility to pay, it's delivered in a collaborative and appreciative manner (including words and phrases like "congratulations," "please," and "thanks for bidding"). In support of a fast transaction, notice how it entices the win-

End of eBay Auction: The Hypnotic Eye orig. 1960 1-sheet - Item #3307121885   _ ☐ ✕

File   Edit   View   Insert   Format   Tools   Message   Help

To: high-bidder@email.com

Cc: dlprince@bigfoot.com

Subject: End of eBay Auction: The Hypnotic Eye orig. 1960 1-sheet - Item #3307121885

Congratulations!

You were the high bidder in this auction. Your item total is $64.20 ($59.99 plus $4.20 USPS Priority Mail).
If you wish to have this item insured, please add $2.20 to the total amount. If you wish faster delivery via
USPS ExpressMail or international delivery via USPS GlobalPriority mail, please contact me.

For fastest service, you may pay via PayPal by posting the total amount to my account ID of dlprince@bigfoot.com.
I will ship immediately upon confirmation of funds received. If you prefer, you may pay via money order, cashier's check,
or personal check by sending payment to the following address:

Dennis Prince
1234 Anystreet
Anytown, CA, 12345

I provide immediate shipment for money order and cashier's check payments. Personal checks will need to clear first.

Please remit payment within 10 days of this notification to gain fastest delivery of your item and to retain your
high-bidder status.

Please reply to this email message so I'll know I was successful in reaching you. Please also provide your
mailing address so I may prepare your package.

Thanks for bidding!

Dennis
eBay ID: dennis_prince

Figure 11-2   Customize your end-of-auction message for best results.

ner to pay quickly to gain "immediate shipment." A message like this will typically get the ball rolling in the right direction.

Once satisfied with the tone and content of your custom EOA message, save it. Create a template for quick use whenever you need it. Save it as a simple text (.txt) file on your computer's hard drive, then simply cut and paste it into your e-mail program when it's time to notify your next winning bidder. Since time is money, why waste it retyping the same message over and over again?

e B a y T I P :   When you move into high-volume sales, you might wish to consider automated yet customizable e-mail messaging tools as well as eBay's own invoicing tools. Chapter 23 will cover these options in greater detail, including a rundown of the best available tools and their costs.

COLLECTING THE MONEY

At this point, collecting payment should be relatively simple. Thanks to your well-worded sales policy (stated within your item listing) and reinforced by your EOA e-mail notification, the high bidder should have no questions about how payment should be made, when it should be remitted, and what sort of delivery service can be expected. You've done your job for now; it's time for the high bidder to respond. Most bidders will respond to your request for e-mail confirmation, indicating how they will pay, when they will pay, and what special shipping needs, if any, they might require, which hopefully your policy already supports.

If paid via PayPal, BidPay, or another form of online payment you might have employed, you'll receive an e-mail notification indicating your high bidder has paid (see Figure 11-3).

Visit PayPal to confirm funds are in your account, then prepare the item for shipping. It's that simple.

If the buyer elects to send a money order, cashier's check, or personal check, keep a keen eye open for arrival of payment and be sure to send e-mail confirmation to the buyer when the payment arrives. At that point, indicate how and when you will be shipping their item.

TRANSACTIONAL TROUBLES?

What happens if the money's *not* good? Well, once in awhile some transactions will hit a snag and might require a bit of extra effort. In your quest to make a

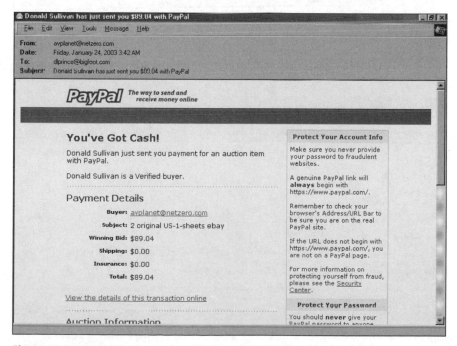

Figure 11-3 PayPal sends e-mail notification of the good news: You've got cash!

fortune, expect the occasional slow payment or bad debt; it's just part of doing business. Of course, your sales policy will have filtered out most payment problems before they occur, having clearly stated your acceptance of the safest and most reliable forms of remittance. But, if a problem does arise despite your proactive efforts, you'll need a plan of action to rectify the situation.

Slow Payment

For whatever reasons, legitimate or otherwise, some winning bidders are slow to pay. Your easy payment methods and prompt action after the auction will get most bidders to pay quickly (and some are downright impressive in their shared commitment to a fast transaction), but a few are less motivated than you'd hope. If you've stated that payment must be received within 10 days and it's been 8 days with no cash in hand, send a reminder to the buyer, reminding him or her of their win and their commitment to complete the deal (see Figure 11-4).

Notice that the reminder message is never threatening and is actually quite forgiving. Just because a payment is slow in arriving (and slow payments are generally the exception, not the rule), it's not necessary to form all manner of suspicious thoughts about your high bidder. Whether the winner forgot to pay, has been away from their PC, or has experienced technical difficulties,

---

REMINDER: End of eBay Auction: The Hypnotic Eye orig. 1960 1-sheet - Item #3307121885

File   Edit   View   Insert   Format   Tools   Message   Help

To: high-bidder@email.com
Cc: dlprince@bigfoot.com
Subject: REMINDER: End of eBay Auction: The Hypnotic Eye orig. 1960 1-sheet - Item #3307121885

Hello,

I haven't yet heard from you nor have I received your payment for this item you won in my auction. Please confirm your receipt of my original notification message and let me know when I can expect to receive payment.

I'm sure this was a simple oversight and I look forward to delivering the item to you. Please refer to the attached original message for all pertinent details for payment and delivery.

Thank you for your prompt attention here.

Best,

Dennis
eBay ID: dennis_prince

-------- attachment follows --------

Congratulations!

You were the high bidder in this auction. Your item total is $64.20 ($59.99 plus $4.20 USPS Priority Mail). If you wish to have this item insured, please add $2.20 to the total amount. If you wish faster delivery via USPS ExpressMail or international delivery via USPS GlobalPriority mail, please contact me.

For fastest service, you may pay via PayPal by posting the total amount to my account ID of dlprince@bigfoot.com. I will ship immediately upon confirmation of funds received. If you prefer, you may pay via money order, cashier's check, or personal check by sending payment to the following address:

Figure 11-4   The friendly yet firm message that reminds winning bidders it's time to pay.

offer the opportunity for that winner to make good on the deal before you consider a harsher approach.

No Payment

If your auction has been visited by that .001 percent of the eBay population, those who just won't pay up, you'll need to take a firmer stance in your attempt to collect your due. If your messages have gone unanswered, your payment clock is ticking down, and your patience is wearing thin, it's time to escalate a bit. Begin with a final notice message as that shown in Figure 11-5.

The "Final Notice" message is direct and to the point. It remains professional but could evoke any number of responses from the former winning bidder (or none at all). The key to the message is it does not leave the situation open-ended ("our business is complete") and indicates your response to the winner's inaction ("contact eBay's SafeHarbor"). The posting of negative feedback has not been used as a threat here (*may* post negative feedback); it's simply been stated as a possible further act on your part. The winning bidder could still possibly make good on the deal and you're wise to keep the door opened, if just a crack, to allow the transaction to be completed successfully. However, when you start managing multiple auctions on an ongoing basis,

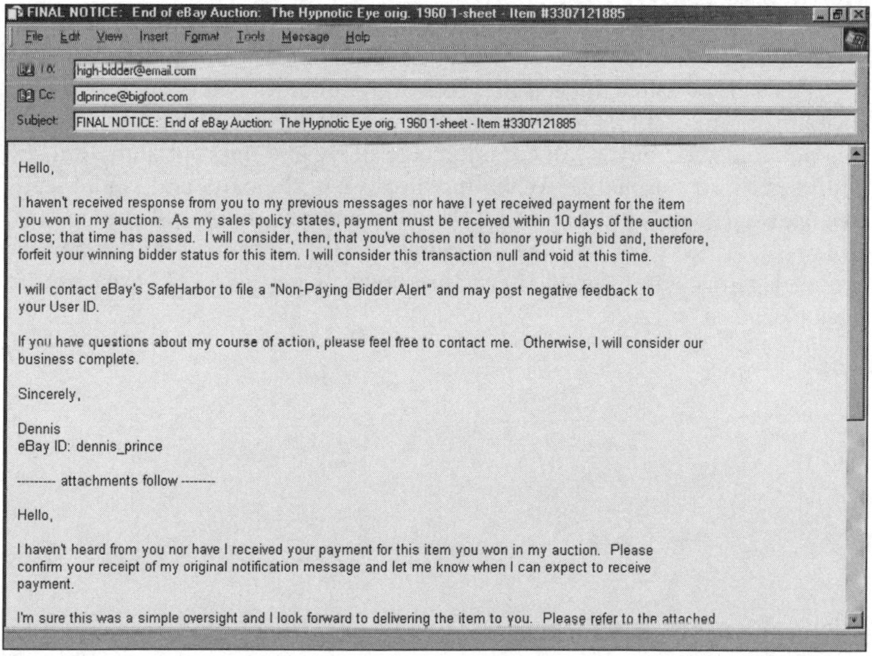

FINAL NOTICE: End of eBay Auction: The Hypnotic Eye orig. 1960 1-sheet - Item #3307121885

File   Edit   View   Insert   Format   Tools   Message   Help

To: high-bidder@email.com
Cc: dlprince@bigfoot.com
Subject: FINAL NOTICE: End of eBay Auction: The Hypnotic Eye orig. 1960 1-sheet - Item #3307121885

Hello,

I haven't received response from you to my previous messages nor have I yet received payment for the item you won in my auction. As my sales policy states, payment must be received within 10 days of the auction close; that time has passed. I will consider, then, that you've chosen not to honor your high bid and, therefore, forfeit your winning bidder status for this item. I will consider this transaction null and void at this time.

I will contact eBay's SafeHarbor to file a "Non-Paying Bidder Alert" and may post negative feedback to your User ID.

If you have questions about my course of action, please feel free to contact me. Otherwise, I will consider our business complete.

Sincerely,

Dennis
eBay ID: dennis_prince

--------- attachments follow ---------

Hello,

I haven't heard from you nor have I received your payment for this item you won in my auction. Please confirm your receipt of my original notification message and let me know when I can expect to receive payment.

I'm sure this was a simple oversight and I look forward to delivering the item to you. Please refer to the attached

Figure 11-5   Last call for the nonpaying winner.

there simply isn't time to deal with a drawn-out exchange nor engage in a personal battle.

Bad Debt

What if the money's no good? Usually, you'll only run into this problem if the winner has sent a personal check (those do still bounce from time to time). In this situation, take the following steps to sort out the problem:

- Contact the buyer immediately via e-mail to explain their check has been refused.
- Avoid accusations; this may be as much a surprise to the buyer as it is to you.
- Politely but firmly request repayment via online payment, money order, or cashier's check, plus reimbursement for the returned check charge your bank may have imposed.
- When the payment is finally received and verified, confirm to the buyer, issue the appropriate thanks, and ship the item.
- If the buyer fails to make good on the payment, consider canceling the transaction.

THE KEY IS COMMUNICATION

To enable the smoothest transaction and highest level of satisfaction for your buyer as well as yourself, keep the lines of communication open at all times. From the point of EOA notification through the receipt of payment, ensure that you and your buyer can communicate freely and appropriately to instill confidence in the exchange. When the money's in the bank and you're ready to ship, keep communicating to set the buyer's expectations and demonstrate you're committed to providing exceptional service. Since your next step in the process is to pack and ship the item, turn now to Chapter 12 and learn how to pack like a pro.

12

Packing and Shipping Like a Pro

When the auction ended, you leapt into action to make contact with the high bidder and collect your earnings. But your job isn't finished yet. Once that payment arrives, you have to do a little more work. The excitement of selling at eBay often overshadows what's really going on: a seller is offering to sell and ship an item to a buyer. After the auction has ended and the buyer has paid, the onus is on the seller to bring the deal to a successful close by getting the item there quickly and safely.

Packing and shipping is something of an art and not to be underestimated or taken lightly. This is the point of the transaction where you, the seller, will establish your reputation in the buyer's mind. Take this step seriously and you'll be recognized as a stellar seller. If you're new to packing and shipping, don't fret over the how's and why's of the process; this chapter will help you determine the best supplies to have on hand, the best way to use them, and the best methods to ensure that the item gets from Point A to Point B safely, to your buyer's delight.

SETTING UP YOUR SHIP SHOP

Believe it or not, many sellers overlook a key element in their packing process—*where* they will pack up their items. You might think you can grab a box, bubble wrap, and packing peanuts, and do your packing anywhere at anytime. Certainly, you can take that approach, but it's not the most efficient way to work, and besides, a transient "ship shop" could result in loss or damage to the items you'll pack.

If you'll be managing a significant number of auctions (and therefore will be packing a lot of goods), you're best advised to establish a designated area for your packing activities. Choose a clean, well-lighted environment that is dry and reasonably free from foot traffic (in other words, avoid folks who may share the same living or working space with you and might tend to move items or abscond with the packing tape). A good ship shop lends itself to easy "staging" of items; it features a sizable flat work area (like a large table or workbench) that keeps the items free from damage and dirt; it provides easy access to all your shipping supplies; and it helps you develop a packing flow or routine that will save you time while ensuring your customers' ultimate satisfaction.

TOOLS OF THE TRADE

Efficiency begins with a well-stocked supply of the packing goods you'll need to ship items. Before that buyer's payment ever arrives, ensure you have the following supplies:

- Sturdy shipping boxes, reinforced envelopes, mailing tubes, and any other containers that will safely transport the items you sell
- Box fill, bubble pack, shredded paper, or other such cushioning materials that will protect the item inside the package
- Shipping tape
- Shipping labels
- Shipping forms such as insurance tags, international disclaimers, and so on
- Shipping tools, including permanent markers, tape dispensers, utility knives, and so on

SOURCES OF SUPPLIES

Although there are costs incurred in stocking a ship shop, you'll be happy to learn the bulk of the materials and supplies can be had for free. For starters, begin with the United States Postal Service (USPS) to stock up on all manner of boxes, envelopes, tubes, labels, and more, to handle the majority of your shipping needs. Besides these supplies being free, they're easy to order right from your PC. Simply go to *shop.usps.com* in your favorite Web browser and navigate to the "Shipping Supplies" area. Order the items and amounts you need to stock up your ship shop then use the simple *checkout* screen to have the items sent to you. Just like the regular mail you receive every day, the USPS will deliver these supplies right to your doorstep.

If you'll be using United Parcel Service (UPS), Federal Express, DHL, or another commercial carrier, look them up on the Internet as they, too, offer free shipping supplies for packages you ship using their services. Of course, you can also get these same supplies at your local carrier's offices or designated partner stations.

Some packing supplies, though, are not free. When it comes to box fill, specialized cartons, and the like, you may actually need to purchase these items. Visit your nearest wholesale or "club" warehouse for better prices on packing tape or specialized envelopes not readily available from the carriers. Visit your local office supply store or shipping office for large bags of styrofoam peanuts and rolls of bubble pack.

eBay TIP: Don't be bashful about picking up such supplies free from time to time. Office places, liquor stores, and even grocery stores routinely throw out reusable packing supplies. Ask around if you see those materials ready for the dumpster, and if they're clean and seem suitable for your packing task, ask if you can take those supplies for yourself.

Don't forget eBay itself; it's full of merchants selling these sorts of packing supplies and usually at better prices than you'd expect. If you're actively buying while selling, be sure to recycle the packing materials that protected the items you received. Most interior packing material can be used over and over again without any significant degradation.

eBay TIP: If packing supplies are costing you money on a regular basis, you can consider recovering that cost in your "shipping and handling" fees. If you're maintaining a high volume of sales, those costs can likely be recovered by adding as little as 25 cents to your shipping fee. Be careful, though, as any cost much higher than that could be construed as a form of final price manipulation.

PACKING PROTOCOL

Although packing is something of a profession, it's a skill easily mastered if you have the right supplies and know how to use them properly. Here are some things to consider as you approach your packing job:

- Think "lightweight" to save on shipping costs but not at the expense of safe delivery.
- Pack items snugly in boxes but don't overdo it lest you damage the item before it ever leaves your site.
- For fragile items, use the "box within a box" method to ensure extra cushion and protection (still mindful of total package weight).

- Use rigid mailers, padded envelopes, or insert cardboard stiffeners to protect flat items.
- Be considerate of the recipient and don't overtape or otherwise excessively seal a package; the item could be damaged as the buyer tries to wrest it free.

With the item ready to ship, send it on its way at the nearest carrier's office or authorized forwarding station. Be sure to retain your receipts, insurance forms, delivery confirmation numbers, and so on; not only will you want to have these important documents when verifying shipment and ultimate delivery, many such expenses might be suitable as a business tax deduction (see Chapter 25 for more details). Once the package is en route, send another message to the buyer to indicate the item is on the way and provide tracking numbers (if available) so the buyer may monitor the package's journey (another free service available from most carrier's Web sites—see Figure 12-1). In your message to the buyer, request a confirmation response to indicate when the item has arrived and if all is satisfactory.

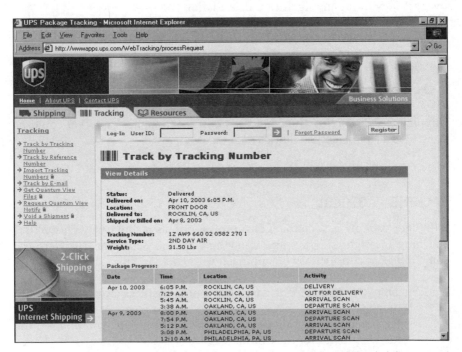

Figure 12-1   Here's an example of the UPS online package tracking service, helping you and your buyer monitor a package's journey.

GETTING SPECIFIC: WHAT ARE YOU SHIPPING?

For added guidance, here are a few rules of thumb the experts use when they approach a particular packing job:

- *Photos or Other Nonbreakable Flat Items:* Use a suitably sized envelope with a same-size piece of cardboard for stiffening. For particularly old or delicate flat merchandise, consider putting the item in a plastic sleeve, then sandwiching it between two pieces of cardboard. Don't just lick that envelope flap; use a strip of packing tape to seal it shut. If the item is particularly large, consider rolling it (if it won't cause damage) and send it in a sturdy (repeat, *sturdy*) mailing tube with both end-caps taped down.
- *Glassware, Pottery, and Other Fragile Items:* Wrap the item in light tissue paper first, then wrap it again with bubble wrap. Put it in an appropriately sized box with a cushion of packing peanuts around the item. Next, place this box inside another box, again using a cushion of packing peanuts around the box within a box. Styrofoam sheets also work great as outer box siding material.
- *Framed Items:* Size matters here, and you'll need to size up the job to see whether it's within your potential to do a good job and whether you'll be able to work with the supplies you have. For starters, if the item is behind glass, it's best to disassemble the piece and pack the elements separately (see the above tips on flat items). Bubble pack and foam sheets are a must here, and you should wrap frame corners with sheet foam to prevent them from puncturing the packing box or causing damage to the piece itself (be it a litho, photograph, or whatever). Although you can find special packing boxes just for framed items, if the piece is too valuable or too unwieldy for your comfort, take it to a professional.
- *Big Tickets:* If an item is too big to handle; if you feel you'd have to improvise a patchwork of packaging; or if you just don't think you'll be able to get it in and out of your car when you're all done, then by all means hand the job over to a pro.
- *The Little Things:* Whether a small piece of jewelry, a stamp, or any other "little" collectible or item that could have big value, be sure it doesn't get lost in the mail. First, protect it: Put the item in an appropriately sized box with the right amount of packing peanuts or foam sheets to cushion it. Next, make it visible: Put that little box into a medium-sized box with appropriate interior cushioning. The second box might add more protection than required, but the goal is to be sure that little darling doesn't fall into some crevice, crack, or piece of mail-sorting machinery after which it might never be seen again.

ADDITIONAL PACKING CONSIDERATIONS

You may have never thought there could be so much to simply packing an item. This discussion isn't intended to overcomplicate the process but does recognize how important it is to you and your customers that the items be shipped and received in satisfactory, undamaged condition. To that end, here are a few more considerations to take into account:

Shake and Break?

One USPS employee imparted this bit of wisdom: "If you can shake it, we can break it." With that in mind, all items you ship should be given the *shake and rattle* test: Before sealing an outer box, hold the flaps closed and give the item a few shakes. Do you hear any movement inside? If so, you might want to add a bit more interior padding until it's whisper-quiet in there. Movement could be the opportunity for items to shift and become damaged during their journey to their new home.

Help Fight Wetness

Other postal and shipping employees tell of water hazards. Somehow, even if there's not a cloud in the sky, items can get wet during transit. Expect that most water damage is irreversible, so take a simple step to ward it off: Put the item in a plastic bag whenever possible. It typically doesn't have to be hermetically sealed, but a simple ziplock bag or a larger poly bag sealed with packing tape is usually enough to keep the wet weather out. Also, experienced handlers recommend that clear tape be used to seal the address label on the package's outside. If that gets wet and smeared, your package might end up in the Dead Mail vault for all eternity.

Don't Overpack It

OK. If a little cushion is good, a lot should be dynamite, right? Not really. Too much interior packing can literally cause an explosion. Remember that boxes will get bumped, stacked, kicked, and tossed about on their sometimes perilous journeys. Use enough interior packaging to keep the item safe and secure, but if the box bulges like an overpacked suitcase, the item that's inside will probably get damaged the moment you seal it shut.

Sealing the Deal

Not only will too much interior packing lead to potential damage, but an overzealous packer might likewise present buyers with something of a challenge as they try to extract their treasure from a practically impenetrable tape-and-cardboard sarcophagus. Seal the item enough to ensure it won't accidentally open in transit, but don't feel you have to extinguish an entire supply of tape, staples, and whatever else to guarantee the item's safety. Many buyers tell of having accidentally damaged an item themselves as they struggled to free it from its packaging. And don't forget, excessive packaging adds excessive weight—which results in added shipping costs.

LITTLE EXTRAS MAKE A BIG DIFFERENCE

If the item is particularly fragile or will fare best if unpacked by a certain method, put special unpacking instructions inside that can be found the moment the recipient opens the package. Also, be sure to include an extra shipping label *inside* the package; often labels will come loose or become unreadable during the journey, or they might get wet. In some instances, packages are opened by the carrier in the hope that he or she will find an extra label to get the item on its way again.

PACKING AS CUSTOMER SERVICE

Be sure to make use of the rate calculators that the different carriers make available on their Web sites (see Figure 12-2). These will help you to be more

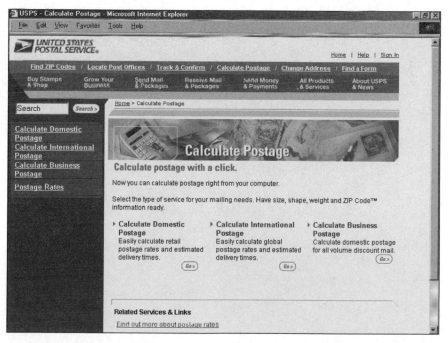

Figure 12-2 Accessed at *www.usps.com*, the postage calculator helps you determine the cost to ship your package.

accurate when quoting shipping costs to your buyers. If you accidentally overcharge the buyer by a dollar or more for shipping costs (perhaps the package didn't end up weighing as much as you anticipated), put a refund in an envelope and seal it up with the item. That sort of honest service speaks volumes to buyers, and you'll feel better knowing you did the right thing.

13

Dealing With Difficult Customers

"The customer is always right." How many times have you heard that? Well, it's a great mantra to utter when you're a customer deserving (maybe demanding?) total satisfaction. How about when you're the seller, though? Sure, most auction sellers work hard to satisfy their high bidders, but there are times when that bidder-cum-customer turns out to be . . . well . . . difficult. In the interest of good business and good customer relations, this chapter provides some sage advice and useful tips for the time when you might find yourself dealing with a buyer who requires more "hands-on" treatment than you had originally expected.

FIX THE PROBLEM, NOT THE BLAME

To be successful with your customers, you're going to have to get to know them—and have them get to know you—quickly. Recall the discussion of the anxiety some buyers and sellers encounter at the end of an auction? While buyers are taking the leap of faith, so to speak, in paying up front, sellers sometimes feel even more vulnerable, fearing the possibly undesirable whims and moods of potentially impatient or irrational buyers. If this sort of situation rears its head, fall back on your clear and concise communication and your straightforward sales policy to help you navigate these choppy waters. Be attentive, though, to the cause of the difficulty you're engaged in with the buyer and determine if it's a response to something potentially troublesome in your policy. If you encounter the same difficulty with more than one customer, it could be an indication that your policy requires some revision. To that end, try to determine why the customer is dissatisfied and otherwise disgruntled with the way in which you're conducting the transaction. Whenever possible, try to be collaborative and sensitive to the customer's needs; make an ally out of the buyer, and you'll stand the greatest chance of steering the deal into a cooperative direction and winding up with a win-win situation.

PERSONALITY PARADE—DIFFERENT TYPES OF CHALLENGING CUSTOMERS

Of course, you never know how a deal might go until you've gotten into the thick of it. As stated before, most buyers will honor the auction agreement without much complication, but there are some who have more peculiar and problematic styles. A difficult deal doesn't necessarily mean a bad deal, nor does it always involve a creep on the other end. To help you be better prepared to the sort of personality that lay behind the difficult deal, keep an eye opened for personalities like these:

- *The Newbie:* Newcomers don't necessarily mean to be difficult to deal with—they're often just a bit uncertain or overanxious when conducting business online. Unless they manifest the behaviors noted in some of the following profiles, just welcome them to the auction space and show them perhaps an extra bit of consideration. Help them learn the ways of online auctioning and you'll help yourself to a smoother exchange. You'll be an ambassador to the new cyber-market they've found, plus you might gain yourself a repeat customer—someone who will come back and buy your items again— in response to your patient efforts.

- *The Antsy Buyer:* This is the one who wants their item fast, fast, *fast.* You might receive pestering e-mails that continually ask, "*When will it arrive?*" Of course, until you have a buyer's payment, there can be no progress. However, use ample communication with this person and clearly state when you will send your next status update (e.g., when payment arrives, when item is shipped). Acknowledge the anticipation of impatient buyers by encouraging them to pay for a shipping method that provides online tracking; they can monitor the progress of their packages themselves while you move on to your other business.

- *The Paranoid Buyer:* Trust is the key for these individuals and, truth be told, they might not trust you. Regardless of your fair policy, your engaging communication, or your professional style, paranoid buyers find dealing with strangers difficult. Quickly, but completely, lay out how the deal will take place and offer them additional services—insurance, package tracking, escrow, or whatever—to help them feel more secure (of course, this will be at *their* cost, not yours). Keep the communication flowing and work to bring the deal to a happy close. Once you've earned their trust, you might have earned a faithful customer.

- *The Postauction Haggler:* Believe it or not, some buyers think there's still opportunity to negotiate a better deal *after* they've won one of your auctions (this is especially true of multiple-item winners). *"How 'bout if I just send you such-and-such dollars for the three items I won?"* Sure, offer to combine items in a single shipment to save on carrier costs but don't go beyond that. Politely thank them for their offer, but just as nicely, state that they need to honor their high bid in accordance to auction rules. If a particular buyer becomes obstinate, stick to your price and policy (this could be a test of your resolve). If the buyer becomes irascible, consider cutting off the deal and reporting them to eBay's SafeHarbor as a nonpaying bidder (refer to the discussion in Chapter 11).

- *Unhappy Harvey:*   Some people just can't be pleased. Whether it's complaining about your sales policy, griping about your shipping charges, or whining about the item they ultimately receive, some folks seem born to be dissatisfied. If you sense this early in the transaction, you might consider letting the bidder off the hook right away and avoiding the whole deal at the outset (they, of course, would have to agree with this move without repercussion). If you've already received payment and are preparing to send the item, be painstakingly clear about your shipping method, guarantees, and return policy. Carefully file all correspondence in this sort of situation; you're blazing a paper trail here (physical and virtual) and you might need to recall it if the buyer simply cannot be pleased no matter what you do. In the case of a return, it's sometimes best to take the item back (in the *same* condition sent), refund the money, and avoid any further encounter with the individual. Check the buyer's feedback rating—he or she might have a history of this sort of thing. It's OK to cancel bids from any bidder with a spotted past or overall negative feedback rating. If you can't please 'em, avoid 'em.

- *The Deadbeat:*   This is the same personality introduced to you in Chapter 11, the one who for whatever reason isn't talking and isn't paying. Simply restated, it's best to establish a time frame for payment receipt within your sales policy and EOA messaging. If the time elapses, communicate your option to negate the sale. When you get into volume selling, you'll have little patience and even less time for this unreliable renegade.

eBay TIP: Although their intentions are never suspect, some buyers simply have difficulty following instructions. Whether they live by a more casual credo or simply don't understand "what's the big deal" about making a timely payment, you'll likely encounter a buyer or two who just don't move very quickly. Exercise patience to the best of your ability but, if this is a buyer who might tend to frequent your auctions, gently but firmly explain you policy in one-on-one correspondence or, if that proves to no avail, consider blocking the bidder from your future auctions. Use your best judgment in these cases.

Naturally, there are some buyers who will embody two or more of the personality styles mentioned here. Don't forget, also, that you should find difficult buyers to be a very small percentage of your customer base. The point of exploring these more difficult types, though, is to understand what may be driving their behavior (be honest in asking if the problem could be your policies and engagement style) and strive for meeting on the common ground. With just a bit of effort, you'll find you can usually resolve problems quite quickly.

SHARE THE OWNERSHIP

Remember, it takes two to transact—a deal can only be successful when both parties are committed. As a seller, you state your policies and methods up front—no surprises. If there is concern or disagreement on the buyer's part, the two of you have the option to negotiate a *mutually agreeable* solution (you can also stick to your original policy if you choose). Whatever agreement you reach, though, is ultimately a deal that's owned by both parties in the transaction. So long as you, the seller, hold up your end of the bargain, there's no room for the buyer to contest the agreement.

DIFFUSE THE SITUATION

One of the basic tenets of customer service is kill 'em with kindness. While you should never completely yield to anyone—neither your policy nor your principles—you can head off caustic situations by showing understanding and a willingness to make the deal work. If a buyer becomes irritated, quickly ask what the problem is—often, it's nothing but a simple misunderstanding. If the buyer won't settle down and seems bent on arguing with you, it might be best to respond with, *"Perhaps it would be better if we cancelled this deal."* Whether the buyer seemingly doesn't like you or is trying a harsh tactic to weasel out of a commitment, you're probably better off to cancel the deal and sell to someone else.

A WORD ABOUT LEAVING NEGATIVE FEEDBACK

When things get ugly, most everyone throws out the threat: *"I'm posting negative feedback on you!"* Longtime eBayers know the value of their feedback rating (you'll be shown how to get the most of yours in Chapter 15) and many will go to great lengths to maintain a spotless record—and some bothersome buyers know this. As a seller, threatening a difficult buyer with negative feedback isn't necessarily an effective way to coerce compliance. As demonstrated in the Final Notice e-mail shown in Chapter 11, communicate your option to post negative feedback but expect you could receive the same in return. Though you shouldn't feel unjust in speaking your mind in the public forum (that's why Pierre created it), take a moment to ask what the negative feedback you might post could truly achieve. Give it some thought first then do whatever you feel will serve you best, both now and in the future.

RISING ABOVE IT ALL

Finally, if you have been through somewhat of a bumpy experience with a buyer but the deal comes off smoothly in the end, recognize that fact and thank the buyer for working with you. Although we often would like to lash out at that hard-to-please so-and-so, a professional manner always leaves you standing in the best light. Chalk it up to the further development of your customer management skills.

14

Satisfaction Guaranteed—
Keeping Customers Happy
and Coming Back for More

You were introduced to many of the auction-going personalities in Chapter 13. This chapter discusses another personality type that will pose a different set of challenges as well as afford interesting opportunities to you. Now that *you're* the seasoned seller, it becomes your duty to usher in newcomers to the auction experience and, for some, it poses a sort of dilemma for the new age. On the one hand, sellers like you want to actively attract the interest and patronage of online newcomers, while on the other, you must anticipate the possibility that you'll need to work harder with these uninitiated buyers in the cybermarket.

While not all "newbies" (as they're affectionately named) are problematic, many sellers agree that working a sale with a first-time auction-goer or online buyer can require some extra effort, extra explanation, and occasionally extra patience. However, if you're prepared to assist a neophyte through the sometimes perplexing world of e-commerce, you'll find yourself in prime position to adopt a long-term customer for your efforts.

GET TO KNOW YOUR NEWBIE

When you encounter someone who's new in town, put your best foot forward while mentally preparing yourself to help them through a process that could be quite foreign and even intimidating to them.

For starters, be prompt in all of your communication and be prepared to answer additional questions regarding your terms, methods, and policies.

Then, remember that some of these new shoppers might find conducting long-distance business with complete strangers a daunting and uncertain undertaking. Your punctual responses and polite answers to their questions will assure them you are there to assist with their purchase.

Of course, be on the lookout for the occasional dark cloud—you know, the buyer or bidder who's looking to scam and scamper. The undesirable elements are out there, and if your newbie turns out to be this sort of charlatan, be sure your terms-of-service (TOS) cover your expectations of timely payment and so on. If the newbie is trying to be clever, cut that one loose and move on.

eBay TIP: Most of all, when sizing up and making first contact with newbie shoppers, remember that you're going to make an early impression upon them about how the online marketplace works. Guide them through the transaction, guard against shenanigans, and encourage them to come back again.

Newbie Shopping Habits: Under Control or Out of Hand?

Of most interest to sellers should be the shopping habits of a new bidder. Although it's difficult to evaluate a newcomer's activity in fixed-price venues (outside of your own), if you're meeting them in the online auction spaces, a seller can quickly ascertain whether the new shopper is adopting one of two common buying styles:

- *The Super Cautious:* Some new shoppers won't buy much at all (either in dollar amount or in the number of items concurrently bid upon) until they can gain a certain level of comfort and familiarity with the online process. If they have good first encounters and believe the cybermarket to be a venue of success for them, they'll typically loosen up and get a bit more active in future pursuits.
- *The Super Shopper:* Other new shoppers find online shopping to be a veritable playground. Although their enthusiasm is appreciated, a quick check of their virtual shopping cart or auction bid history might reveal they're committing to a hefty tally. So what? So you'll want to act fast to ensure your item will be quickly and fully paid for, lest your new customer finds he or she has overcommitted their present bankroll.

Of course, these are pretty much the two extremes and you can expect a good many newbies to fall somewhere in between.

eBay TIP: Although some might argue it's not a seller's business to know about how, when, and how much a newcomer bids or buys, those who've been selling on a regular basis understand that it's worth noting how newbies are shopping and how to engage them to ensure the deal comes to a successful close to both parties' ultimate satisfaction.

A Satisfying Opportunity

It's wise to recognize the special opportunity to aid and build rapport with new shoppers. There's certainly little time for intense hand-holding of newcomers (a seller *must* attend to other customers, after all), but consider these methods of engagement and approach, some of which have already been touched upon earlier in this book, which can be especially helpful in ensuring a win-win transaction with a newbie:

- *Set the Tempo.*   Many new buyers aren't exactly savvy to the protocol of online buying; they might be overanxious, or they might be undercommitted. Working with good e-mail communication and your well-thought-out TOS, promptly get the exchange in motion once a sale has been decided. Demonstrate your tried-and-true professional business process, and newbies will know they're working with a real pro—someone who'll reliably guide a smooth transaction.
- *Be Their Guide.*   It's also good practice to help newcomers (*your* new customers) better understand how online fixed-price and auction sales work. Remember, if you're there to assist them, chances are they'll remember you, your products, and your good business style. That's usually the formula for earning repeat business.

Embrace the New Attitude

At the end of the day, a seller's bottom line is determined by the amount of care extended to customers. Though it's certainly not just newbies who frequently require additional attention, the opportunity to lend a hand to a wide-eyed newcomer is where lasting customer relationships are formed. Take the time to understand and assist newbies and you'll likely become their seller of choice.

KEEPING YOUR BUYERS INFORMED

An informed buyer is generally a happy buyer. As an online seller, strive to do your best to keep your buyers in the know throughout the entire transaction process. From timely EOA messages to updates on an item's shipping status, the more a buyer knows about the deal in process the better he or she will feel about doing business with you.

Service with a Smile

Some sellers say they get too bogged down by sending multiple e-mail updates to their customers, and some even make it a policy to provide minimal or no e-mail contact (feedback is enough, they contend). However, sellers who forgo this kind of helpful customer service risk causing unnecessary concern for buyers, especially newbies, who might panic if they don't hear from sellers once their payment has been sent.

Receiving a brief status update via e-mail can be very reassuring to buyers. Take the extra time and let your customers know how the transaction is progressing. Remember—a lack of communication and "virtual" silence can scare off potential repeat buyers.

Key Interaction Points

The first step in keeping your buyers informed is to send an EOA notice after the auction ends. Once the auction finishes, make the contact as soon as possible—this also will reassure nervous buyers. Beyond the customary EOA notice, you also should consider sending these customer-satisfying status updates:

- When the payment has been received
- When the payment has cleared (if applicable)
- When the item is shipped

Realistically, it doesn't take much effort to send this sort of simple update yet it speaks volumes to your customers and will help them remember you well when they come back for another satisfying auction experience.

e Bay TIP: Are all of these e-mail updates too much to expect from a seller who might list hundreds of auctions at any given time? Perhaps. High-volume sellers in particular might not have the time to offer this kind of detailed follow-up and follow-through. On the other hand, some of the interaction points needing buyer contact might take place within a short time span and won't require multiple e-mails. For example: "I received your payment on Tuesday, your check cleared on Friday, and I sent your package this morning." Whether it's one e-mail or multiple messages, the bottom line is to make sure that your customer is being kept in the communication loop and isn't left in the dark regarding whether an item has been shipped or a check has cleared.

Additional Considerations

Here are two other considerations for helping buyers stay informed: Be sure to update your item descriptions with any additional information or photos, and respond quickly and thoroughly to all user queries and e-mails. Just as you "checked out" sellers when you were buying, you might be similarly "under review" by a prospective bidder. In short, keeping buyers abreast of an auction's progression will make you a standout seller. How far you want to take it depends on your own personal sales philosophy as well as the time you have available for supplemental e-mail contact. But let's face it: The more comfortable the buyer feels about you as a seller, the smoother the transaction will be, and the greater the likelihood that this same person will bid on one of your auctions again.

DEALING WITH DAMAGED GOODS

Sometimes a bit of post-sale trouble creeps up on sellers in the form of damage claims. Sooner or later, one of your buyers might receive a broken item or—worse yet—might not have received the item at all. The reality is that despite your best efforts items will sometimes get damaged in transit. If such a claim comes your way, don't fret—*act!* Here's what you can do if there's a disgruntled buyer out there who demands satisfaction for a good transaction gone awry.

Exercising Damage Prevention

Before considering what you'll do if an item you've sold at auction is received damaged (or isn't received at all), consider the things you can do to prevent damage and protect both yourself and your buyers ahead of time.

First, consider the value and/or rarity of the item you're selling. If it's price rivals your monthly mortgage payment, consider using an online escrow service. Not only will escrow ensure that payment is made before you ship the goods, it also demonstrates your willingness to ensure that the customer is satisfied before you ultimately collect your funds.

Of course, be very clear in your sales policy about how you manage returns and refunds. In the case of damage claims, be sure your policy is explicit regarding how you and the buyer will work *together* in the unfortunate event that an item becomes damaged or lost in transit (often dictated by the chosen carrier's damage claims process). By making your policy clear before the bidders bid, you'll provide yourself a sturdy foundation to stand upon if trouble arises, one that the buyer shouldn't claim ignorance to.

Cover Your Assets

Since it's ultimately the carrier who will be involved if an in-transit problem arises, make sure you and your buyers agree to the shipping method, tracking, and insurance services you'll use. Encourage speedy shipment methods, online tracking, and adequate insurance protection for valuable items. If the buyer elects to "save a buck" and opts out of such protections, be sure it's clear to him or her regarding who will bear the loss if the package is damaged or unrecoverable (some sellers will cover such situations in an effort to provide 100 percent guaranteed satisfaction—you need to decide if that will be your policy as well).

A Broken Item, Not a Broken Relationship

The following point can't be emphasized enough: in the event of damage, focus on the situation at hand, not on debasing one another. Your up-front establishing of how the transaction will work, what special payment and shipping services you'll use, and what sort of guarantee or recourse you'll offer in the event of trouble comprise the true matter at hand. Through collaboration, you and your buyer can resolve the problem and hopefully retain the ability to transact again in the future.

TRANSFORMING CUSTOMERS INTO REPEAT BUYERS

There was a time not long ago when a good variety of merchandise was the only hook needed to attract eager consumers to online sales and auction venues. Those days, however, are over. Today, more and more online retailers have recognized the equal importance of the "customer experience"—how well the customer is served, how comfortable the customer feels, and how often the customer returns. It's no longer a matter of goods alone; today serving your customers well and gaining their loyal and repeat patronage is critical to the long-term health of your business.

The Staggering Statistics

These days online shoppers are interested not only in *what* they will be served but equally *how* they will be served. If you invest your efforts only in the particular merchandise you offer, ignoring your responsibility for the quality of the customer's shopping experience, you'll soon find you're lagging behind your competitors. Don't believe it? Here are some revealing statistics presented by Vicki Henry, CEO of Feedback Plus, Inc., on why customers *don't* return:

- 68 percent leave because of rudeness or indifference.
- 14 percent judge by first encounter.
- 9 percent prefer competitors.
- 5 percent buy from friends.
- 3 percent move away.
- 1 percent die.

Remember, with the millions of items online up for sale or bid on any given day, it's highly likely that other sellers will be offering the same sort of things that you have on the block. If another seller greets the customers with a bigger smile and a more attentive policy than you do, they may win the customers that you just ignored.

Setting the Stage for Follow-Up Business

A second sale is dependent upon how well the first one went. With competition running high at eBay and elsewhere, sellers who are in this business for the long haul need to be sure that when they serve a new customer, that customer will be compelled to return for more.

In most business scenarios, repeat customers are cheaper and easier to serve since they've developed a trust in you and your operation, and you've established an awareness of how they manage themselves. It's in your best interest to delight your customers at every turn, persuading them that you're the "seller of choice." Initially, this may take some extra effort, but in the long run your efforts will certainly benefit your business. So what sorts of things can you do to keep your customers coming back? Consider these core customer satisfying techniques:

SAY "THANK YOU" REPEATEDLY   For starters, understand that good customer service is all about attitude. If you truly value your customers and their contribution to your bottom line, you can't help but be thankful. So go ahead and thank the customers who come to shop for your wares, even before they've purchased anything. If you're forthcoming with your desire to answer their questions, allay their concerns, and treat them with respect, they'll likely see that you're committed both to your business and to their satisfaction.

Tell them, "Thank you for your interest in my merchandise," "Thank you for your bid," "Thank you for your fast payment," and "Thank you for your business." These are the first steps in building good and hopefully long-lasting customer relationships. Too many merchants and businesses take their customers for granted these days, and your thankful attitude will quickly identify you as a bright spot in a sometimes cold, impersonal, and occasionally unfriendly marketplace.

OVERDELIVER ON WHAT YOU PROMISE EVERY TIME   Keep in mind that any seller who merely meets customer expectations can easily be matched and replaced by another seller offering the same level of service. But when you *exceed* your customers' expectations, you're more likely to be remembered and sought out when customers come back looking for more. How can you overdeliver? Recall these simple methods:

- Enclose a trinket with an item. Simple baubles like "thank-you" cards, small toys, candy, bows, or even a cleverly designed business card will add a special touch and show that you care about your customers beyond their purchases. Also, think about including a little extra that relates to the item purchased. For instance, one seller I know who sold used DVDs always sent along a free packet of microwave popcorn.

- Upgrade the shipping or provide free shipping. When those bidding wars ensue and you make out much better than you expected on an item, consider surprising the high bidder with upgraded or free delivery. *That's* definitely an extra that's always remembered.
- Ensure that your items always will be regarded as "better than expected." Remember to be careful in grading and consider slightly undergrading your items so that your buyer will be pleasantly surprised at how much better than expected the item appears upon receipt.
- If there's ever a problem, don't delay in resolving it. Although many sellers fear being abused or exploited by unsavory buyers, it's not worth risking your reputation by being hard-nosed. Take care of the customer quickly, whether by way of replacement or refund, and keep a smile on your face throughout the process.

Sweat the Small Stuff Always   If you're looking to pull well ahead of the pack, you'll need to do more than everyone else. Of course, there's not much to listing items, providing basic communication, and shipping merchandise—which is all pretty much the *modus operandi* of the industry. But your customers' delight is in the details, and when you take note and take action on the oft-overlooked minutia of method, you begin to surpass customers' expectations, leaving them delighted while leaving much of your competition in the dust. For example:

- *Choices and Voices.*   Give your customers more options (e.g., shipping, payment methods) and they'll see you're customer-focused. Hear them out when they have comments or concerns about your methods and they'll know you care.
- *Rapid Response.*   Don't keep customers waiting, especially when the auction clock is ticking. If you're typically unavailable to respond, they'll typically be unavailable to do business with you again.
- *Don't Be Satisfied Until Your Customers Are.*   Though you shouldn't relegate yourself to doormat status, you should remain "at their service" until you're sure your customers are satisfied. Only then can *you* feel satisfied that you're doing exceptional business.
- *Emotional Rescue.*   Sometimes your customers have a thing or three to say to you—hear 'em out. Whether they're angry, confused, or whatever, you need to interact closely to determine what you did (or didn't do) that left them feeling out of sorts. Consider an informal survey ("please let me know whether you had any concerns or letdowns in doing business with me") after the transaction, then listen closely if and when they take you up on the invitation.

- *Uncompromising Ethics.* Honesty, sincerity, and compassion will take you and your business a long way. Ask yourself how you'd like to be treated in a similar transaction, and then go above and beyond that benchmark when you serve your customers.

BE CONSISTENT . . . CONSISTENTLY   The key to retaining your customers is to first sustain your own performance in their eyes. That is, conduct yourself and your business in such a way that you're able to exceed customer expectations and overdeliver on promises with *every* transaction. While it's great to hear your customers praise you on an initial transaction, it's disappointing to both of you if they consider a follow-up transaction to be of lesser quality. It's up to you to be sure you can fold in premium customer service methods without them costing you consistency in execution.

When all is said and done, your efforts here will work to gain you what every serious merchant covets: customer loyalty. Understand that *loyalty* is not the same as *satisfaction*. Although satisfied with some purchases, most bidders and shoppers continue to seek out the best deals, exercising their purchasing options. However, through the building of a relationship with a seller who exhibits exemplary attitude and business behavior, buyers often forgo the hunt for a cheaper deal, realizing they're getting the *best* deal from you, the stellar seller. That's loyalty and that's the big payoff for your extra efforts.

CUSTOMER SATISFACTION—THEIR WORDS, NOT YOURS

"Sure my customers are satisfied—just ask me and I'll tell ya." Although this seller-centric sentiment may sound funny, there's more truth in it than many would want to admit. It's a trap that's easy to fall into: believing your *own* praises. Experts often remark that to truly excel in customer satisfaction, a seller needs to have a passion to serve customers, leaving it to them to decide when they've been satisfied.

"Real customer service comes from the heart," notes one veteran seller. "If you don't truly and deeply value what the customer means to your business' health, you may as well not bother." These comments underscore the need to let the customer—not you—determine what's satisfactory. It's one way to ensure that you remain totally customer-focused. For better or worse, you don't give out the grades here, the customer does. The wise seller keeps a pulse on his or her customers' satisfaction as a way to understand which direction the business is going. And at the end of the day, it's an undeniable truth that customer service should become and remain a seller's top priority in the effort to develop lasting customer relations and further your potential to find your online fortune.

15

Building and Maintaining a Stellar Online Reputation

The past several chapters have offered advice and insight into how to stay atop your auction matters, how to best engage your bidders and buyers, and how to keep the transaction on track for a successful close. Through those efforts, you have presented yourself as a committed seller intent on providing good products and great service, through it all establishing a name for yourself within the eBay community. Your good name, then, is among your greatest assets at eBay—so keep it polished, keep it prominent, and promote it with pride. This chapter illuminates the importance of your eBay reputation, helps you get off to a good start in building an excellent eBay feedback rating, and brings to light the additional elements that can make you a stellar seller, attracting and holding customers while creating loyalty in the virtual marketplace.

UNDERSTANDING eBAY'S FEEDBACK FORUM

In addition to inventing the online auction to begin with, Pierre Omidyar likewise possessed the vision to recognize the value and importance of a good online reputation. In 1995 the Internet was a flurry of online "personalities," computer-savvy users and *'Net surfers* having adopted virtual personas used in communing with fellow *'Netizens*. When it came to trading in the virtual space, Omidyar anticipated the hesitation of some who would feel less than confident in dealing with strangers; he saw the value of putting a reputable face with a virtual name. The result: eBay's Feedback Forum.

The Origin of the Feedback Forum

Simply enough, the Feedback Forum was (and is) a virtual public notice board where buyers and sellers could share their comments, good and bad, about their transactions with one another. Those serious about advancing their auction opportunities were conscientious in their dealings to better ensure they would receive good marks from others. Those less than sincere in their auction exploits were quickly exposed to the rest of the community. That's what it became—a community. Thanks to the Feedback Forum and the community's eagerness to utilize it, eBay for the most part developed as a safe venue for online trading.

How to View a User's Feedback

Anywhere you encounter another user's ID at eBay (most often on item listing pages in the form of either seller or high bidder), you'll find a parenthetical number to the right of that ID; that's their numeric *feedback rating*. Click on that number and you'll be able to view the details of that user's feedback (see Figure 15-1).

As shown in Figure 15-1, a feedback summary is provided to aggregate the results of feedback posted for the user from other users (this example happens to be a current picture of my feedback rating). On the left side of the screen, a quick tally is presented highlighting the number of positive, neutral, and negative feedback comments posted to the user's ID. A positive comment

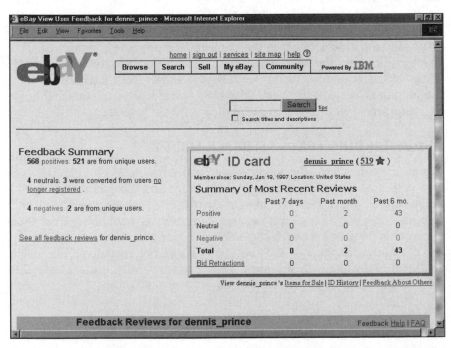

Figure 15-1　Click on any user's feedback rating to view his or her feedback summary.

gains one point; a neutral comment gains no points; a negative comment sub-tracts one point. Understand that feedback can only be posted between regis-tered users who have been recorded by eBay as buyer and seller in a closed auction; no anonymous or non-auction-related comments can be posted. Also, a single user who might post numerous comments, positive or negative, will only be counted as one numeric rating (positive or negative) to be tallied in the recipient user's feedback rating; this prevents feedback padding. Your best friend posting hundreds of nice comments about you or an irate adver-sary dropping many detracting comments will only be counted as a single point in your overall rating.

The right side of the screen shows the eBay ID card that summarizes the tally of feedback received within the past six months. This is particularly use-ful in determining the most recent trends in a user's actions and behavior as reported by other users who have dealt with the individual. Feedback left at eBay is permanent, and though follow-up comments or feedback responses can be posted by the recipient, the original mark will stand. This can be some-thing of a disappointment if you receive a negative comment accidentally (I got one that way) or from an incensed ingrate who is later banned from the site (I got a couple that way, too). Don't let that fact deter you, though, as your overall record will prevail over a couple of unfortunate incidents.

eBay TIP: eBay allows users to designate their feedback as "private," meaning that it cannot be viewed by other registered users. This is a mistake, obviously, since blocking feedback from other users' view implies that there's something to hide. To instill confidence in other bidders and sellers, avoid flagging your feedback as private.

How to Post Feedback at eBay

If you've just completed a transaction (either as seller or buyer), revisit the item listing page and click on the text link to *leave feedback,* either "to seller" or "to bidder," as appropriate (see Figure 15-2).

Looking at Figure 15-3, you can see the form that will be displayed for inputting and posting feedback. Simply enter your comment, select the type of feedback you're giving (positive, negative, or neutral), and click the "leave comment" button at the bottom of the screen. Notice that eBay issues an advisement on this page that "you're responsible for your own words," cau-tioning you against posting libelous comments, and encouraging you to seek resolution if there is a dispute. Your comment and its cumulative numeric result will be added to the user's feedback rating. The actual comments posted for a user can be reviewed by any other registered user by scrolling down and clicking through the successive pages of the feedback screen.

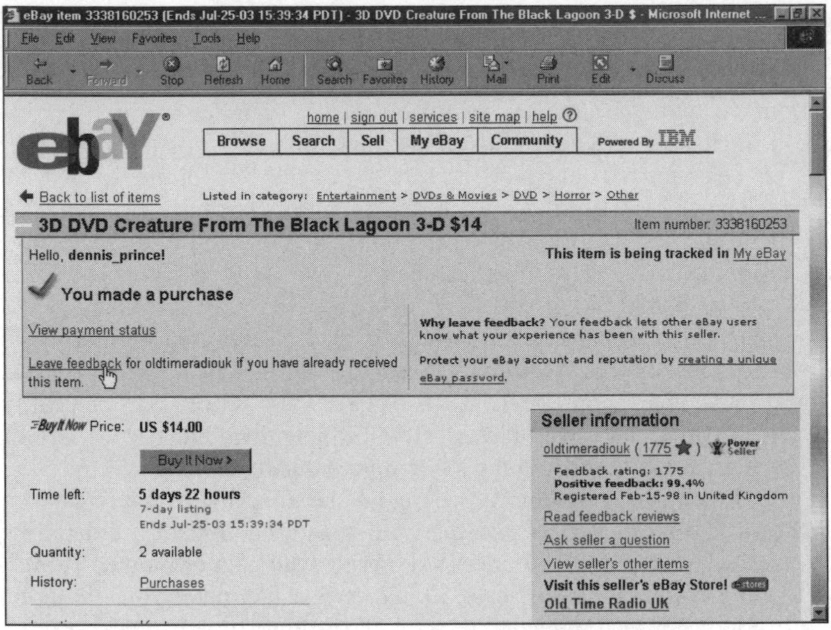

Figure 15-2   Revisit the item listing page to leave feedback to buyer or seller.

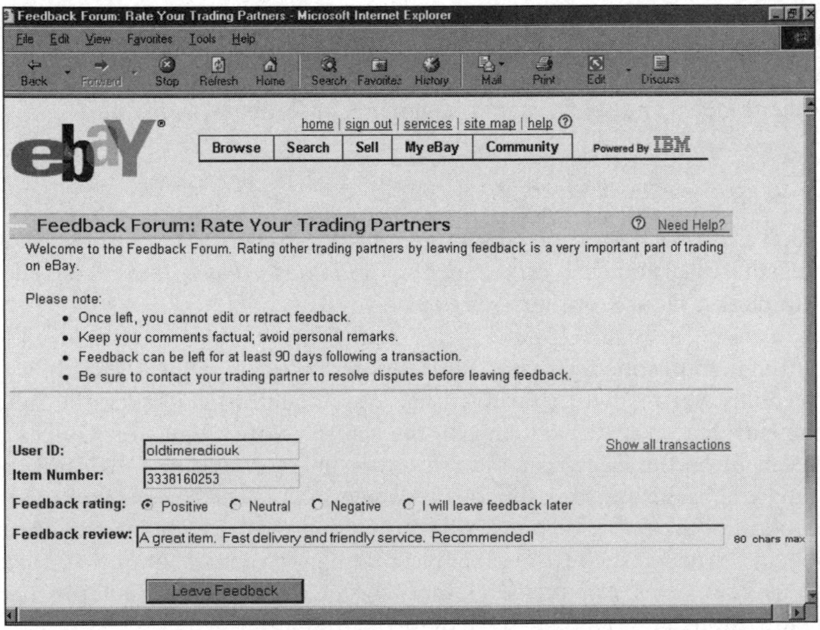

Figure 15-3   Enter a feedback comment in the feedback form page.

BUY FIRST TO ESTABLISH YOUR GOOD REPUTATION

New sellers face something of a catch-22 dilemma: how can they present themselves as reputable before they've done any business to establish a feedback rating? It's true that buyers may be hesitant to bid on your auction if your feedback rating is zero. Your best approach is to become a good buyer first. Positive feedback, being relevant for both buyers and sellers, can be accumulated if you bid and buy first to earn those initial feedback points. Be certain to post positive feedback for the sellers with whom you've had successful transactions, in anticipation that they will respond in kind. Once you've earned an aggregate value of ten positive points, eBay will award you your first feedback star, visible alongside your feedback rating number. Although the actual feedback comments will show you've only been buying, the rating will successfully indicate that you are committed and conscientious in your dealings.

MORE ABOUT YOU AT ABOUT ME

If you haven't already created an "About Me" page at eBay, this is the time. When you're new to selling and are eager to share your intent and aspirations to offer great items bolstered by great service, an About Me page allows you space to tell prospective shoppers a little more about you. Consider including a picture of yourself (there's no need for an eBay transaction to be a "faceless" encounter) and offer some information about the sorts of goods you'll specialize in. Tell as much about yourself as relates to your envisioned auction activity and you'll give bidders a better feel for who you are.

REPRESENT YOUR MERCHANDISE, REPRESENT YOURSELF

The manner in which you offer your items often speaks volumes about you. That said, it's important to always present clear and accurate item descriptions to best represent yourself. Here's how your item descriptions reveal more about *you* than you may have first thought:

- Complete item details will show that you understand the items you're offering, and that you recognize the relevant information bidders will need to consider. These will serve as signs of your thorough approach to presenting items for sale.
- Accurate item details likewise indicate you're either an expert in what you're offering or are conscientious enough to properly research each item you present.
- When you provide thorough item condition details, you show that you're forthcoming, honest, and committed to helping the bidder make a well-informed decision when bidding on your goods.

- Good grammar still counts, and by demonstrating good communication skills you represent yourself as a professional who's attentive to details.

Making the Grade

Experienced sellers know how important accurate item representation can be, not only for the sake of making an immediate sale but also for their own long-term reputation. *Item grading,* however, remains a gray area in online selling, a subjective assessment that if not properly understood and communicated could become a contentious matter between buyer and seller. Unfortunately, there are no uniform, universally accepted grading definitions for all kinds of merchandise. Different terms are often used to describe the condition of different items such as furniture, stamps, glassware, or trading cards. If this multitude of terms isn't enough cause for concern (and it is), *similar* terms are used over a variety of items yet these don't represent the same "state of being" in each item category. Therefore, accurate and responsible use of grading terms becomes something of a *learned* discipline with application of a stated grade often depending upon the experience of the seller.

The bottom line, though, is that bidders are looking for high-quality items, especially vintage goods. As they're willing to pay high dollars for top-quality merchandise, they're looking for sellers who are accurate and dependable in their grading techniques. So, when it comes time to advertise your goods, consider these guidelines when communicating the condition:

- Use the recognized grading terms for the item. Steer clear of off-the-cuff terms like "super condition," "really nice," and "great specimen." Avoidance of accepted terms will make you appear inexperienced or potentially dishonest.
- Accompany the grade with a full disclosure of the item's condition and details. Help the customer decide if your assessment of the item seems reasonable.
- If you're on the fence about where an item truly grades out, consider using "half-grades" (Very Fine +, Near Mint −).
- Carefully consider *undergrading* your item. Without taking too much away from the item, let buyers know you're using a strict grading system, then grade down a half-step. This usually results in subsequent feedback from buyers proclaiming that your items arrive "better than described"—exactly the sort of good PR you want.
- Be sure to apply a suitable offering price (if using a reserve or stating a "Buy It Now" price) to the grade you select. A noticeable mismatch in price compared to condition will not sit well with bidders.

Bidders are seeking out new sellers of desirable goods and will make note of those sellers who seem to be most dependable in terms of item grading. By properly representing your items, you'll develop a reputation for being honest and reliable in all sales.

Your Expertise on Display

When you present yourself as an expert or authority on the items you sell, you further embellish your online reputation as a seller who can be trusted and consulted. Bidders and buyers at eBay are looking for experts when they search through the auction listings, hoping to find a seller who knows what's what and sells items that are properly described and accurately represented. Being regarded as an expert helps you and your reputation in the following ways:

- Being an expert in what you sell will give you confidence in *how* you'll sell and at what prices you'll offer your items.
- Being an expert helps you find the proper customer pool—those actively searching for and buying certain items—and provides you with a better understanding of those customers' wants and needs.
- Being an expert helps you write better item titles and descriptions as well as provide better images that astutely present the critical views to your buyers.
- Being an expert helps you to anticipate changes in demand, supply, and your customers' expectations.
- Being an expert helps you answer your customers' questions quickly and accurately.
- Being an expert helps you to fend off dishonest buyers (as well as dishonest sellers)—you're forearmed with the facts and knowledge to best avoid a scam.
- Being an expert gains you the respect of your customers, who realize you know your stuff and can be fully trusted.

If you're already an expert in a certain sort of item or commodity, you're already ahead of the game. If not, take extra time to research the items you'll sell; research items like them that have already sold; and turn to other sellers and seller's guides to fortify your knowledge. Soon you'll find that you've developed your own expertise and can confidently present knowledge to your potential customers—and earn the highest price for your various goods.

THE ART OF FEEDBACK AT eBAY

To bring this discussion full circle, return to the foundation of your online reputation—the eBay Feedback Forum. The key to making feedback work at eBay is participation; it's the only way you can build and buoy your auction reputation. If you've had a good experience with a buyer or seller, you'll want to reward that person with positive feedback. If you've had a bad experience, you might levy a negative comment. If you're less than tickled but not quite ticked, opt for the neutral comment. Regardless, be sure to leave feedback. Serious users who covet a stellar reputation will work hard to do right in every deal, hoping thereby to build a chart-topping rating.

But *why* does feedback matter? If it's just the opinions of average people on the Net, what noticeable impact can it really have? The answer springs from the need to feel safe and confident in a trading environment. How safe do you feel sending money to an absolute stranger? How safe does that stranger feel sending one of his or her valuable treasures to an unknown buyer? Wouldn't you feel better if you could learn a bit more about the people you'll be dealing with? Granted, feedback can't *make* anyone behave a certain way, but it can help others make decisions about who they'll deal with and who they won't. Your stellar reputation will definitely ease your efforts at eBay and will position you to stand out in a positive light.

PART 3

TECHNIQUES FOR BOOSTING YOUR SALES

16

Keys to Better Auction Listings

Now that you have a foundation of the how's and the why's for auctioning at eBay, it's time to turn your attention to the true matter at hand: *selling anything and making your fortune*. It's true that every item has its buyer and every seller can command his price, especially at the expanse known as eBay. Nevertheless, the fruits of your labors will be much more plentiful if you employ deliberate tacks and methods to your activities. Beginning with this chapter, you'll learn the keys to better auctioning and gain the insights that will differentiate you from an "average" seller. This advanced discussion begins with matters of improving your auction listings using a couple of very simple yet highly effective methods.

KEYS TO USING KEYWORDS

Recall the discussion in Chapter 5 about effectively searching for and finding items based on keywords? Here's where you, the seller, craft the best title possible to draw in the most bidders. As you can imagine, when it comes to the titles of the items you post for sale or bid, your eventual success often depends upon how carefully you choose the words in your item title. Since you're limited to only 45 characters in your eBay item title, it's up to you to make optimum use of the precious verbal real estate to literally make every word count.

Getting the Most Hits

Your first task is to ensure your items can be found easily. Since you're competing with 14 million other active items on any given day, your immediate challenge is to ensure your item has the best chance of showing up on bidders' search lists. Therefore, begin by including as many pertinent key words that shoppers are likely to search for (perhaps those words that *you* specified when you were searching). Identify the words and terms that are commonly used in searches for your item, including the most effective word combinations. As a rule, you'll want to include brand name, origin, year (or time period), and manufacturer of the goods you're offering. Depending upon what you sell, color, size, and other such attributes might also be elemental information to include in your listing titles. When in doubt, search eBay yourself to determine how items like yours are being listed and which listing titles tend to attract more bidders and better prices.

Check Your Spelling

Buyers and sellers continually lament lost sales and missed purchasing opportunities due to misspelled keywords. Be sure to spell correctly, especially when items like yours feature intentional spelling variations or are identified by words that are commonly misspelled. Many sellers go so far as to include common misspellings in their item titles to better ensure their listings will be included in a greater number of search results. Buyers, too, search for these commonly misspelled words to ensure desirable—albeit misspelled—goods don't get away.

Perfunctory Punctuation

Did you know that punctuation marks such as hyphens, parentheses, and exclamation marks can actually sabotage your sales? Dependent upon the search tool being used, a keyword search for "Jadite" might actually ignore titles that include punctuated variations like "Jadite!" or "(Jadite)." Some eBay searches will associate punctuation as part of a word and, in the literal sense, will not recognize the keyword match. It's never safe to assume bidders will universally utilize eBay's specialized search commands, and the onus is on you to ensure that simple searches will retrieve your item. Whenever possible, avoid tacking punctuation onto an item title keyword, or you run the risk of having your goods inadvertently passed over.

eBay TIP: When listing an item, you'll see that eBay specifies asterisks, quotation marks, and special HTML tags are not allowed in item titles. If included, these elements would be misinterpreted by eBay's listing process program and result in an item title that could be virtually unreadable.

Stick to the Facts

Don't waste your valuable title space (it's limited to 45 characters or less) on words that do little to describe the item or properly identify it to the discriminating buyer. Words like "cute," "adorable," and "desirable" do little to attract, let alone convince a buyer. And words like "rare" and "hard to find" are not only superfluous (especially when buyers are already aware of the scarcity of an item) but sometimes have the effect of exposing a seller's attempt to justify a higher price. Subjective words like "awesome," "unbelievable," and "must see" could seem to be enticing but usually just succeed in wasting space. Lastly, visual come-ons like "L@@K" and its ilk are nothing short of obnoxious and should definitely be avoided.

Abbreviated Profits

Abbreviations may make sense to you—may even be recognized among purveyors of certain products—but they could cost you a sale if they fail to show up on keyword search result lists. Unless the abbreviations you employ are commonly used by your buyers, it's best to avoid spontaneous contractions or concatenations whenever possible.

> **eBay TIP:** If you have title space to spare, it is a good idea to include the full name of the item as well as any recognized and well-used abbreviations, this enabling you to find more potential bidders regardless which naming convention they use in their searches.

SO HOW ABOUT AN EXAMPLE?

To sum it all up, a good item title is specific enough to capture the attention of your potential bidders but also is general enough to attract the curiosity of folks who happened to stumble across your listing (either in a related search result or while browsing the categories). To that end, consider a new item to be put up for bid bearing this title:

IT CONQUERED THE WORLD 1956 Lobby Card #2

This title is 41 characters in length (spaces count!) and, while it may appear simple, it effectively captures the following key search keywords:

- The title of the film (in clearly visible capital letters)
- The year of the film
- The precise description of the sort of item (a lobby card)
- The numeric identifier of the item being listed (lobby card #2)

You'll be tasked with providing similar information in your item titles and may need to try different variations of information offered until you lock in to the most effective keywords. You'll know you've created a successful title when you start to receive a larger number of hits.

WRITING BETTER DESCRIPTIONS

Once you've attracted bidders with your well-crafted item titles, you need to convince them your item is the one they simply must bid on. Your bidders need all the right information, and your item description is where they'll look to determine if they can bid confidently. While an item description shouldn't become a book-length dissertation, it likewise shouldn't be a scant offering of ambiguous facts. In reality, the item description is where the seller makes the "pitch," so to speak, in an effort to encourage bids. The information presented should be as well-researched and duly thought out as was the item title. Staying within the theme of movie memorabilia, consider this description for another lobby card:

> From 1956, here's an original 11 × 14 lobby card from the drive-in classic of alien invasion, *It Conquered the World.* This film starred Peter Graves (of *Mission: Impossible* fame), 50's scream queen Beverly Garland, and tough guy Lee Van Cleef. This is lobby card #2 of the original U.S. set of eight. It features a great color photo of Peter Graves confronting another actor in a street scene of panic and confusion. This card also features excellent border graphics of the alien invader and the film's original logo. The surrounding white border features the standard National Screen Service (NSS) proprietary information. It's printed on the standard heavy pulp paper as were all lobby cards at that time. This lobby card is in excellent condition. Although issued 44 years ago for the film's original release, this lobby card has fared extremely well. All corners are slightly soft with one showing a tiny bit of paper loss. There is a barely noticeable quarter-inch tear in the left border, but no paper loss there. The white border shows very light handling soiling and is refreshingly free of any pinholes or tape residue. This card is a clean, vivid specimen that's striking to look at and will be a welcome addition to any vintage horror collection.

After reading a description like that, hopefully you too are ready to bid. Although this description may seem rather exhaustive, recognize that it answers virtually all questions a discriminating collector/bidder may have. Consider what this description achieves:

- It provides the date of item origination.
- It offers information of the actors and actresses who starred in the film (which would come up in a more specific search).
- It states the number of the card and its country of origin.
- It verifies authenticity of the item (reference to NSS markings).
- It identifies the media (paper style) the item is printed on.
- It exhaustively describes the condition of the item without ambiguous term use or misuse.

Although images will be included in this particular listing, the description alone could paint a very accurate and assuring picture of the item, sight unseen. See also how the information provided imparts the seller's expertise in this sort of item, reinforcing the discussion from Chapter 15.

SIMPLE HTML FOR SPECTACULAR RESULTS

As mentioned briefly in Chapter 7, HTML (or HyperText Markup Language) is the lingo of the Internet and is responsible for the majority of fancy Web pages you see and use online. Although most commercial pages are quite complex in their construction, it's possible for you to harness some of the eye-catching effect for use in your eBay listings. Don't think you need to be a seasoned computer programmer to use HTML. If you can type simple text, you can insert the clandestine little keys that will enable your listing to spring to life.

HTML Tags Anyone Can Use

HTML commands that enable text and image effects are referred to as *tags* and are simple notations that are inserted into a regular text listing or document. These tags are simple alphabetic characters embedded between the "< >" signs. Appearing before and after portions of text, these tags will enhance the look or positioning of that text beyond the simple typeset you'd otherwise see. A tag (e.g.,) precedes the text to be enhanced, and then a closing tag that contains the forward-slash (e.g.) will ensure the effect is not continued to the rest of the text that follows. Here are the most common tags you can use to achieve professional looking results:

FONT TAGS
- bold results in **bold.**
- <i>italics</i> results in *italics.*
- <u>underline</u> results in <u>underline</u>
- <font size=12 color=black face="comic sans"> results in text that LOOKS LIKE THIS. This font will remain in use until you insert the </font> tag or specify another similar font equation with different settings.

PARAGRAPHS, LINE BREAKS, AND LISTS
- <p> will produce a paragraph break.
-
 will produce a line break (similar to a carriage return).
- <li> will generate a bullet mark before the text as in a bulleted list.

INSERTING IMAGE URLS AND OTHER WEB LINKS
- <img src=http://www.geocities.com:80/Hollywood/Boulevard/itconqlog. gif"> will insert the specified image into the text.
- <a href="http://cgi.ebay.com/aw-cgi/eBayISAPI.dll?ViewFeedback&userid= dennis_prince">My Feedback</a> provides an active (clickable) link labeled "My Feedback" to direct you to my eBay feedback page.

- <a href="mailto:dlprince@bigfoot.com">eMail Me</a> provides an active link, labeled "eMail Me" to immediately create an email message to my address.

There are a good many more tags available for use in HTML and, if you feel you want to gain a better understanding of the language, grab just about any book that discusses introductory or intermediate HTML coding. For the purposes of your eBay listings, though, these are the essential tags that will make your listing more visually pleasing and useful to potential bidders.

HTML in Action

Turning our attention back to the "It Conquered the World" lobby card, Figure 16-1 shows how I inserted HTML-enhanced text into the eBay description block in the item listing form to prepare my item for auction.

eBay TIP: Immediately below the description block on the listing form, you'll find a text link that allows you to preview the results of your HTLM exploits. If the text or tags require minor modifications, close the preview window and make the necessary adjustments.

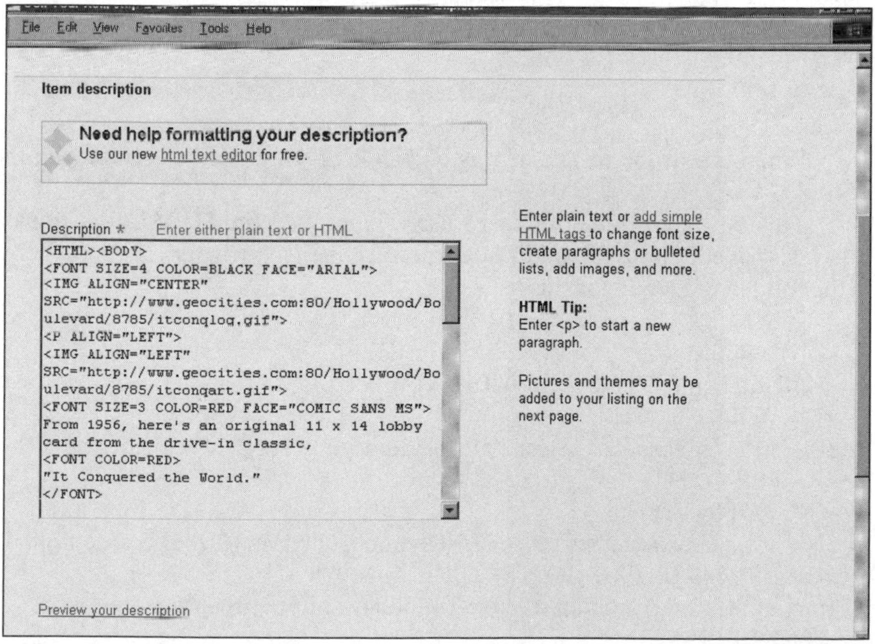

File Edit View Favorites Tools Help

Item description

Need help formatting your description?
Use our new html text editor for free.

Description *   Enter either plain text or HTML

```
<HTML><BODY>
<FONT SIZE=4 COLOR=BLACK FACE="ARIAL">
<IMG ALIGN="CENTER"
SRC="http://www.geocities.com:80/Hollywood/Bo
ulevard/8785/itconqloq.gif">
<P ALIGN="LEFT">
<IMG ALIGN="LEFT"
SRC="http://www.geocities.com:80/Hollywood/Bo
ulevard/8785/itconqart.gif">
<FONT SIZE=3 COLOR=RED FACE="COMIC SANS MS">
From 1956, here's an original 11 x 14 lobby
card from the drive-in classic,
<FONT COLOR=RED>
"It Conquered the World."
</FONT>
```

Enter plain text or add simple HTML tags to change font size, create paragraphs or bulleted lists, add images, and more.

HTML Tip:
Enter <p> to start a new paragraph.

Pictures and themes may be added to your listing on the next page.

Preview your description

Figure 16-1   Use the item description field to directly enter HTML-enhanced text and images.

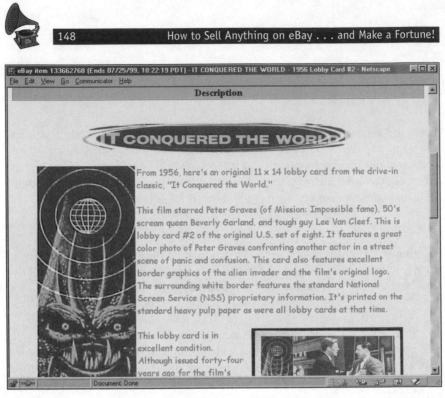

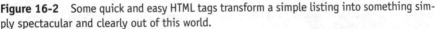

Figure 16-2 Some quick and easy HTML tags transform a simple listing into something simply spectacular and clearly out of this world.

When listed, the results of this particular listing can be seen in Figure 16-2.

This particular auction makes use of many of the HTML tags previously described, plus a few additional enhancements. For your reference, here is the full HTML code for this listing:

```
<HTML><BODY>
<FONT SIZE=4 COLOR=BLACK FACE="ARIAL">
<IMG ALIGN="CENTER"
SRC="http://www.geocities.com:80/Hollywood/Boulevard/8785/itconqlog.gif">
<P ALIGN="LEFT">
<IMG ALIGN="LEFT"
SRC="http://www.geocities.com:80/Hollywood/Boulevard/8785/itconqart.gif">
<FONT SIZE=3 COLOR=RED FACE="COMIC SANS MS">
From 1956, here's an original 11 × 14 lobby card from the drive-in classic,
<FONT COLOR=RED>
```

```
"It Conquered the World."
</FONT>
<P>
```
This film starred Peter Graves (of Mission: Impossible fame), '50s scream queen Beverly Garland, and tough guy Lee Van Cleef.
```
<P>
```
This is lobby card #2 of the original U.S. set of eight. It features a great color photo of Peter Graves confronting another actor in a street scene of panic and confusion. This card also features excellent border graphics of the alien invader and the film's original logo. The surrounding white border features the standard National Screen Service (NSS) proprietary information. It's printed on the standard heavy pulp paper as were all lobby cards at that time.
```
<P>
<A HREF="http://www.geocities.com:80/Hollywood/Boulevard/8785/itconq.gif">
<IMG ALIGN="RIGHT"
SRC="http://www.geocities.com/Hollywood/Boulevard/8785/itconq2.gif"
ALT="It Conquered Lobby Card">
</A>
```

This lobby card is in excellent condition. Although issued 44 years ago for the film's original release, this lobby card has fared extremely well. All corners are slightly soft with one showing a tiny bit of paper loss. There is a barely-noticeable quarter-inch tear in the left border, but no paper loss there. The white border shows very light handling soiling and is refreshingly free of any pinholes or tape residue. This card is a clean, vivid specimen that's striking to look at and will be a welcome addition to any vintage horror collection. Click on the image here to see a larger view.

```
<P>
```

High Bidder will please prepay plus shipping costs (calculated at close of auction). Payment must be received within 10 days of auction close else transaction will be considered null and void. Payment by PayPal, money order, or cashier's check will gain immediate shipment of item upon payment receipt. Personal checks gladly accepted but will need to clear (approx. 10 days) before item can be shipped. All items shipped via USPS Priority Mail or ExpressMail. FedEx delivery is available upon request and for additional fee. Insurance and delivery confirmation if available at additional cost if not already covered in shipping method selected. If insurance is declined, buyer assumes responsibility for damage or loss. All items guaranteed to arrive as described with refunds cheerfully granted if item received is materially different than as listed. Items must be returned within 10 days of original delivery and are subject to inspection prior to issuance of refund. If there are any questions regarding these terms and conditions, please contact me via e-mail before bidding. Thank you for your interest in my auctions.

```
<P>
Check My eBay
<A HREF="http://cgi.ebay.com/aw-
cgi/eBayISAPI.dll?ViewFeedback&userid=dennis_prince">
feedback
</A>
and bid with confidence. Thanks for bidding.
</STRONG></FONT></BODY></HTML>
```

At first glance, this looks like quite a bit of work, but in actuality the real work resides in the first HTML listing you create. Once that's perfected, you can save the document for reuse and modification to be applied to future listings. In other words, you can create an HTML template that's ready on demand.

Does HTML Really Make a Difference?

While simple listings can be undeniably effective, a bit of well-placed style can certainly enhance your item's presence as well as the bidders' shopping experience. Utilize some simple HTML coding to add special fonts, colors, simple backgrounds, and interspersed images in a way that compliments your items and entices visitors to stop, look, and bid. It's the same subtle tactic used by marketing professionals, and it works. When used in moderation, your custom listing designs can lure otherwise apathetic shoppers from being disinterested drop-bys into becoming motivated buyers.

HTML Gone Bad

Of course, too much of a good thing can backfire in your face. Sooner or later, every seller bows to the temptation of seriously jazzing up their sales listings to the point of excess. Whether you've just learned HTML, found a great bunch of animated images (dancing hamsters or what have you), or simply feel you have to have the nicest display in the cyber-market, it's not uncommon for some to get a bit carried away. If you become obsessed with painting too grand a picture in your item listings, here are the risks you'll run:

- You could detract from the actual item you're offering. All the special HTML effects can upstage the very item you hope to sell.

- Your listing could take too long to load. All the extra features eventually pile up and require a certain amount of download time (especially animated images). Bidders are generally disinclined to wait more than 10 or 15 seconds before leaving your slow-loading listing.
- Excessive design could unwittingly communicate that you're eager to distract a bidder from the actual details of the item.

For best results, utilize HTML sparingly. When used properly, HTML can effectively break up large blocks of text, improving the readability of your item. With a discreet amount of design and appropriate embedded images, it can work in your favor to entice bidders to cast a bid for the item that, in plain format, may have lacked the sort of visual excitement and "hook" to positively sway bidders.

WHAT ABOUT eBAY'S LISTING FEATURES?

Arguably, there's an alternate path to visual enhancement for your items: using eBay's listing features and themes. Granted, with just the click of a mouse, you can employ use of eBay's canned designs and templates to brighten up your items. From my position, though, I tend to avoid these features for one simple reason: they incur additional fees. It may seem trivial to worry about an extra dime, quarter, or dollar when listing an item, yet when extrapolated to tens or hundreds of items, this becomes profit-prohibitive and fortune foolish. While I encourage all users to test and try the different eBay offerings, in my opinion, some elements are simply fluff. Look ahead to Chapter 26 for a full discussion of controlling auction costs and improving your fortune potential.

17

Boost Your Sales with Better Photos

In the early days of eBay, finding an actual image to accompany an item up for auction was a real treat; today, it's an absolute necessity. To attract more bidders and earn higher prices, you need to serve up quality images every time. Bidders aren't as prone to take risks on poorly presented items, and with the vast number of items to choose from at eBay every day, they won't settle for items sporting low-quality pictures. In this chapter, take note of how to take better pictures and how to avoid having your auctions summarily dismissed as apparent halfhearted attempts. Even if you're not a professional photographer, taking good photos is easier than you might expect, and the bids those photos will attract is well worth the extra effort.

IMAGING EQUIPMENT

First things first: good images are the product of good equipment. Before you concern yourself with *how* to take better photos, focus on how well equipped you are for the task.

Digital Cameras

Digital cameras are definitely the tool of choice these days, thanks to their portability and versatility. When shopping for a digital camera, pay close attention to the following features that contribute to better images:

- *Image Resolution:* This is the most important factor in determining which camera you should purchase and how much you can expect to pay. Low-priced VGA cameras (offering only 640-by-480 pixels) are inexpensive but won't give the detail and clarity your bidders are looking for. Instead, aim for at least a 2.1 megapixel (1600-by-1200

152

pixels) model. Go for even higher resolution if you can afford it. The higher the pixel count, the sharper and truer the image.

- *Lenses and Focus Mechanics:* Look for a camera that offers both auto and manual focusing, with a real bonus being zoom capability for illuminating tiny details with crystal clarity.
- *Ease of Use:* The simpler the controls, the better. Fighting and fumbling with a camera will not only be frustrating but will usually result in less-than-stellar images.
- *Tripod Mount:* Most cameras have these by default, but be sure. Mounting your camera on a tripod reduces blurring caused by shaky hands.

Digital cameras have gotten significantly less expensive than when they first appeared on the scene, yet a good camera will still cost between $150 and $300; a bit pricey, yes, but well worth the investment due to the camera's versatile nature.

e B a y T I P :   Although the topic will be covered fully in Chapter 25, understand that some of the equipment purchases you make to support an eBay business might qualify as tax write-offs. If you'll be serious about conducting a "business for profit," the equipment and other necessities that support that profitable venture are often expenses that can be deducted from your annual taxable income. Perhaps that will help take some of the sting out of purchasing the imaging equipment discussed in this chapter.

Digital camera prices will vary depending upon the extras you might desire as well as the method of image storage and retrieval (internal memory sticks or 3.5-inch floppy disk storage). Try several different models before you decide to purchase one.

Scanners

Digital scanners are generally the second-best choice for making auction images unless you deal strictly with flat items (such as lobby cards and the like) where the scanner actually becomes the preferred imaging equipment for its ability to deliver even sharper detail than a camera. Scanners are becoming better and better and their prices keep dropping lower and lower. As with cameras, use image resolution as your guide to which models will deliver the best results (1200 × 2400 dpi is the lowest "dot per inch" resolution you should settle for today). The bonus of scanners is that they serve multiple uses. Many scan directly from 35mm slides or negatives, allowing you to easily digitize pictures from last year's Disneyland trip when you're not listing auction items. As for prices, scanners are a great value with the mid-range models priced at about $100 to $175.

Traditional Cameras

And don't forget conventional 35mm cameras. Although they lack the convenience of photographing direct to a digital source, many film processors (online and off) will develop your pictures direct to downloadable online files or to an easy-to-use CD-ROM. If you've photographed several auction items using a 35mm film camera, it's now easy to convert those to digital images ready for auction use.

SETTING UP A SIMPLE PHOTO STUDIO

Don't just plop an item on your desk or drop it on the garage floor and start snapping photos—you'll likely end up doing it disservice by introducing background elements that will detract from the item's overall appearance, not to mention exposing it to all manner of dirt or damage. Rather, find a spot in your home or apartment (or wherever else you'll be working) to create your own designated photo studio.

Setting the Stage

You don't have to commandeer the spare bedroom or begin renovating the garage to establish your private atelier. All you really need is a few feet of dedicated working space. Purchase one or two parson's tables (the inexpensive kind you find in the bed-and-bath stores) and situate them side by side. If you'll be photographing larger items, get a piece of half-inch plywood that can straddle the tables or a pair of sawhorses; it doesn't have to be a fancy setup to be effective—just stable and sturdy.

Dolling Up with a Simple Backdrop

With your studio surface in place, you now need to establish a background that will best compliment your items and provide a professional appearance. A good choice for establishing a background is a length of inexpensive material in a solid color (with off-white, black, or dark blue offering the best contrast results). Tack the material to a wall or in a corner to form a backdrop, then drape it over your work surface (see Figure 17-1). You now have a consistent background color that will show off the item without showing it up.

Light Source

A key consideration to any photography is lighting. While it's not terribly difficult to establish good lighting, it's almost certain death for an image (and an auction) if the lighting is terrible. Here are a few lighting tricks the professionals employ to get high-quality images on an amateur budget:

Figure 17-1 An inexpensive parson's table, some dark velvet, and an empty corner make for a simple but stellar photo studio.

- *Go Natural:* Photos taken in natural sunlight usually produce the best results with regard to reproducing details and true colors. If the sun is shining, photograph outdoors.
- *If It Must Be Artificial:* Use incandescent bulbs (60 watts or less) for best results. Higher-wattage bulbs tend to oversaturate the item with light, giving it a washed-out look. Also, stay away from fluorescent lighting; it gives your images a yellow-green tint and usually misrepresents the coloring of the item.
- *Control the Light:* Aim the light where you need it to get the best results. If you're working outdoors, use a reflector (something as simple as white poster board or a mylar auto sunshade) to direct sunlight at your item. If working indoors, purchase three automobile worklights and suspend them above and on either side of the item (again, being careful not to blast too high a wattage at it).

As simple as that, you have a professional-quality photo studio at a cut-rate cost. Experiment with the different elements and with your camera's settings until you have the perfect balance to gain consistently superlative results.

TOUCHING UP YOUR ITEM IMAGES

Although you're now equipped to properly light, accentuate, and photograph your items, it still may be necessary to do a bit of postphotography touching up. Whether you need to crop, color-correct, or just sharpen up some fuzzy edges, here are some tips to help you decide when and how to polish up your pictures.

Determining When Touch-Ups Are Necessary

Try as you might, the images you shoot sometimes need just a bit of tweaking to properly represent your items. These should be minor adjustments, though, not wholesale reworking. If the image you're working with seems to require significant modification, you're better off rephotographing the item. However, barring a complete restart, here are the sorts of attributes of an image that can be easily adjusted without scrapping the whole shoot:

- Images that are excessively bright, overly dark, or oversaturated with color (see Figure 17-2)
- Images that do not properly represent the actual appearance of the item (problems usually related to coloring and brightness)
- Images that include unnecessary or distracting background elements that should be cropped out (see Figure 17-3)
- Images that are simply too large and should be resized prior to using in an auction

 eBay TIP: Beware! If your image editing results in the concealment of blemishes or defects, stop immediately. You'll want to steer clear of those fabled "touched-up photos" that mask an item's true appearance, serving only to mislead bidders into believing they'll be receiving something significantly different from what you really have to offer. This is not to say that altering item images is an exercise in deception. However, many sellers have unintentionally misrepresented their items in their honest effort to provide customers with a clearer and more colorful picture. To avoid this accidental occurrence, always compare your final image to the actual piece and ask yourself if the image looks *better* than the item itself; if it does, you've edited too much.

Editing Tools

Photo editing software comes in a wide variety of prices and accompanying features. If you want the Cadillac of applications, look no further than Adobe's *PhotoShop.* It's the application that the pros use (and commands a

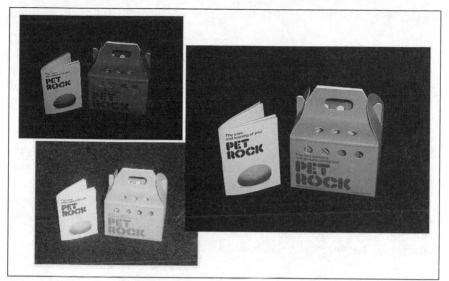

Figure 17-2   Too dark, too light, just right (on the right!).

professional's price of around $600). If a more economically priced applications will suit you better, look at Jasc Software's *Paint Shop Pro*, Microsoft's *Picture-It*, or MGI's *PhotoSuite*—each is generally available for $100 or less and can deliver the fundamental photo editing features you'll need. The truly frugal among of us have found many *shareware* and *freeware* versions of these

Figure 17-3   Too much clutter around your item is distracting and unprofessional.

applications and others ready to be downloaded from the Internet right into your computer.

eBay TIP: In case "shareware" and "freeware" are new terms to you, they're functional computer programs or applications that are free—that's right, free—for you to download from the Internet into your PC. By definition, shareware programs are of the sort you can download and try for free to decide whether you like them or not. For a nominal fee, you can then download the full-featured version to use (the shareware version of the program usually is missing some features of the fee-based version). Freeware is free to use and typically has all of the features the programmer intended to provide. To find out more about shareware and freeware, as well as to find a ton of programs you can try or have free of cost, visit *www.tucows.com;* it's the preferred download destination on the Web that features safe (virus-free) applications that are easy to transfer to your PC.

Though these free products might have a limited use period or are equally limited in their capabilities, free downloads are a great way to test-drive an application before you invest in it. And don't overlook any decent image editors that may have actually come preloaded on your computer or in a CD-ROM accompanying the digital camera you purchased.

Fine-Tuning the Fine Details

So what exactly can you hope to correct if your image doesn't represent your item just right? By using one of the image editors previously mentioned, here are the most common image enhancements you can make with just a few clicks and drags of your computer's mouse:

- *Brightness and Contrast.* If your image is too dark, washed out, or rather murky, work with the brightness and contrast controls to draw out details and brighten the color tones (see Figure 17-4).
- *Color Saturation/Hue.* If the lighting you used cast an odd tint on your item's natural coloring, this control will allow you to independently adjust the red, green, and blue levels. With only minor adjustment, you can restore the actual coloring of the item that was otherwise misrepresented in your unretouched photo.
- *Sharpen/Edge Enhance/Smooth.* After making other adjustments, you might find the need to add crispness to your image, or conversely, soften what might have emerged as harsh edges. Using these controls, you can bring out blurred detail or smooth out jagged edges. Be careful, though, as this adjustment can often result in giving your image that dreaded "touched-up" look.

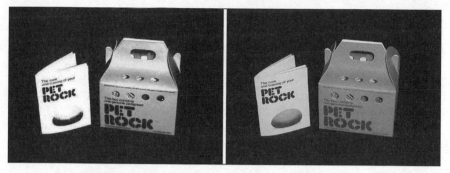

Figure 17-4 The washed-out image on the left was easily corrected, utilizing brightness and contrast adjustments, to become the image on the right.

Size Matters

Finally, don't overlook the importance of being equally attentive to the size of your photos. Online shoppers can be an impatient lot and few are inclined to wait around while a "fat" image creeps onto their computer display. Rather than risk losing a sale, be sure your images load fast by keeping the file sizes at or near the 30K mark. Start with your camera: work image adjustments down from ultra-fine detail to medium quality (which still renders a nice photo). You can also use image editing applications to resize larger images (but watch out for image degradation). And, you can find image compression software (programs that essentially squeeze large files down to a manageable size without sacrificing picture quality) like WinSoftMagic's Advanced JPEG Compressor that can get those files down to size and speedier to display.

More Help—Free!

Naturally, the different image editors use different terminology and manage their features uniquely from product to product. If you're looking to become a real expert with the editor you've selected, hit the Internet and search for Web sites that offer free help. A search on the name of your image editor will typically reveal multiple sites that offer simple tips and even some impressively thorough tutorials.

PICTURE IMPERFECT: EIGHT COMMON IMAGING MISTAKES TO AVOID

While there's no denying that quality images will boost bidding rates and potentially increase your sales prices, it's equally true that poor photos can quickly undercut your best efforts, alienating and even angering potential bidders. To make sure you steer clear of this digital minefield, here are the eight most common blunders that tend to afflict sellers' online images:

1. *Poor Lighting.* If the lighting is dim, the image detail can be grossly underrepresented. Equally, an item too brightly lit will result in a severely overexposed image. Refer back to the lighting tips presented earlier to avoid this problem.

2. *Blurry Images.* Fuzzy images are an annoyance and reflect lack of attention on the seller's part. Always check the focus before you shoot and, if you have a jittery hand, use a tripod for a true "still-life" image.

3. *Excessive Glare.* A close cousin to poor lighting, excessive glare can be the result of an overlit item, yet is usually caused by improper flash usage. Shoot items from an angle (left, right, over, or under) or wait until you can photograph outdoors.

4. *Lack of Cropping.* Few bidders are interested in scouring an image of your messy desk in search of the item you purport to be selling. Crop your images to cut out anything that distracts from the item—that includes the kids or the kitten, no matter how cute they may be.

5. *Reflective Surfaces.* There's an infamous image making the rounds on the Internet of a chrome tea kettle reflecting a full view of its immodest proprietor. If you've seen this picture, then you know why you need to take care when photographing reflective items that might reveal distracting or even embarrassing elements opposite them. Shoot these at an angle and across from a neutral background.

6. *Bad Backgrounds.* Forgo overly-fancy backdrops or garish colors—they only distract from your item. Choose neutral or complimentary background colors to really make your item stand out.

7. *Confounding Combo-Shots.* Some sellers think it a good idea to photograph multiple items in a single image; they should think again. Other items adjacent to the one you're selling will again distract the potential buyer away from what you're really offering for sale.

8. *Lack of Close-Up.* Ever looked at images of jewelry or small collectibles where the item is too tiny to clearly discern? Avoid this frustration by getting closer to the item (watch the focus) or by taking full advantage of your camera's zoom function (see Figure 17-5).

Certainly, none of these are truly *fatal offenses,* and many can be forgiven by tolerant buyers. Still, take the opportunity to learn from past mistakes of others to further improve your item images and give your auctions the best profit potential.

Figure 17-5 Lost somewhere in this terrific photo studio is a little item begging for a much-deserved close-up.

IS ALL THIS EFFORT REALLY WORTH IT?

If ever you doubt the value of taking and providing good images of your auction items, consider this sentiment shared by longtime auction enthusiast and friend Gretchen Hakala: "I'm annoyed by sellers who post bad images—it's sloppy and shows the seller must not be too concerned with quality." It's a poignant testimony that shows how image quality has a direct reflection on the seller's perceived style. Hakala continues on, offering this sobering insight about the effect of poor images in an auction: "I might take a chance [and bid] on an item that has a poor image simply because I'm pretty certain I'll get it for a good price—I know most other bidders won't bid at all because of the lousy picture and I wind up with a better deal." If that's the case, then poor images really *do* cost sellers in the long run and could stand between you and your fortune.

18

Selling Strategies—Tried, True, and Groundbreaking

You've probably already noticed that this book is full of strategies for getting the best possible prices for items you sell on eBay—strategies for the most eye-catching images, the most intriguing listings, the most successful sales policies, and much more. Think of this chapter, then, as the gold of auction mining: the time-tested strategies that will yield better results to your efforts.

Ask any eBay expert about strategy, and they'll generally tell you the secret is not so much in the tool itself, but rather in the way that you use it. Forget the come-ons you might see where a CD-ROM peddler is promising to unveil all the closely guarded secrets of the eBay PowerSellers (those who maintain a sales volume of at least $1000 per month); the secrets aren't really secret at all, they're simply well-founded business techniques that most newcomers have yet to apply. There are, however, a few unique approaches to marketing and selling at eBay, techniques you may never have figured could make a difference to your eBay bottom line. This chapter, then, offers the insights you've been waiting for, the methods and means to set yourself apart from the others as you edge ever closer to your financial goals.

IT ALL STARTS WITH TIMING

As the old saying goes, "timing is everything." Although it may sound a bit trite, when it comes to online auctioning, savvy sellers have found that strategic timing—in terms of *when* and *how long* an auction will run—can have significant impact on their ultimate success. The questions to answer, therefore, are: what is the best day of the week to list or end an auction?; how long should an auction run?; and which is the magical hour for ending an auction? Those are the questions; these are the answers:

The Long and the Short of It

Before listing, you need to calculate which day you want your auction to end. This in turn will dictate the starting day for your auction. As you recall from Chapter 7, eBay offers several choices for auction length, ranging from 3 to 10 days (sometimes even longer). Remember this, though: if an auction is too long (such as the 10- or 14-day epochs), it might be forgotten during its lengthy run. If it's too short, however (as in the 3-day quickie), it might not generate any momentum before it ends. In general, it's best to run auctions for a 7-day stretch. Granted, this can be a long wait for sellers anxious to close a deal; however, by having an auction encompass a full seven days you can best reach people who browse the Internet and eBay only on certain days of the week (believe it or not, some folks still have limited access to a computer). Most important, the 7-day listing will span both weekend days (if started on a Saturday or Sunday) when auction traffic is generally higher.

What a Difference a Day Makes

Although opinions vary, Sunday is still considered the best day to end an auction. Start and end your auction on a Sunday and you tap a full week and weekend's worth of exposure. Again, Saturdays and Sundays tend to bring out bidders, accommodating those who don't enjoy the luxury of surfing the 'Net at their workplaces.

Are there bad days on which to end an auction? Well, Fridays can be challenging since your listings won't benefit from the weekend surge. And, folks who sneak off for early weekends might be away from their computers on Fridays and Saturdays. By ending an auction on a Sunday, though, you can still entertain those folks who've been away for most of the weekend yet are ready to go online upon returning home Sunday afternoon or evening.

eBay TIP: Surely you'll hear others exclaim such-and-such day is the *best* day for auctions to close. Be sure to experiment with closing days to see what suits your bidders best and be willing to be flexible enough to adjust that closing day if certain situations (such as holidays) dictate.

And how about those holidays? Most sellers agree that it's best to avoid ending auctions on a holiday (especially holiday weekends). Since most of us are either traveling or otherwise occupied by festivities, the traffic at auction sites will typically be light.

eBay TIP: Incidentally, the 14-day auction was created to accommodate the national holidays, allowing a seller to list an item before the holiday occurred and able to maintain the auction activity for another week after the big event has passed. While this scheme seems good in theory, 14-day auctions haven't proven to be a boon to sellers.

Tapping Into the eBay Rush Hour

Perhaps the most crucial consideration in timing strategy is choosing the hour your auction will start and ultimately end. By and large, the best time to start or end an auction will be in the evening hours when potential bidders are better able to browse for extended periods of time, having better chance to notice your new listings as well as allowing them to be "in attendance" to bid during your auctions' final minutes. Be sure to consider time zones in all this, offering West Coast citizens enough time to get home from work without making East Coast citizens stay up all night. (Hint: between 6 P.M. and 8 P.M. Pacific Time is the safest bet.)

 eBay TIP: As you decide on an ending time for your auction, keep in mind that eBay runs it's auctions based in the Pacific time zone.

Choosing Bidder-Friendly Times

You can see that smart auction timing takes your customers' surfing and bidding habits into account, trying to accommodate their schedules by and large. In fact, many sellers have reported receiving kudos from their customers for running auctions that tend to be easy to bid on thanks to their customer-considerate timing.

USING COUNTERS TO CHART YOUR SUCCESS

One of the best ways to determine how well your auction listing efforts are paying off is to monitor the amount of traffic your items are attracting. A simple tool that's been available for some time is the *online counter*. When listing an item at eBay, you're able to select a free counter that will be displayed for all to see or hidden, if you choose, for your eyes only. Here's some insight into counter use and how to distill the information you might gather.

Why Count?

I once read the following sentiment about online marketing: "Fifty-percent of my advertising doesn't work. I just don't know which 50 percent." Though relatively clever in content, there's truth to this statement as sellers struggle to determine when and where their auction enticements are most effective. The best way to gauge the appeal of your listings and adeptness of your sales strategies is to quantify the public response—that's where counters come into play.

Counters can tally how many people have visited your eBay listings. With each time a particular item is viewed, the tally is incremented. In this way, you'll see how much relative activity an item is generating, helping you to determine which items seem to be the most popular (by way of comparing the counter "hits"). Immediately, you'll be able to identify those items that draw more attention from lookers and bidders and those which seem to languish undisturbed on the virtual shelf. This might provide valuable insight to which attributes of the listing (style, category, timing) are responsible for attracting the most traffic for your items, which item key words seem to get the most search hits, which pricing strategies seem to lure more potential buyers, which days of the week see the most counter increases, and, overall, which combined approaches seem to be working best for you. Armed with these raw statistics, you're in a much better position to make well-reasoned adjustments as the numbers dictate.

Do the Numbers Ever Lie?

Understand that a high number of counter hits doesn't necessarily ensure a successful sale or higher auction bids. In fact, an item that receives a high number of hits but still doesn't sell might indicate your price needs revising, your description needs revamping, or perhaps your images need sprucing up. Be especially watchful of an item whose images take an extraordinarily long time to display (did you overdo the HTML?). Visitors may have decided not to wait around even though their attempt to view the item was tallied.

More to the point of counter accuracy, the free counters at eBay are often limited to providing simple *page views* (the number of times the item page has been looked at). While this is generally useful, the most granular and most telling statistic would be that of *unique visitor hits,* that is how many *different* visitors have viewed the item (as opposed to the same visitor viewing your item page several times or more). Don't expect to get this sort of data integrity from eBay, though. Generally, to gain this sort of specific information, you'd need to purchase specially-developed online tracking software and use it at a commercial Web site of your own (a topic of discussion taken up later in Chapter 27). If you're not yet considering starting your own online business outside of eBay, it may be too soon for this.

Better Seen or Unseen?

Here's where the discussion often picks up—the argument over whether it's better or worse to include visible counters on your item pages (recalling that you can elect to have the counter visible only to your eyes). One faction argues that a visible counter can help motivate buyers and bidders, citing that a high number of counter hits will indicate to shoppers that the item is potentially high in demand; a subsequent buyer might be prompted to take the item quickly before someone else snatches it away.

From the other side comes the argument that visible counters might dissuade a buyer or bidder for a couple of reasons. First, an item with a high counter value might indicate belief that something's wrong with the item; if the current bid doesn't reflect a high value in concert with the high counter rate something could be amiss. In a bidding scenario, a high count might foretell of a bidding war that will likely ensue, a competitive showdown that many buyers choose to avoid. And if the count is low; well, that could also indicate a perceived problem with the item, or it might act as enticement to bargain hunters.

Either way, there are pros and cons to utilizing visible counters. It's wise to use invisible counters at the outset as you can learn which items and sales approaches seem to be most popular, without tipping off or otherwise influencing your bidders. Then, experiment with making those counters visible and determine if they have a positive or negative effect on your sales.

Strength in Numbers

Whatever your approach, using counters makes good sense and will help you learn more about "online marketing" as well as your growing online customer base (repeat bidders). And while some statistical data can be a bit misleading, any sort of numerical results can typically aid you in honing your approach to improve your auction income.

THE POWER OF PERSUASIVE PRICING

With 14 million items available every day, competition among sellers at eBay is stiff. Don't throw up your hands in despair just yet, fearing the only way to lure bidders is by dumping your great stuff at giveaway prices. Truth is, high sell-through and healthy profits can both be yours *provided* you're using the best pricing strategies.

Know How Your Items Fare

The preamble to proper pricing is to understand how your goods will measure up in the competitive auction marketplace. Therefore, consider these core tenets of smart pricing: present supply and demand, condition and completeness of your goods, your investment value in your goods, and your realistic sales goals. Research current and closed auctions to ensure your pricing strategies will compliment, not contradict, current trends in auction sales. You'll find this to be the critical information that determines if what you want to sell is what the bidders want to buy—and at which price.

How Low Can You Go?

Naturally, bidders are looking for a bargain and your task is to entice them with a low minimum bid that practically screams, "Take me home, cheap!" Half the fun of online auctions is the gamesmanship of back-and-forth bidding, and low starting bids will start the ball rolling. Once a bidding volley ensues, thwarted bidders often return to reclaim the item they've likely taken "emotional possession" of, frequently battling hard to bring home the win, even ignoring that the current market value might have already been surpassed. If you've done your sales research thoroughly, you can safely attract those bargain hunters while ultimately achieving present market value (and sometimes beyond) for your item.

Is Higher Better?

Sometimes, higher-quality or highly desirable goods might be ill-served by a low opening bid that could conjure thoughts of "at that low a price, there must be something wrong." A higher opening bid can work wonders to effectively communicate your item is the real deal. It caters to the truly discriminating buyers (especially those who search specifically for higher-priced offerings) and showcases your knowledge and confidence in the fine goods you're offering. However, don't stall the bidding with *too* high a price. Rather, keep that starting price below present market value: try an opening bid price that falls between 50 and 75 percent of current market value. Bidders will see that you understand your item's value, yet aren't opposed to allowing their competitive bidding to set the final price. Savvy buyers rarely let a desirable item sell too cheaply.

RESERVE BIDS

If you're unsure about getting a reasonable price or recovering your investment in an item, apply a reserve price to it. Establishing a secret reserve price (it's never displayed in your listing) is an option available to you during Step 3 of listing your item. Reserve prices, as you'll recall from the discussion in Chapter 1, are preestablished sales price limits in which you're not required to sell your item at the auction's close if the high bid fails to reach your reserve price. This allows you to ensure you can protect your level of investment or belief of value in an item and not have to sell at a price you would consider too low. Although some bidders are put off at the mere sight of a reserve price auction, sometimes it's your best bet to avoid a significant loss. But like the high opening bid strategy, set your reserve slightly below market value whenever possible to allow for the auction process to ultimately decide the final sales price. If you get greedy or drop a reserve on *every* auction you list, you'll incur the stigma of being an overpriced seller who has little knowledge of (or faith in) the bidding market.

Buy It Now: A Quick, Noncompetitive Alternative

There's definitely a population of eager buyers who aren't interested in competitive bidding nor inclined to wait for an auction to run its course. Instead, they prefer a quick purchase, plain and simple. Likewise, some sellers also prefer the fixed-price format of eBay's "Buy It Now" listings (see Figure 18-1) as a way to mitigate the risk of relinquishing items too cheaply, avoid use of the secretive and oft-maligned "reserve" price, and generally effect a rapid transaction. Recall you were given the opportunity to designate a Buy-It-Now price on Step 3 of listing your item, the stage in which you designated your opening bid price (refer to Chapter 7).

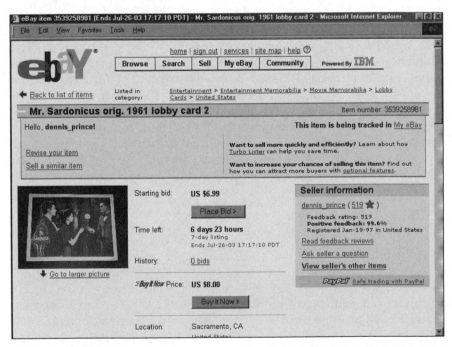

Figure 18-1   When the Buy-It Now option is in use, you'll see the "take it" price listed just below the Place Bid area.

If you're not certain when you should employ the Buy It Now feature, consider these situations:

- Your item is in demand and you've found the current market value to be acceptable; offer to let buyers take it at that price and be done with it.
- Your item is in *high* demand and you stand to gain above market value from a buyer who doesn't wish to lose out in the bidding wars any longer.
- Your item is of "time-boxed" demand (e.g., seasonal or trendy goods) and a fixed price sell ensures the buyer of receiving it in a timely manner.
- You're in no particular hurry and can afford to set fixed prices to see if the market will bear a potentially higher price.

e B a y T I P : Remember that you can make use of the Buy It Now price within a traditional auction at eBay. Establish your opening bid, a reserve if you feel the need, and then suggest a Buy-It-Now price too. Some bidders will decide it's best to take the item for the reasonable fixed price you're offering, resulting in a fast purchase for them and a quick sale for you. If not, the normal bidding can ensue. Usually, the Buy-It-Now option disappears once a bid is placed on an item that included the fixed price alternative. However, if the seller also stipulates a reserve price in the listing, the Buy-It-Now price remains available until normal bidding meets or exceeds the Buy-It-Now price. Once the reserve is met, the Buy-It-Now option then disappears.

Let the Bidders Decide

In the end, your best bet is to give the buyers what they really want: options. Whether they choose to battle other bidders for your goods or elect to buy your items outright, give them the opportunity to decide for themselves. Though this doesn't imply that *every* item you offer has to be presented in dual strategy, utilize the different methods in an effort to ultimately give bidders the power of choice.

SALVAGING UNSUCCESSFUL AUCTIONS

When you're new to auctioning, it's natural for you to step into eBay with high hopes for high bids, and most sellers will usually achieve a high level of success. However, when your hopes are high but the bids aren't, you might wind up with an occasional "unsuccessful" auction. Whether your reserve price wasn't met or even if nobody bid at all, there might still be a way to drum up a sale even after the final gavel has struck. Here are a few strategies to employ to bring success to your "unsuccessful" auction.

Ringing Up the Reserves

Believe it or not, one of the easiest postauction sales to make is when your auction's reserve price isn't met. Whenever you have an auction close without the reserve price being met, it's good customer courtesy to contact the high bidder as a form of closure. But, as you're thanking a bidder for his or her interest in your item, you might ask if they're still interested in buying it. Oftentimes, bidders are willing to make a deal. In a polite e-mail, ask the high bidder if he or she would like one more chance to purchase your item:

> Thanks for bidding on my item. Unfortunately my reserve price of $40 wasn't met (you were only $5 away). If you're still interested in the item at this price, just let me know before I relist it. Thanks!

Divulge your secret reserve price to let the high bidder know how close he or she might have been to winning. The bidder may take you up on your reserve price (try throwing in free shipping to help clinch the sale) or the bidder may counteroffer a lower price. Don't get greedy here—if the counteroffer is reasonable and you're truly interested in making a sale, work with the bidder. If you have enough margin to work with and are willing to negotiate, you still might make a decent profit.

The Easiest Sale You'll Make

Sometimes the buyers will come to you. If a buyer contacts you after your "unsuccessful" auction's ended, asking if you're interested in making a deal, consider their inquiry. Though some buyers might try to swoop in and take advantage of you (offering an offensively low selling price perhaps), many are legitimately interested in striking a reasonable deal. Reply promptly and be prepared to negotiate a bit—remember that if the buyer was interested in paying your original price, he or she would have bid during the course of the auction. And, don't be surprised if a high-bidder gives you the old "suggestive selling" routine in reverse: "*Got anything else like this?*" It's a real bonus when the bidders start knocking on *your* door.

APPEALING TO BUYERS' SENSES

Here's a strategy you may never have considered: oftentimes, sellers overlook the importance of appealing to their buyers' senses. That is, in all the flurry of listing goods and managing sales, it becomes easy to overlook these small but significant nuances of selling items. Therefore, selling to senses, so to speak, will help you improve your offerings, ensure high levels of customer satisfaction, and keep those buyers coming back for more. Here's how:

Sight

Clearly, first impressions are lasting ones. If an item you have to offer is dusty, dingy, or generally just a bit dilapidated in appearance, see if you can clean it up a bit. And while brushing off the dust and wiping away the soil is typically a good idea, take care in your cleaning. Some sellers have damaged items in their efforts to add a bit of polish (such as attempting to remove old price tags, stains, or what have you) and some buyers proclaim that removing an item's natural "patina" is a definite no-no. Therefore, clean when it makes sense—when there's no risk of devaluing the item—to give the item a best possible appearance (find out how other sellers and collectors shine up similar articles). If you're not sure, provide a full disclosure of the item's present state and the potential for polishing, then leave it for the buyer to decide if a cleaning is in order.

Smell

Sometimes the nose knows what's inside a package long before the eyes ever get a glimpse. Take special care to please this sense as buyers are often more than disappointed when an item brings along a stench that wasn't bargained for. If an item has a musty odor from moisture exposure, let it be known. If you're a smoker and your items have absorbed the odor, let that be known too. Whatever the situation, if your goods have a certain "air" about them that could be potentially offensive, be certain to state it up front.

Touch

Usually, touch isn't a sensation that proves too troublesome. Of course, items that are rough, sticky, or whatever—and shouldn't be—necessitate full disclosure. The same holds for furniture or other items that might have been worn smooth over years of use or could have the telltale rippling or warping that comes from moisture damage; these situations should also be properly explained at the outset. Many buyers will close their eyes and run their hands over an item to detect variations or imperfections that their eyes might miss. Be sure there are no tactile surprises in store for your customers.

Sound

Naturally, when you're selling audio-related items (such as old records, tapes, radios, and so on), you'll want to fully describe the aural qualities of the goods. But, beyond these obvious sound-related items, give consideration to any sounds *any* of your items might make. If it rattles, is something broken? If it squeaks, does it need to be lubricated? Again, no sense is to be taken for granted when selling to and satisfying your customers.

Taste?

OK, this is the one sense that you might not need to cater to as carefully as the previous four. Still, some rock, gem, and coin collectors have stated that their taste buds can offer the final determination about an item's authenticity and lineage. You probably can't offer a taste-test up front but just be aware of this form of buyers' authentication.

Making Sense of It All

Although it might have sounded a bit far-fetched, appealing to your buyer's senses is just another consideration to be given as you manage your listings and strive for your fortune. Remembering that online sales prevent buyers from fully experiencing an item as they would in person, therefore work to present as much positive sensory information as possible when listing your goods, and then be doubly certain that there will be no negative sensory surprises when the goods arrive. This is a strategy that will certainly set you ahead of your peers.

KEYS TO RELISTING

If, for all your efforts, your item simply doesn't sell, don't consider throwing it out just yet. Now knowing about the effect and impact of sales strategies, you're in the best position possible to reevaluate your approach while further refining your selling expertise. Therefore, always give consideration to an item's second life through relisting.

Review, Revise, and Remarket

On every eBay item page, just above the item description, there is a text link that reads, "Relist this item." Click that link to navigate through the same listing forms as when the item was originally posted for auction. All of the original listing information is still contained within the listing forms, but when relisting you may consider making some changes. Perhaps you need a change in approach and strategy as you prepare to reposition your item. To that end, consider these key relisting opportunities:

- Review your auction title for clarity and maximum "hit" keywords (for buyers' searches).
- Review your auction category and determine whether it was the best choice, the only choice, or if there's a better choice available.

- Review your auction description to be sure it's informative, accurate, and enticing.
- Did you offer images of the item?
- Was your minimum bid price or reserve price set too high? Can you adjust it down or forgo the reserve, trusting the current market to bring you a reasonable price?
- Was this the best time to list? Review the time, day, and season of your auction and determine if an adjustment is in order.
- How many times have you relisted (if this isn't just your second go-round)? Is it possible there's simply no interest in your item at this time? (Yes, this is a rare but plausible conclusion at times.)

There is a value about a failed auction: it communicates that your approach, somehow and somewhere, didn't quite work. Be very open, perceptive, and flexible with each of your auctions. In many cases, it's a fine-tuning procedure where you're stabilizing your business approach and adjusting your offerings. Relistings allow you to tinker with your listing approach until you can lock into your customer base in a way that has you bringing in the bids at a maximum success rate.

19

Building and Managing Your Inventory

With expert sales strategies powering your auction results you must now turn your attention to ensuring that your inventory of goods doesn't dwindle and dissipate. Some successful sellers have enjoyed terrific sell-through rates only to be caught unprepared when their stock of auctionable items virtually evaporates in short order. To make a long-term run at auctioning, sellers need to establish reliable sources of replenishment or else face the dreaded out-of-stock dilemma. In this chapter, you'll learn how to keep your shelves fully stocked at all times and effectively manage that online storeroom to ensure your auction income is never interrupted.

SETTING YOUR GOALS BEFORE STOCKING YOUR SHELVES

eBay is a terrific venue for cleaning up the house and yard and bringing home a few extra dollars. However, if you aspire to become a serious seller—to be in this for the longer term—you'll want to take a more focused approach to developing and growing your business potential. Once you get into that league, *inventory* is your product—and acquiring and maintaining that inventory by way of an inventory plan is what keeps you operating profitably. In establish this inventory plan, be sure you have clear answers to these questions:

- Are you selling for the long haul or is this just a one-time stint?
- How much inventory do you already have (possibly made up of your own possessions), what return might it bring, and how long will it sustain your selling activity?
- How much capital (expendable cash or access to it) will you need to establish your inventory of goods?

- What sorts of goods do you want to sell? Will you generalize or specialize in your inventory?
- At what prices can you purchase goods and what profit percentage can you expect to achieve?
- How popular are the items you want to sell and what kind of inventory turnover can you reasonably expect?
- How (and where) will you store your inventory, and does it require any special environmental conditions (temperature, humidity, etc.)?
- How many listings do you want to stage each week or month and what levels of inventory will you need to support that?
- What is the lead time to replenish your inventory?
- Will the items you sell be seasonal, selling best at certain times of the year as opposed to sustained levels year-round?

After having gotten the hang of auctioning at eBay, you'll want to seriously concern yourself with these inventory matters, ensuring that the goods you need are fully considered beforehand without having your aspirations of fortune depending on whatever items you might be able to hastily scrounge up.

IDENTIFYING SOURCES OF SUPPLY

Where do long-term sellers find all that great stuff to auction? Actually, it's rare for sellers to rely on a single source of goods; most have learned to seek out a variety of sources to keep their auctions running at full tilt. Here are some of the key places you'll want to investigate for potential inventory, including some you may have already considered and some maybe not.

Secondhand Goods

You've heard the stories: someone made a hundred bucks on a bauble they paid two bits for at the local flea market. Though it's common knowledge that online auctioneers have turned flea markets, garage sales, and thrift shops upside down in their quest for auctionable goods, the fact is that these are still very viable sources of inventory. With some of the initial auction fever having waned (casual sellers discovering how much work is required in steady auctioning), sellers are again finding buried treasures at these discard depositories. Though you won't want to rely solely on these secondhand venues, they're still worth a regular visit.

Inventory for Under a Buck

Surely, there's one of those funky 98-cent-type stores near you. If you haven't yet visited it, do so—there are some decent finds within (and don't forget to visit *www.99centwholesale.com,* too). Often, manufacturer's overruns or discontinued merchandise can be found at these stores. Just because the retail market has turned its back on these goods doesn't necessarily mean the auction market has. Many sellers have admitted these stores house some great items that cost less than a dollar yet can net profits of $5 or more. You'll have to be selective and you'll need to visit regularly since much of the inventory changes from week to week. But, with the frequent good finds to be had, it would be foolish to turn your nose up to these cut-rate supply headquarters.

The Online Source, of Course

One of the most convenient places to find inventory is on the Internet itself. Without ever leaving your computer you can research, locate, and procure the kinds of goods that you've found are selling well at eBay. Many importers and wholesalers maintain an online presence in an effort to reach a greater audience of buyers, as are you. Don't overlook the potential of searching by specific item keywords, which will usually turn up additional commercial and private sources. And remember to constantly peruse the auction listings themselves for even more low-priced inventory. It's commonplace for sellers to proclaim they've landed great bargains at eBay, then, with a bit of sales strategy applied to a new listing of their own, turn the goods over in the same venue for a healthy profit (I do this constantly, by the way).

eBay TIP: Some sellers can maintain steady auction activity by purchasing huge lots of merchandise, by the pallet full or box load, often at incredibly low prices. They then sell each item individually for a healthy profit. If this is what you're interested in doing, look in Chapter 20 for information on how to buy big.

CARE AND STORAGE OF YOUR INVENTORY

Not all inventory is created equal, nor should all inventory be treated the same. As you continually research what sorts of things might sell for you at eBay you should also be sensitive to special requirements or considerations for the goods you'll handle. Matters of item size, item value, fragility, and so on will need to be considered as part of your work in acquiring, maintaining, and selling your goods. Therefore, take a look at this list of considerations as you determine whether your inventory will require any special care and handling:

- *How big (or small) will your items be?* If you're selling furniture or other large items, you'll be faced with the need for a larger storage area than if you're selling knickknacks.

- *Do your items require climate control?* All items are best stored in clean, dry environments, and some items will need special care in regard to humidity and exposure to sunlight.
- *Does your inventory require authentication?* If you're dealing in truly rare and collectible items, you might find your customers will be wanting irrefutable proof of originality before they'll drop big dollars. Authentication can cost extra and is a cost you'll need to figure into the overall cost of your goods to ensure that your eventual income will cover your outlay. (Incidentally, visit eBay's site map for a link to authentication services.)
- *Can your inventory be secured?* Though you needn't distrust friends or family, you will want to be able to close up your inventory area to ensure nothing is inadvertently moved or misplaced. And, of course, truly valuable items such as jewelry and the like should be locked up for safety's sake.
- *How large will your inventory grow?* Though you may start off with lower expectations, many sellers who find their rhythm tell of storage facilities that are quickly outgrown. Keep expansion in mind and be prepared to deal with overflow from your initial storage solution.
- *Will storage cost?* Some sellers have so much inventory that they have to move much of it to offsite storage facilities. Keep those costs in mind as you estimate your selling expenses and profit expectations.
- *How accessible will your inventory be?* If your items are stored offsite or in the attic, always work to keep them relatively easy to reach. Clambering over boxes or being unable to access an offsite facility could become inconvenient and time-consuming.

While maintaining a steady supply of hot-selling inventory is always the goal for the enduring online seller, never fail to plan how and where you'll store your goods before you commit to either a box full or a boxcar load of items.

KEEPING TRACK OF YOUR INVENTORY

A well-organized inventory will be a key asset to you as you make your fortune grow. Employing the use of either a spreadsheet application (see Figure 19-1) or inventory ledger, here are the details you'll want to record:

- *Item Number.* Develop a simple numbering scheme to make item identification easier—and make sure you always assign a number to incoming items.
- *Item Name.* What is it?

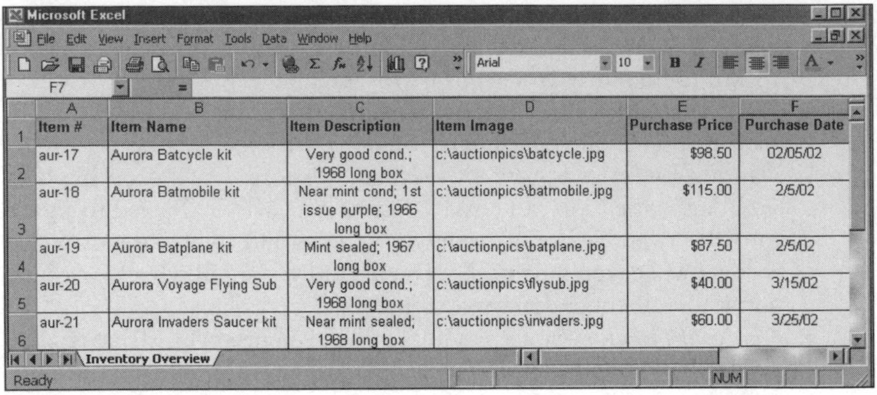

	A	B	C	D	E	F
1	Item #	Item Name	Item Description	Item Image	Purchase Price	Purchase Date
2	aur-17	Aurora Batcycle kit	Very good cond.; 1968 long box	c:\auctionpics\batcycle.jpg	$98.50	02/05/02
3	aur-18	Aurora Batmobile kit	Near mint cond; 1st issue purple; 1966 long box	c:\auctionpics\batmobile.jpg	$115.00	2/5/02
4	aur-19	Aurora Batplane kit	Mint sealed; 1967 long box	c:\auctionpics\batplane.jpg	$87.50	2/5/02
5	aur-20	Aurora Voyage Flying Sub	Very good cond.; 1968 long box	c:\auctionpics\flysub.jpg	$40.00	3/15/02
6	aur-21	Aurora Invaders Saucer kit	Near mint sealed; 1968 long box	c:\auctionpics\invaders.jpg	$60.00	3/25/02

Figure 19-1   The spreadsheet program on your computer makes keeping inventory records a breeze.

- *Item Description.*   Detailed enough description that highlights unique attributes of the item.
- *Item Image.*   Though this takes a bit more effort up front, an image will make identification all the easier. It will also be useful when it comes time to list your item—the image is ready to use whether it's a hard-copy photo that you'll scan or a link to a digital image that you'll later upload.
- *Item Cost.*   How much did you pay for it? (Don't forget to keep all of your receipts for potential tax deduction purposes.)
- *When Purchased.*   This helps you keep track of how long the item's been in your inventory.
- *Where Purchased.*   You may have stumbled on a great source of inventory and will most likely want to visit it again.
- *Estimated Resale Value.*   This can be subjective, but try to refer to generally accepted market values by reviewing price guides, talking with other sellers and collectors, and researching previous auction prices.
- *Storage Area.*   Where is it now? If you keep inventory in several places (as many sellers do), you'll want to minimize time spent hunting down an item.

Of course, you should tailor this list of information to best meet your own specific needs, but be sure you have sufficient data to enable you to accurately identify, retrieve, and list any item in your inventory.

REINVESTING WISELY

The key to building any fortune is to put your earnings back to work for you. At eBay, this means utilizing your auction profits and diverting some of that income back into growing your inventory. Knowing the stocks you have today will not last forever, consider how you'll keep that supply of goods in steady replenishment. Though you may not have thought this out as you embarked on this fortune hunt, here are some things to think about as you reinvest in your auction future.

- First and foremost, invest only at a price that provides you the opportunity to make a reasonable profit upon resale.
- Tie your reinvestment decisions to what you've learned in your ongoing market research, electing to invest only in inventory that has a proven market.
- Target a percentage of your auction income for immediate reinvestment in inventory. If you're in this for the long haul, you need to let the business (rather than your personal funds) carry the burden of inventory reinvestment.
- Try to invest in goods that you can successfully resell within three months. Avoid having your operating profit tied up too long in inventory that may not provide the return you hoped for.
- Seek to build an emergency reinvestment fund for times when sales may slow or, better yet, when a rare opportunity to buy big presents itself.

Yes, it takes money to make money, but if you've chosen your inventory carefully, maintained it faithfully, and reinvested astutely, you'll be halfway home on the path to your fortune.

20

Buying for Resale

To be a truly successful seller and an expert in maintaining inventory, you'll need to become an equally adept buyer. By now you can see that one great buy or even an attic full of stuff isn't going to be enough to support your auction business (and it is a business) for an extended period. In order to ensure you can maintain an inventory of tempting and profit-bearing goods, you'll want to be sure you embody the traits of a savvy reseller and employ the uncompromising tactics of sound reinvestment to keep your business operating comfortably in the black.

THE RESELLER'S RESOLVE

To be a good reseller, it's important to approach that part of your eBay activity with only the purest resale objectives in mind. If you're not certain what criteria successful resellers apply to their inventory purchase, consider these differentiators:

- Resellers value an item for its ability to generate another sale, to broaden their offerings, and to ultimately entice more bidders.
- Resellers are in business to sell and thus avoid becoming emotionally attached to their resale merchandise.
- Resellers will buy new and different sorts of items if they sense a trend beginning, if their return buyers continue to ask for such items, or if there's a viable opportunity to expand the appeal of their offerings to a larger buying public.

Though it may sound a bit cold to approach auctioning and inventory management in such a "distanced" fashion, recognize that fortunes aren't made by buyers who keep all the items they've purchased, or make buys without a strong market to justify the investment. If you're in it to make a fortune, you're in it as a businessperson—cool and calculating.

CASTING A CRITICAL EYE ON REINVESTMENT

Operating under this sort of objective, profit-bearing mindset, approach each inventory purchase or profit reinvestment by first asking yourself a few questions about the sales potential of the goods you may acquire:

- Can you purchase an item or items at a price that assures you a reasonable profit?
- Can you resell the item relatively quickly? You don't want your money tied up in inventory for too long.
- Is there demand for the item that has been proven in the online auction arena?
- If you're dealing in collectibles, do you know which items are more elusive and which are more common? You'll want to hunt down the elusive items to make larger profits. (Hint: Talk with other sellers and dealers to learn what their customers are most eager to purchase, then explore the availability of those items for yourself.)

Of course, there's no way to be 100 percent certain in every purchase you make regarding the resale potential of those goods, but by casting an arguably "critical" eye on the items you might buy for turnover, you'll maintain that steely and objective mindset that will drive you to make better decisions before committing to a purchase.

THE PERCENTAGES DON'T LIE

As a final litmus test, you should strive to acquire inventory that will yield at least a 75 to 150 percent return on your investment. Consider how manufacturers and retailers make their profits by achieving a similar (if not better) return. To attain your desired bottom line, you'll need to operate in much the same manner. Don't scoff at these percentages, though, as they are highly achievable if you carefully identify and source your inventory purchases. Beyond the percentage return, seek out either a good mix of items that appeals to many customers or narrow your offerings to a focused set of items that are sought by serious buyers (if you can achieve both, all the better).

FINDING LOTS TO SELL

At this point you may be wondering where other sellers are finding the sorts of low-cost, high-profit items under discussion here. Actually, the goods are probably closer at hand than you think. First, consider the outlets in your local area (places like Cargo Largo or any of the dollar stores). If there are other closeout warehouses in your area, be sure to check those out. In fact, browse your local Yellow Pages for wholesalers, liquidators, and importers. To truly broaden your reach, though, go online to find even more suppliers of goods. Consider these:

- *Close-Out Networks.* Visit www.bizbb.com/CloseOutNetworks for a wide variety of goods that have been discontinued, overrun, and otherwise closed out.
- *Speedy Liquidators.* Serving as buyers and sellers of wholesale merchandise, visit www.speedyliquidators.com to see the wide offering of goods they have to offer.
- *5-Star Closeouts.* Located at *www.5starcloseouts.com,* here is yet another outlet for wholesale consumer goods with new merchandise arriving every week.
- *eBay.* That's right, even eBay is a great source for low-cost, high-quality goods that are ready for bulk purchase and immediate resale. Be sure to visit the "Wholesale Lots" link in the eBay categories to see who's selling lots (see Figure 20-1).

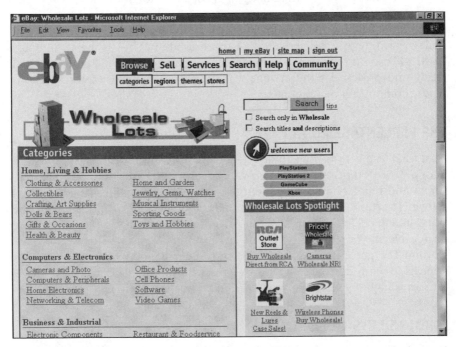

Figure 20-1 The Wholesale Lots category on eBay will link you to even more brokers and manufacturers offering bargain-priced inventory.

Of course, these are just a few of the outlets available to you when it comes to finding great resale merchandise. Be sure to visit your favorite Web portal (such as *www.google.com*) and perform searches using keywords like "wholesale," "closeout," "liquidators," and so on. You'll be amazed at the amount of inventory ready and waiting for you.

MORE INSIGHTS INTO BUYING ON SPECULATION

To continue our discussion of which items will yield the greatest return on your investment, let's delve a bit deeper into the matter of speculation. Good buyers are constantly on the lookout for that diamond in the rough whether it be a hot new collectible or a timeless favorite. Moreover, they have learned how to snatch such items from a variety of sources without tipping off the competition (other sellers). Here are the key factors at play when reinvesting in inventory really pays off.

Know Your Stuff

Knowledge is power, and it will be the strength of every one of your speculative purchases. If you'll be speculating on items about which you're already an expert (you know the commodity inside and out, including past activity, current trends, and future potential), you're already ahead of the curve. If your expertise is a bit light, be sure to fully research what you'll buy. Use trade papers, collector's guides, the Internet, and even eBay itself to acquaint yourself with the item of investment. Become well-versed in the history, manufacturing dates, variations, and reproductions (if any) of the items you will invest in.

Then research the sellers who are currently dealing in these goods (especially pertinent if you seek to acquire the inventory within the confines of eBay). Determine how long a seller has dealt in this sort of item and what expertise he or she seems to have. If you're purchasing outside of eBay, say from a dealer at a show, responding to a classified ad, or standing at someone's garage sale, you'll need to be prepared to make quick, on-the-spot assessments of authenticity and potential value. In these situations, if the item's inexpensive, you might not have much to lose in making the purchase. However, if it seems costly and you're just not sure, you might wish to pass or at least get the seller's contact information for a chance at a later purchase—after you've done more homework. The key here is to never rush into a costly purchase lest you get burned.

eBay TIP: If I had a dollar for every time I overheard someone visiting one of my garage sales excitedly mutter to a friend, "I can sell this for a lot more at eBay," I'd have an additional fortune in my coffer. Truth is, most of the items I drag out onto my driveway are those that didn't fare well at eBay; I've already tried that market and found the market isn't buying. These folks who think they're about to rob me blind likely haven't done *their* homework, else they'd know that what I'm offering for a buck or two is truly a castoff. I just smile and gladly take their money.

Remember Your Limits While Testing the Seller's Market Prowess

Regardless of how desirable an item is or whatever its profit potential, you'll need to ensure you buy it at a price that allows a profit to be realized. Although this is a bit repetitive to what has already been mentioned in this chapter, it's perhaps the single most important point that is forgotten during inventory purchases. Again, you're best served when you can obtain an item at a "wholesale price," that is, roughly 60 percent below the current retail value, always striving for the 75 to 150 percent return on your investment. This doesn't mean you'll always get this sort of price, and clearly it's your prerogative to earn less, but this margin should be your goal. How much you relax that target can only be driven by how much profit you wish or need to make.

How About a Haggle?

Of course, good haggling skills are a must in situations where you'll be making a direct purchase from a seller. Quickly assess how much the seller knows about the items and how fairly the items are priced. Never insult a seller with an obnoxiously low price—remember that seller might be trying to make the same profit you have in mind. After a bit of back-and-forth maneuvering, you may wind up with a better price than you originally anticipated—or you may need to abort the purchase if the seller is fixed on a price that offers little room for your profit potential.

If you're speculating at online auctions, your best bet is to set maximum bids—and not exceed them—that will allow you the profit margin you desire. While it's true that sniping often brings in good prices, it might also incite impassioned bidding on your part, causing you to exceed your investment limit. Good alternatives are to bid early in an auction and then forget about it, or to utilize sniping services like eSnipe.com. Though you might be outbid often, you might also find EOA notices coming your way, bringing tidings of great deals. Of course, if you have the willpower to stay to your limit during a live snipe, enjoy the truest thrill of reinvestment and snipe away.

     eBay TIP: As a final but critical point, try to avoid rampant speculative buying. If you're grabbing everything in sight, you might lose sight of how much you're spending. Even if you are getting great deals, your outgo could quickly exceed your income. Try to keep a balance between sales and purchases, with the best situation being that where a designated percentage of your auction profits are reinvested in future speculative purchases.

ESTABLISHING THE PROPER FLOW FOR YOUR MERCHANDISE

A final consideration to guide you in inventory purchases is determining ultimately how, when, and at what rate you'll offer up your goods. A sort of "cousin" to the timing strategy of listing items for auction, this is where, as you buy for resale, you determine the best time to offer the inventory you've invested in. For fun, I refer to this inventory turnover principle as knowing when to "flow, show, or stow your stuff." Here's how it works:

Flowing Your Inventory

Obviously, the key to profiting from an invested buy is selling when demand (and prices) are highest. Look for events (historical, film, media) that will make your item particularly sought after—then sell! Sometimes the best time to sell is immediately after purchase. If you're holding a trendy item that is virtually impossible to obtain, demand will be high. However, if you hold on too long, the demand might bottom out and you'll be stuck with a fad gone bad (anyone remember Beanie Babies or Furbies?).

Showing Your Inventory

Some of your best sales happen when you're not actively selling. If you have some great items that you're holing up, pop them up for view on a Web site of your own. You can easily obtain free Web space from a variety of hosting sites (e.g., Yahoo/Geocities, Juno, AngelFire, or your ISP) where you can easily link from an HTML-enhanced eBay listing, then show off your cool stuff for any visitors to see. Frequently, bidders or potential customers will ask if the items are for sale, which could spell great direct-sale profits for you.

Stowing Your Inventory

Some items you speculate on will need time to "mature" to reach their highest value potential. If you're buying items like limited-edition sculptures, Christmas ornaments, or character icons, you might need to hold on to these for a while before their ultimate value can be realized. Figure that most pop-culture items need around 20 years to reach maturity—the point when younger folks of that day have also matured and now feel a tug of nostalgia for reminders of days gone by. Therefore, find good storage for these items—someplace dry, dark, and solid. Believe it or not, the time will click by sooner than you realize, and suddenly you're sitting on a nice nest egg of the items people are clamoring for.

The key to buying for resale is to be extremely knowledgeable about the potential profit that items can bring to you. When you consider buying in large quantities, you'll need to be relatively sure you can move that inventory within a reasonable amount of time (around three months), can free up your invested money, and can realize a profit that supports your fortune-finding goals. There is no secret to this approach, really, and there are very few secret stashes or stones unturned as some might have you believe. The success in buying for resale is knowing what to buy, when to buy it, and when to sell it.

21

Identifying Trends: What's Hot and What's Not

The key to gaining the best profits possible at eBay is the market potential of your inventory. The past several chapters have dealt with those goods you'll sell and those additional goods you'll invest in to continue selling, but there is another faction of inventory that rounds out the keys to finding your fortune: locating those goods that are in demand at eBay and avoiding the goods that aren't. Unfortunately, there's no secret formula, nor are there any crystal balls in use that will ensure every item you'll be purchasing will be high on every bidders' want list. However, by applying the strategy and insights already discussed and adding a bit of perceptive prowess, you can develop your own method—perhaps even intuition—for finding what will be hot and what will be "squat" at eBay.

UNDERSTANDING ONLINE SALES MINING

Just as you wouldn't begin a treasure hunt without some sort of map or plan for where you'll search, you likewise can't expect to know which are the most desirable goods to go after until you've gotten some direction for where to begin looking. The trick to this planning is to begin with the information you have. Then go further by analyzing it and letting it lead you in the right direction. Sure, you can put your trust and hope into accidentally stumbling upon a fortune, but it makes better sense to leave nothing to chance, especially when you face the prospect of investing your profits into additional goods. So when it comes to knowing what to sell, how to sell, and where to sell, it becomes imperative to actively drill deep into the online sales market and let the cyber-statistics guide you on your way to the best possible results.

Data on Demand

Perhaps one of the greatest contributions of the online marketplace (next to the ease with which we can all buy and sell goods) is its volume of real-time sales data, readily available day in and day out. This is the core of the "data mining" potential, enabling sellers like you to seek out products similar to yours and determine the mood of the marketplace for such items.

Start your mining by finding out who's selling the sorts of items you'll offer. First, check their minimum bid prices as well as their Buy It Now prices to see which sellers' strategies seem to be attracting the highest bids or most lucrative fixed-price sales. Next, check the bidding activity to see which items are commanding the most active bidding. When you zero in on the listings that are generating the greatest "buzz," take note of the listing categories being used, an indication of where most buyers might be congregating. Beyond price and category, take a careful look at the listing title (watch for all-important keywords), the listing description, the images presented, the seller's sales policies, and the seller's feedback. In short order, you'll be able to ascertain which sellers are successful, which products are drawing activity and garnering the best prices, and what overall sales style seems to attract the most customers.

eBay TIP: Understand that *how* you sell an item is as important to your success as *what* it is you'll sell. Sometimes, what's hot at eBay are those goods that seem to languish about, unattended by other sellers who fail to recognize the proper marketing that will hoist those items out of the bowels of the site and high up on the most-wanted lists. By minding the market climate for certain goods and then offering those sorts of items thoughtfully, strategically, and in a way that caters to current market desires, you stand the best opportunity to tap into current trends.

But what about other sales destinations on the Web? Be sure to expand your data mining to the various "store" venues (such as at Yahoo and Amazon) and search those listings, too (see Figure 21-1).

You may find it helpful to perform a search engine query to comb the entire World Wide Web in order to locate merchant sites run by folks just like you. Standing in the customer's shoes, ask yourself how well each destination you encounter motivates you to inquire further and possibly compels you to buy. Check carefully to determine if the site is being regularly updated or if it appears to have been overrun by virtual cobwebs. Don't be bashful about contacting the shop owner via e-mail to ask specific questions about his or her operation and merchandise.

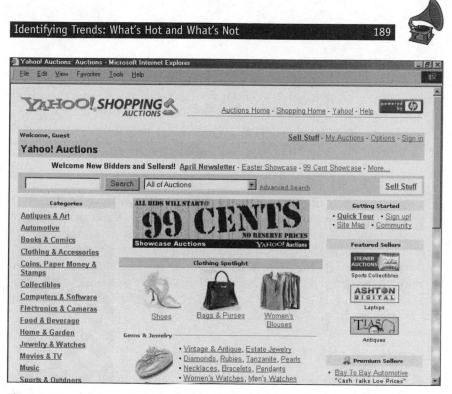

Figure 21-1 Yahoo.com hosts auctions and serves as another source for monitoring market trends.

History Rarely Lies

The most telling statistics, naturally, are those found in the past. Again, the online marketplace has plenty of information to offer here. At eBay, take a careful look at completed listings, seeking out final selling prices as well as determining if prices are holding steady or are experiencing upward or downward trends. Be particularly attentive to listings that seem to appear as "spikes" or "dips" in the market (with a final price being either unusually high or low); closely scrutinize these listings as you seek to determine what contributed to the spike or dip (was the item miscategorized, priced too high at the outset, poorly presented, or just not in demand?). This sort of sales history data is a bit more difficult to cull from fixed-price or independent merchant sites. Some sellers provide sales history (and you should too when you venture into the merchant realm) whereby you can ascertain what goods they've dealt with in the past and how much activity they've seen over a period of time. Again, inquire (politely) about recently sold items if you have questions.

Tallying Up the Counter Once Again

Another way to gauge the appeal of products and their accompanying sales strategies is to quantify the public response by way of a counter. Look for counters—either at eBay or at fixed-price venues—to ascertain the popularity or attractiveness of an item up for sale. Although these counters don't necessarily indicate *unique* page views or site visits, they are a good indicator of whether the seller's style and strategy seems to be successful with potential customers. If the counter numbers are low, then something in the seller's methodology could be amiss.

Mine Your Own Business

While you're actively sifting through the offerings of others around you, don't forget to carefully examine your own offerings as well. Keep close track of *your* sales history, determining where your items sell best, when they seem to be in greatest demand, and which transactions have encouraged customers to make return visits. By regularly watching others while monitoring your own results, you'll develop the conclusive data that will help you successfully navigate the ever-changing online marketplace and make wise decisions regarding which goods you should continue to invest in.

LEARNING TO ANTICIPATE THE NEXT WAVE

The crux of this discussion is how to find new material to put on the auction block that will have bidders clawing at one another for the chance of ownership. Naturally, you want to buy these items cheap and sell high to secure your fortune. The problem is that other sellers are trying to do the very same thing. So, how do you beat them to the punch and bring in the hottest merchandise? Moreover, how do you ensure that the items you buy won't be yesterday's news when you go to list them, leaving you with nothing but a cluttered inventory hold? Good questions, all. Here are some answers:

Perennial Favorites

Certain items always seem to do well in the auction market; you need to be aware of what those items are and whether you should be offering them. The real opportunity lies in your potential to specialize in a few select "hot" commodities so you can develop that valuable expertise as well as being sure you're not running your auction activity in a sort of hit-or-miss fashion. When you specialize, you have the opportunity not only to become intimately familiar with certain items (which your customers will definitely appreciate) but you also position yourself favorably to detect new buying or collecting trends before the mainstream populace catches on. In the competitive eBay selling world, this puts you ahead of your peers.

These perennial favorites, then, include such things as original advertising materials, books, coins, china depression glass, dolls, entertainment memorabilia, sports memorabilia (see Figure 21-2), hi-tech collectibles, and toys.

Figure 21-2 Sports memorabilia like these limited-edition 2003 Sacramento Kings team bobblehead restaurant premiums are examples of the sorts of items that are always in big demand at eBay.

Of course, there is much more that generally stays high on collectors' and buyers' "must have" lists, yet the items just mentioned typically remain in high demand and can lead you to discover other related items that are equally desired.

eBay TIP: When you're researching the hot items, be sure to review eBay's category listings page and notice the number of items in the various category headings and subheadings. Immediately, you'll notice in which categories the bulk of the items are being listed. To spot the current trends, further investigate headers and subheaders.

Trust the Experience of Others

While very few of us have a truly innate and infallible intuition for identifying those items that will lead the next megatrend, it is possible to get the jump on the competition by merely keeping an open mind to the input and experience of others. Therefore, recognize the tremendous value of forming relationships and even friendships with other sellers, collectors, and commodity experts. As you deal at eBay, you'll meet more experts than you ever dreamed possible— some being sellers from whom you might buy and others being buyers to whom you might sell. Almost everyone at eBay has some level of expertise about something, and by remaining diligent to uphold positive transactions with these folks you have the opportunity to also learn from them in ways that will help you understand what's hot and what's not.

Beyond eBay, recognize the value of being more attentive to what's selling in your local area. When visiting major retailers, take time to observe what seems to be selling well and what isn't. Take note of where marketing dollars are being spent, and in what manner (or "angle") the seemingly popular items are being pitched. Of course, the proof of popularity is in the results, so take the time to observe which promotions are highly successful and which appear to be lost causes. This is perhaps one of the best ways to determine mass market mentality—while riding the coattails of someone else's investment (that is, the retailer's marketing dollar).

Next, visit smaller retailer establishments, and especially secondary-market shops (those that re-sell used goods). Ask the store owners what buyers seem to be seeking and what items seem to be in short supply. In addition, be sure to read up on trends in the local and national trade papers and collectibles magazines. Search the Internet for specialty Web sites that cater to certain commodities and market trends. If these publications offer e-mail updates or product notifications, consider opting in to that distribution as an additional source of free information.

Distrust Your Bias

One of the biggest challenges for sellers eager to determine which items are popular in buyers' minds is to maintain a clear vision of what the buyers are really buying, as opposed to what you, the seller, are most interested in. To develop a truly astute understanding of merchandising trends, you need to be able to recognize everything that is selling, not just those items that interest *you* the most. So often a seller will look right past popular items because he or she has little interest in them. Consumers, however, may be buying up those goods at a fast and furious pace. To be successful in detecting trends, sellers need to develop a wider scope of vision, recognizing *anything* that is in demand regardless of their own personal view of the goods.

FOLLOW THE FICKLE MARKET

When preparing to identify and invest in "hot" goods, be sure to anticipate how quickly the market can fluctuate. Ultimate success comes when you can buy before the market spikes and sell just as the market begins to peak. Be especially watchful for fads and trends that early on deliver great profits, then quickly bottom out as the mass of sellers attempt to cash in—only to flood the market and devalue the price of the goods. To this end, it's unwise to buy when the market is already peaking, when your investment cost may already be at a point that will prevent a decent level of profit and, as supply eclipses demand, actually results in future selling prices dropping lower than your original purchase price. Besides the surge in supply, anticipate the potential effect of current events and changing public opinion and how those might positively or negatively affect item demand and selling prices. Watch for upcoming events that could increase the value of some goods (such as new product launches, technology developments, and even movie releases) and likewise might render other items as cold as yesterday's breakfast.

GETTING THE JUMP BY PRESELLING

Sellers who've been successful in navigating product trends at eBay and elsewhere have learned another strategy in careful inventory management: the less they have tied up in inventory that might or might not sell, the more effectively they can profit as consumer interest spikes, and likewise avoid losses when demand dips. The secret is to offer items *before* the inventory investment has been made. But, without inventory on hand, there's nothing that can be auctioned—or is there?

Whether selling items yet to be released or managing sales through a partnership with a third-party supplier or distributor, some sellers have learned that *preselling* items at eBay can be a smart move. It's not uncommon to find presale listings on eBay for items such as collectible figurines (see Figure 21-3), trading cards, toys, and even event tickets. It's not easy to effectively presell, though, and it requires special attention to ensure the item the high bidder wins *will* actually be available to successfully complete the sale. This advanced sales strategy has been noted to be highly effective in capitalizing on ever-changing market opinion. Here are some things to consider if you're interested in managing your auction inventory using this more dynamic method:

Introducing Dynamic Inventory Management

Dynamic management of goods for sale (often referred to as "just-in-time" inventory—you receive just the inventory you need just as you've sold it) can put you ahead of the curve in the marketplace. By establishing reliable inventory sources (wholesalers, distributors, or manufacturers), it's possible to let that source of supply manage the inventory for you, whether offering you the ability to order and presell unreleased and much-anticipated items, maintain a source of goods without having to purchase what you haven't yet sold, or even drop-ship (that is, your supplier will ship directly to your customer) sold items directly to your buyers without the need for you to ever see or handle the merchandise. It's the same method of "supply-chain management" that big businesses utilize every day.

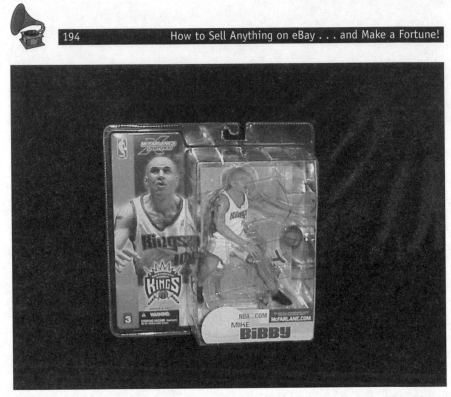

Figure 21-3 New sports items like this Mike Bibby action figure were actively being presold prior to the figure's scheduled March 2003 worldwide release.

The key, of course, when selling items that you don't physically possess, is being able to count on your suppliers to deliver the goods—quickly and consistently—every time a sale is made. This requires that you keep in constant communication with your suppliers to ensure that *their* inventory is on-hand, is as described, and is always ready to ship. If the supplier is subject to constantly changing inventory (such as liquidators) or prone to frequent out-of-stock situations (backorders), then you'll be faced with having to inform your buyers that the goods they just won aren't readily available, if at all. Therefore, if not managed and monitored closely, your source of presell supply might become a supply management nightmare that will frustrate both you and your customers.

Understand eBay's Rules

Understanding the real potential of managing auction sales and inventory in this dynamic method, eBay has come forward to establish how preselling is to be managed at their site. By site policy, eBay allows presales provided the seller can deliver the goods within 30 days of the auction's close. As a seller, you'll need to be absolutely certain that you can uphold this stipulation. Without proper compliance, it's possible that presale listings could be unceremoniously canceled without warning and your online efforts could be quickly thwarted.

Disclosing the Details

The key stipulation of eBay's rules—and one that every seller should commit to—is the full disclosure that an auction item is being offered on a "presell" basis and is not yet "in hand" from the seller's perspective. eBay's policy, in fact, goes so far as to require that sellers disclose presales information in an item's description (see Figure 21-4) using an HTML font size of at least 3. (No tiny print that might serve to mislead bidders or misrepresent the items up for bid.)

More to the point of preserving your good reputation, it's in your best interest to be absolutely certain that bidders and buyers are fully aware that presell goods are not presently in your possession and there may be a longer-than-usual delivery time due to the fact that the goods are on order or will be delivered by a third party. If you ignore such disclosure, you risk all sorts of postauction backlash including buyer dissatisfaction, negative feedback, demands for refunds, and even escalation to eBay's SafeHarbor or consumer protection agencies.

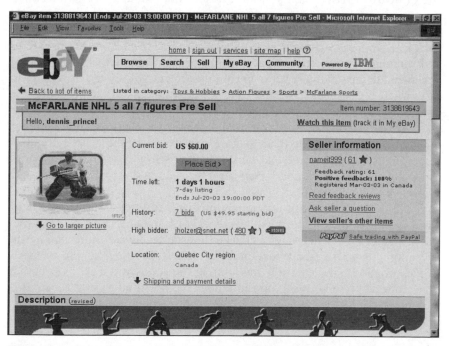

Figure 21-4   This seller clearly states in his item title that these very desirable action figures are offered on a presell basis.

eBay TIP: Visit the Federal Trade Commission's Web site for more information related directly to the matter of proper guidelines and legal statutes for offering presale items. The FTC's *Business Guide to Mail or Telephone Order Merchandise Rule* (which incorporates preselling online) can be found at this Web address: *http://www.ftc.gov/bcp/conline/pubs/buspubs/mailorder.htm*

Ensuring Customer Satisfaction

Here's the heart of the matter of striving to offer hot items in a presale methodology: do you stand behind everything you presell, and are you committed to the customer's 100 percent satisfaction? If so, then you'll need to go to extra lengths to ensure that your customers will be absolutely delighted with their presell purchases. Although it's within your right to state that all sales are final, such a policy isn't well-suited to the sale of goods that you don't own at the time of listing. Whether an arriving item is different from how your supplier (and ultimately, *you*) described it or it arrives damaged or late or doesn't arrive at all, you must absorb the fallout to avoid alienating your customers.

Be ready to accept returns and deliver refunds. If shipping inventory back to a supplier, you might need to navigate some special return procedures and you might be required to pay a return or restocking fee of some sort. If you intend to pass along any fees to your customers, you should only do so in cases where a customer has changed his or her mind about the purchase, but not due to any reason of item misrepresentation (that's *your* liability).

Although some sellers have tried to blame problems of item delivery, quality, or content upon their suppliers, it becomes the seller's ultimate responsibility to guarantee that whatever they sell is "as advertised" in all aspects of the phrase. If not, buyers have the right and responsibility to take protective counteraction.

Although no one can unfailingly predict every trend and market shift when seeking to identify the next "big wave" of hot items, there are nevertheless many steps that can easily be taken to hone in on buyers' wants and needs. By continuing your regular auction research, testing strategies and methods to present goods, and carefully investing in the goods you'll sell (sometimes on a strategic presell basis), you can unlock the potential to read the market and stay in pace with (and ahead of) the auction-going trends.

22

The Forbidden Zone:
What You Can't Sell at eBay

While you've now seen that practically anything and everything offered at eBay will find a buyer, there are some items that for good reasons shouldn't (and according to the site's rules, can't) be offered for bid. Whether inappropriate, immoral, illegal, or in unforgivably bad taste, eBay has deemed certain goods off limits. Therefore, familiarize yourself with the sorts of items you can't sell, and equally important, the sorts of items you shouldn't buy at eBay.

ITEMS eBAY FORBIDS

No doubt while listing an item for sale at eBay you have seen a text link that describes the sorts of things eBay has prohibited. Simply put, if you attempt to sell this stuff and are caught, the eBay Patrol may shut down your auctions, might revoke your registered status, and could possibly turn you over to law enforcement agencies for actual prosecution. Yikes! Make no mistake: when they say "forbidden," they mean it.

In actuality, eBay states some items fall under one of three categories: *prohibited, questionable,* and *potentially infringing.* Right away, be sure to understand what is absolutely forbidden to list. Here's the rundown on these illicit items:

- *Alcohol.* Alcohol is generally forbidden for auction because of the complex taxation, import, and licensing rules that govern it. Unless you're bidding at a licensed site and dealing with sellers licensed to deal in alcohol (such as at a site like Winebid.com), the rules generally state that alcohol auctions will be promptly closed by the site.

- *Firearms.* Though firearms are sometimes considered a type of collectible (for period pieces), eBay has had to unequivocally forbid auctioning of any mechanism originally designed to fire some sort of projectile. There are, however, some sites (such as ArmsBay.com) that are properly licensed and specialize in auctioning such items.
- *Fireworks.* These are illegal in many states and in many other parts of the world. They are, therefore, not eligible for auctioning.
- *Drugs and Drug Paraphernalia.* Illegal goods, plain and simple.
- *Human Parts and Remains.* Yuck, right? At eBay, it started with the human kidney auction back in 1999. Since then, no body parts. However, at eBay the rules do state that selling skulls and skeletons for educational purposes is allowed.
- *Animals and Wildlife Products.* Excluding, perhaps, a warehouse find of vintage Sea Monkeys, dealing with the sale and shipping of live animals is typically left to the pros (animal handlers and such). Adhering to edicts set forth by the U.S. Fish and Game Service, eBay does not allow the sale of live animals or animal parts unless expressly noted (for instance, sale of some taxidermic items, pelts, and so on might be allowed if strict conditions are adhered to). If you're considering this sort of item, read the full disclosure of what's allowed—and what isn't—before you venture forward.
- *Stolen or Counterfeit Goods.* They're stolen. They're illegal. They aren't allowed for auctioning. This should be obvious.

With the most obvious items explained, here's the quick list of additional prohibited items:

- Catalog and URL sales
- Counterfeit currency and stamps
- Credit cards
- Embargoed goods and prohibited countries
- Government IDs and licenses
- Links
- Lockpicking devices
- Lottery tickets
- Mailing lists and personal information
- Plants and seeds
- Postage meters
- Prescription drugs and devices
- Recalled items
- Satellite and cable TV descramblers
- Stocks and other securities
- Surveillance equipment

- Tobacco
- Travel (allowed but limited due to local travel regulations)

If you disagree with the banning of these items or simply want to learn more about why they're disallowed, visit eBay's site map and drill into the links that more fully explain these items and why they've been prohibited.

The lists of "questionable" and "potentially infringing" items are significant yet aren't *completely* forbidden, depending on the situation. As a seller, it's your duty to understand the site's rules about these additional items and to make sure that what you sell isn't illegal, infringing, or even unnatural. Again, carefully review the explanations eBay has provided to ensure you don't stray into the forbidden zone.

WHO SAYS THESE ITEMS ARE FORBIDDEN, AND WHY?

So why has eBay gone to such great lengths to blacklist so many items from sale? Well, aside from some of the more obvious items, eBay cites these reasons:

- Since eBay never actually possesses the goods for sale, it is unable to verify the legality or appropriateness of questionable or potentially infringing goods.
- Many goods that might be sold are subject to local statutes that differ from state to state and country to country.
- For health, environmental, and agricultural reasons, some goods would violate import or export statutes.
- In some cases, eBay might actually incur liability for the sale and subsequent effects of certain goods.

DEALS, STEALS, AND "GRAY MARKET" GOODS

Taking the informed buyer's perspective, it's important to understand whether what you might bid on is forbidden or questionable. Certain items are perennial favorites of backroom sellers. When you're buying, you might be surprised to find that you could be bidding on illicit goods. What kinds of things might be offered by unsavory sellers? Here are the most common examples:

- Computer software
- Electronics (small and midsized)
- Music (CDs and cassettes)
- Movies (VHS and DVD)
- Pornographic material (though not necessarily stolen, often the content of some of it *is* illegal)

- Knock-offs (illegal copies of name-brand items)
- Printed matter (undisclosed copies or restrikes)

Of course, there are more ways to proliferate bad merchandise than you'd probably care to imagine, but those just listed tend to be the most common, largely due to their relative ease of handling as well as their profit potential.

When you're buying, it's up to you to identify items that might be bogus or stolen (and therefore forbidden). When you search the auctions for items to bid on, exercise the following due diligence to make sure you're not courting eBay contraband:

- Check the seller's feedback rating first! Are there any comments that might indicate trouble?
- Compare the potential selling price of the item to what the market usually bears; if it's *too* cheap, remember the old saying about things that are too good to be true.
- Pay close attention to the item's description and determine whether any key information has been omitted. Is the description blatantly incorrect in terms of the item being described? Is the description evasive in a way that makes you wonder if the auction's on the level?
- Contact the seller to ask questions. If you don't receive a reply, or receive a very curt and uninformative reply, think twice about bidding. (If nothing else, this could simply indicate a seller who might not be very responsive and might not manage the postauction activity to your liking; a warning flag for a different problem.)
- Study the seller's policy: does it contain harsh or potentially unreasonable terms (short payment period, no returns or guarantees, and no good explanation for the policy)? Does the seller seem to be in an unusual hurry to sell and wrap up business?
- Most important, be knowledgeable about the items you might bid on and be aware of their potential for being stolen or illegally reproduced material. It's not such a good deal if you end up with inferior merchandise that isn't even worth the "bargain" price you paid.

THE ABCs OF COPYRIGHT

Copyright is usually a gray area in the minds of folks who buy and sell stuff, either at online auctions or elsewhere. It makes up the bulk of the "potentially infringing" category of goods. Whether it's music, software, promotional materials, or similar items, copyright can become an issue more often than most people realize.

First, the official definition of copyright as presented by the U.S. Copyright Office goes like this:

Copyright is a form of protection provided by the laws of the United States (Title 17, U.S. Code) to the authors of "original works of authorship," including literary, dramatic, musical, artistic, and certain other intellectual works. This protection is available to both published and unpublished works.

But what does that mean to you as you buy and sell at eBay? Simply enough, it means that any copyrighted material that is duplicated for multiple sales yet is not being sold by the originator or licensee of the work is most likely infringing on a legal copyright registration.

Who's licensed to sell copyrighted material? The answer depends on who the copyright owner (the originator of the work) has authorized to distribute the work. Typically that means someone who has been granted a license to reproduce and sell the work in a "tangible medium of expression" (such as a CD, a DVD, a book or magazine, a poster or lithograph, or even a dramatic work).

Are infringing items, then, being regularly offered at eBay and elsewhere online? Absolutely. Can the legal copyright owners or licensees claim infringement? Absolutely. Does every infringing sale get noticed and acted upon? No. But don't let the sheer volume of items being exchanged lull you into a false sense of security (or obscurity). These days, people are diligently hunting down bootleggers and frauds who make a living on the originator's work without a license and without sharing the income with the originator. Musicians, filmmakers, writers, and the like are all working to take a bite out of infringement, and auction sites especially are working alongside them to keep trading legal to the greatest extent possible. That's why copyright is such an important matter.

YOUR CHECKLIST TO AVOID POSTING INFRINGING ITEMS

Here are some guidelines to use to determine if the items you wish to auction will be deemed lawful and legitimate:

- Avoid selling unlicensed items manufactured by yourself or others that bear legally registered logos or trademarks that you don't have permission to use.
- Avoid selling counterfeits (knockoffs) made to specifically resemble licensed items, including the use of logos, markings, or other trademarked details.
- Avoid selling promotional items that are marked "Not for resale."
- Avoid selling bundled software that is delivered with computers.
- Avoid selling live recordings (audio or video) for which you do not have express permission from the performer or license holder.

- Avoid selling items that are unreleased, or "beta" versions not intended for public use or display.

DOESN'T EVERYONE INFRINGE JUST A LITTLE?

The question is: will you get caught for selling copyrighted material when you're not the owner or aren't licensed to do so? Maybe and maybe not. Perform a search of eBay and you'll likely find a generous offering of such material with nary a mention of the original copyright owner or licensee. Quite often copyright owners will turn a blind eye to such things, realizing the amount of work it would take to track down, halt, and prosecute every violator.

Believe it or not, some content owners see the secondary market that exchanges copyrighted material as potentially good for business. Though legally this is discouraged and disallowed, the word-of-mouth potential and greater dissemination might bolster public awareness for an artist, a musician, or whomever. Provided it's not a situation that truly gets out of hand and becomes outright piracy, some content owners will consider it part of the business and a form of free marketing (of course, you don't know which copyright holders are inclined to this lenient sentiment).

Be cautious, though, since some content owners are adamant about protecting the rights (and potential income) of their work. In fact, many such owners are working directly with eBay to monitor listings and to identify infringing items. If such items are found, the penalty to the infringing seller can be as simple as a *cease and desist* order (a "slap on the hand" that instructs the seller to discontinue such sales both now and forever)—but it might involve stiff fines or even imprisonment. In more blatant cases of piracy or fraud, content owners are working with federal agencies to conduct sting operations to ferret out and fully prosecute hard-core offenders.

WHAT IS eBAY DOING ABOUT COPYRIGHT INFRINGEMENT?

eBay got significantly more involved in policing its listings amid claims of rampant fraud and illegal and infringing sales back in 1998. To maintain a safe and legal trading environment and to prevent its portal from becoming an absolute nest of thieves, eBay has taken these steps to keep its listings on the up-and-up:

- eBay has posted explicit policies regarding items that are disallowed for auctioning.
- eBay provides listings of prohibited, questionable, or infringing items as guidance to sellers who want assistance in determining if their items are potentially problematic.

- eBay actively monitors certain categories of items in search of illicit goods.
- eBay regularly shuts down auctions of disallowed items.
- eBay regularly suspends sellers who are in clear violation of site policies in these matters.
- eBay has teamed up with organizations such as the National Consumer's League, content owners, and the FBI to take further steps against violators.
- eBay maintains its right to turn over user information to official agencies when requested as part of an investigation or potential prosecution.
- eBay has even solicited the help of the auction community to assist in identifying and reporting offending listings.

THE AGENCIES WHO TAKE ACTION

So who's getting involved in bringing auction offenders to justice? You might be surprised to learn how visible online auctions have become in the prosecutorial community. Here's just a small list of organizations who are presently involved in scrutinizing listings and their proprietors while simultaneously assisting buyers and eBay itself in matters of the goods for sale and the proper practices in selling them:

- NCL (National Consumer's League)
- BBS Online (Better Business Bureau)
- RIAA (Recording Industry Association of America)
- MPAA (Motion Picture Association of America)
- SIIA (Software and Information Industry Association)
- FTC (Federal Trade Commission)
- INTA (International Trademark Association)
- FBI (Federal Bureau of Investigation)

Clearly, with the heightened visibility of online auctions, many national law enforcement agencies, content owners, and consumer organizations are just as active at these sites as are bidders and sellers (though for clearly different reasons).

THE AUCTION VIGILANTE

Communities of involved members are what make many auction sites successful. However, some people have gone a bit overboard in deputizing themselves to strike out and rid the auction streets of targeted "undesirables." Although their intentions might be good, their methods of attack get muddled and can become as undesirable (sometimes more so) as those they purport to be policing.

To start, understand what creates an auction vigilante (what I've often referred to as the *Net Cop*):

- Some users feel the need to step in to help eBay deal with wrongdoers (a good intention, initially).
- Some users respond (sometimes overzealously) to the site's appeal for community members to get involved in helping police the auction place.
- Some users feel eBay doesn't do enough to thwart auction misdeeds.
- Some users feel eBay can't or won't act fast enough to execute justice online.
- Some users feel the need to be needed; an exaggerated desire to be wanted or perceived as important.
- Some users are bored and want something to do—seriously.

So though you're minding your own business and attempting to steer clear of trouble, a Net Cop might tap you on the shoulder and inquire about your purpose for being here. Here's how you may be approached:

- You may get unexpected e-mail messages from strangers who don't seem to be potential bidders, inquiring about an auction and the item's origin.
- You may hear from an anonymous user (using a vanilla e-mail account such as HotMail) informing you of an auction site's policies or current laws that conflict with an item being auctioned.
- After you bid in an auction, you may get a message warning you about the seller and urging you to reconsider and withdraw the bid.
- After you post an auction, you may receive a threatening message warning you to halt the auction or risk being "turned in" to auction administrators and even law enforcement.
- If a host site cancels an auction, you may get a message from another user, claiming responsibility for the cancellation.

Clearly, the activities practiced by Net Cops range from helpful advice to unwanted harassment. Take the friendly contact as just that: friendly. However, if you're uncomfortable with how some unannounced vigilante has gotten involved in your business without being authorized by an auction site or official agency, here's how you can respond:

- Ignore the contact. Remember, some are just bored or looking for an excited response. File the message away for the time being and go about your business.

- Politely respond to the sender and ask their purpose and authorization to contact you. They might be trying to help you or they might be trying to rattle you.
- Report any bothersome, harassing, or threatening messages to the hosting site immediately.
- Report any individual (or e-mail address) to proper authorities whenever you suspect someone is posing illegally as a law enforcement or agency official.

Although this information paints Net Cops in a pretty poor light, there are some involved community members who are responsible and conscientious when patrolling the auction sites. In fact, eBay generally encourages all community members to become involved and not turn a blind eye or deaf ear to obvious misdeeds (recall, this is the core tenet of ensuring eBay's Feedback Forum remains successful). Just remember to keep it within reason and turn matters over to the properly authorized individuals if a real problem arises.

Although you may never have considered all this, these are the ins, outs, ups, and downs of dealing in forbidden items at eBay. Be familiar with—not fearful of—the site's policies and guidelines and always be aware of the items you'll offer and whether they cross the sometimes fuzzy line of what's considered illicit at eBay.

PART 4

BUSINESS SPECIFICS

23

Becoming a Business and Managing High Volume Sales

By this time you're probably realizing your fortune will be acquired not by just selling *anything* at eBay but also by selling a high volume of anything. This section of the book now brings us full circle to the original discussion of how you will define "fortune" and how willing you'll be to invest effort and resources into earning that fortune, whatever your timetable. Every one of us would like to get rich quickly and at eBay, though you might not become rich overnight, you can hasten your results by moving more goods through the auction space.

This chapter, then, begins the next phase of your fortune-finding trek—helping you to get more results from your auctioning efforts by further exploring your motives and commitment, then helping you gain more from your listing activity by showing you how to list more items in less time. If you're ready to take the next step, this chapter will further guide you in your journey.

PASTIME, PART-TIME, OR FULL-TIME?

Although you might not be ready to proclaim your ultimate purpose just yet, this is the perfect time to look in your future to determine what you're looking to gain at eBay and what you're willing to invest to do so. The common question from newer eBay users is whether this can be a reliable single-source of income. The answer: it depends. There are many factors that will determine how you will approach an auction "business," including those driven by the economy and marketplace and those driven by your own personal motivations. The good news, though, is that auction at eBay is such an adaptable enterprise that you can pretty much make of it whatever suits you best, either casually buying and selling or feverishly moving merchandise (and you can flip-flop between these modes whenever you like). But, to provide some food for thought, consider how auctioning can fit any lifestyle and which opportunities and challenges you may face as you decide whether you'll do this for fun or profit.

The Happy Hobby

If you've defined fortune as being that opportunity to buy and sell as you choose, lounging about in your bathrobe and slippers, earning a few dollars here and there and finding some great items for yourself along the way, then you've adopted the hobbyist's approach to auctioning. This approach is perfect for those who wish to utilize eBay in the fashion of being a pleasant pastime that can yield some very promising rewards in terms of gaining a modest amount of income, acquiring some terrific items, and enjoying the aspect of interacting with interesting people along the way.

Are there drawbacks to the hobby approach? From a pure business standpoint, a hobbyist is not able to take advantage of certain tax breaks that the bona fide businessperson can use. According to the United States Internal Revenue Service, tax deductions for business expenses can only be legally claimed if the effort maintains an operating profit for every five years of activity, and income activity must be properly reported using the appropriate small business/sole-proprietorship income tax filing (see Chapter 25 for more about taxes). Further, if a hobbyist attempts to "fake it," claiming to be a business in order to deduct expenses, the IRS likewise stipulates that if said "business" reports an operating loss for more than two years in every five year period, that operation will be deemed a hobby, ineligible for deductions and possibly liable to pay taxes and/or penalties on undeclared income.

eBay TIP: Though your initial intentions may be to operate as a hobby, don't be surprised to find yourself drawn into the profit potential of eBay and other online selling. Many of today's ardent sellers began as hobbyists but found the fortune awaiting them too good to pass up. The benefit, though, of beginning from a hobbyist's mindset is the approach allows you to slowly ease your way into the entrepreneurial fray and deliberately decide when and where to ratchet up your efforts. In this way, many hobbyists develop real-world expertise and are better poised for success when they turn their attention to becoming more serious in their auction endeavors.

The Part-Time Proprietor

So when the business bug first bites you, the natural response is to investigate running your entrepreneurial effort on a part-time basis. This approach is best for those who aren't willing to play the high-stakes gamble of forsaking all other forms of income and rely solely on auction and other online income. I usually recommend that eager entrepreneurs (and hobbyists-turned-home-business-persons) operate on the part-time basis for at least three to six months. All the while, keep that day job, whatever it may be, for these good reasons:

- You can be more at ease venturing into self-employment if you maintain the safety and security of a regular paycheck protecting your everyday living expenses.
- A part-time endeavor will be relatively risk-free as you determine whether online auctioning will suit you in the long run.
- You'll be able to safely determine whether you have the motivation and mindset to maintain and manage a home-based business before fully committing yourself.
- You'll be able to take advantage of company benefits from your regular employment while testing the waters of self-employment, determining whether the income you gain will be able to support the cost of those benefits.
- You'll have the opportunity to begin keeping business records at an activity level that allows for experimentation and change as you seek the best method that suits you.
- Your part-time profits can be stashed away as a financial foundation to ultimately be reinvested in a full-time venture, should you decide to make that transition.

Truly, taking a part-time approach when courting an online business makes sense in order to avoid the anxiety of having to ensure fast and steady income to support your living expenses. Working at it part-time also enables you to use the extra income as just that—extra, while also permitting you to increase or decrease your activity as needed.

The Full-Time Fortune

If you're ready to make a go of it, then lace up your shoes and get ready to run. Many have been quite successful operating an auction business full-time, especially those who had developed a good understanding of the sorts of activities required to maintain a steady income. If this is to be your path to fortune, be sure to understand what sorts of activities full-time sellers engage in, day in and day out, week after week:

- Stage and photograph new items to sell.
- List plenty of items regularly (at least 100 items every week).
- Source and acquire new inventory regularly.

- Keep clear and concise business records to measure outlay versus income (determining if a true profit is being realized).
- Keep current with product trends and market shifts in demand.
- Attend to bidder inquiries quickly.
- Monitor and manage current listings (especially if changes are required in midauction).
- Respond to completed auctions and engage the buyer to begin the payment-for-goods transaction.
- Prepare and package items sold.
- Arrange for carrier drop-off or pickup as needed.
- Follow up on EOA messages and late payments.
- Return to the start and do it all again (and again and again).

Certainly, this isn't an insurmountable list of tasks to manage, yet it's no cakewalk either. There's much to do to maintain a full-time auction endeavor, yet, if your heart and mind are properly focused, this can equally be the fortune fantasy so many would-be entrepreneurs have dreamed of: a business you can run from your back room that can be as far-reaching as the fabled four corners of the globe.

To make the transition from part-time to full-time business, you'll need to prepare yourself to commit to the ways and means of going into business for yourself. Here are some of the tasks that will greet you:

- Be sure you are extremely well versed in the methods and manners of online auctioning and are clear about the tasks and duties you'll need to manage along the way.
- Ensure your credit is good with banks and other financial institutions while paying down as much outstanding consumer debt as possible before potentially cutting any previous regular income flow.
- If you have a spouse or other partner who's currently employed, determine whether their regular income can serve as a backup or safety net to your business start-up and if you can be added to their benefits package.
- Strive to save a cushion of 6 to 24 months' living expenses to fall back on in case your start-up efforts are slow to gain momentum.
- Leave any previous employment on an "up" note and seek a letter of recommendation from your manager or supervisor (this might be useful if you decide to apply for a business loan).
- Set realistic business goals, and track your progress every step of the way to ensure you're executing to plan.
- Believe you can do it!

Make no doubt about it, going into business for yourself can be the most stressful, yet most rewarding, of experiences. If you're fully prepared, have created a sound plan, and have the appropriate level of funds to back you up, you're ready for the plunge. In fact, those sellers I've spoken with who had regretted going into an auction business full-time confessed they hadn't planned properly before making their move. These days, it's clear that eBay and other forms of e-commerce aren't simply fads and aren't showing any signs of weakening in their mass appeal. Therefore, be deliberate in your preparations and recognize that you have time to fully consider a thorough approach to auctioning; you'll be in the best possible position to make the leap if you've taken the proper steps in preparing to earn your full-time fortune.

BULKING UP YOUR BUSINESS WITH BULK LISTING

Now that you've given full consideration to how you'll approach growing your eBay business, consider how to most easily increase the volume of item listings at eBay. No matter what volume of activity you wish to maintain in your auctioning, the simple fact is you can earn more for your effort if you can list more items in less time. One way to achieve greater results for your listing efforts is to employ eBay's bulk listing tool, Turbo Lister. This application allows you to create bundles of item listings in a single screen, avoiding the need to navigate the numerous steps in listing a single item. If you want to make more items available in just a fraction of the usual time, Turbo Lister is the tool for you. Here's why bulk listing makes sense:

- Bulk listings can be created offline as eBay's Turbo Lister application runs directly on your PC without requiring an active Internet connection. You can create bulk listings while on the go, too, using a laptop if you like.
- Bulk listings can be assembled whenever you choose at a pace to best suit your needs.
- Bulk listings can be uploaded in a single effort to start immediately or to be scheduled to start at a later date or time.
- Bulk listings allow you to combine similar items to simultaneously list and effectively cross-sell your goods.

DOWNLOADING TURBO LISTER

The best news about bulk listing at eBay is that Turbo Lister is completely free to download and use. Here's how to do it:

- Go to eBay's site map and seek out the link to Turbo Lister.
- Click on the "Download Now" link to install the program onto your PC (see Figure 23-1).
- Upon successful download, you'll see a new icon on your PC's desktop from which you can easily launch Turbo Lister (see Figure 23-2).
- Upon first use, you'll need to provide your eBay User ID and pass-

word, then verify your registered contact information. On subsequent uses, it's only necessary to provide your eBay password.

- To begin creating a listing, click on the "Create new" button at the top of the Turbo Lister screen (see Figure 23-3).
- Creating Turbo Lister listings is a simple three-step process. Much like listing single items within eBay itself, begin by selecting the auction format in Step 1.
- In Step 2, enter an item title, description, and images (see Figures 23-4 and 23-5).

eBay TIP: Turbo Lister will assume that you wish to use eBay's iPIX image hosting service and will invoke the tool to select images directly from your PC. If you'll be using images that are stored elsewhere, such as at a Web site of your own, you can change the iPIX default choice by clicking the appropriate checkbox when you select the "Change image hosting" link. By doing so, you can specify the Web location where eBay should look for and select the images you'll specify.

- In Step 3 of the process, designate auction particulars including duration, pricing, shipping and payment instructions, and any listing upgrades (see Figure 23-6).
- When completed with Step 3, simply click the "Save" button to complete the listing creation process within Turbo Lister.
- With listings now resident in your Turbo Lister Item Inventory, select those you wish to upload to eBay (simply clicking on the item to highlight it). Determine when you want the auction to begin (the selection buttons at the bottom of the screen allow immediate start upon eBay upload or designating a later start date/time). Click the "Add to Upload" button to transfer the selected items to the "Waiting to Upload" queue (see Figure 23-7).

eBay TIP: Before actually uploading the items to eBay, make use of Turbo Lister's "Calculate Listing Fees" button to determine how much each item will cost in insertion fees. If the fees are higher than you like, you can easily go back and modify some of your individual listing specifics and enhancements.

- From the "Waiting to Upload" item collection display, click on the "Upload All to eBay" button to enact the item transfer (see Figure 23-8).
- When the upload is complete, click either the "Go to the Pending Listings . . ." text link (if you specified a later date/time) or "Go to

My eBay . . ." link (if you selected immediate auction launch) to view the results of your upload (see Figure 23-9).

eBay TIP: With Turbo Lister you can schedule and upload up to 3000 items at a time. Now that's bulk listing!

Clearly, bulk listing makes it easy to manage a large volume of items and allows you to schedule and otherwise stagger when your auctions will begin. While creating your listing collections, keep these important considerations in mind:

- List similar items so that multiple-item bidders can find related goods to maximize cross-selling potential, or list a wide variety of goods to provide a range of items to attract more single-item bidders.
- Upload listings to coincide with peak bidding days and times.
- Always calculate listing fees before uploading to ensure you're aware of the costs.
- Try to stagger the end day of listing collections so you'll be able to tend to end-of-auction activities one collection at a time.
- Be certain you're fully prepared with all shipping materials and other supplies to quickly package and queue sold items that will be awaiting payment.

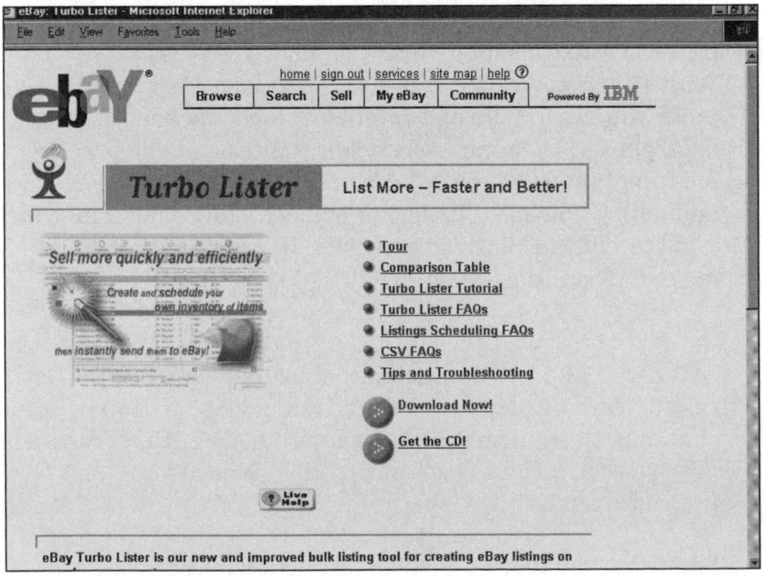

Figure 23-1   eBay's Turbo Lister information page has answers to all your questions plus the link to download the application to your PC.

Figure 23-2 The Turbo Lister "shortcut" is ready on your desktop; just double-click and launch.

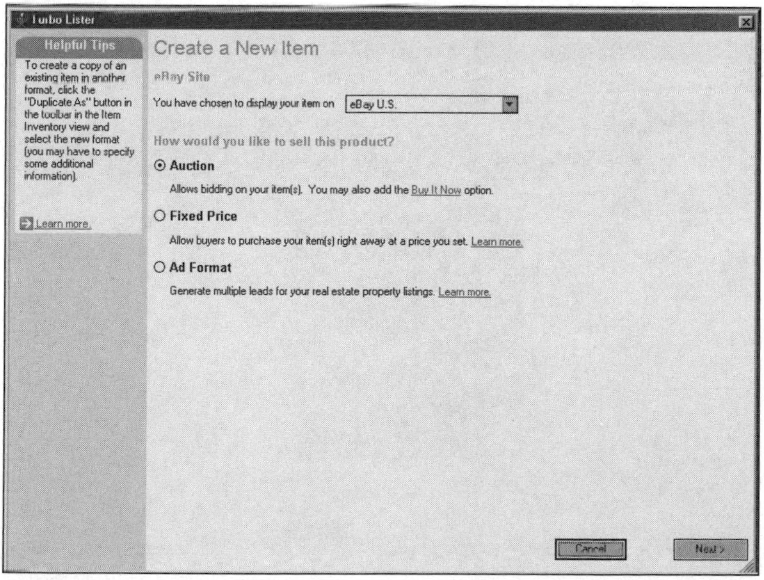

Figure 23-3 Creating items in Turbo Lister follows the screen layout as creating single items within eBay itself.

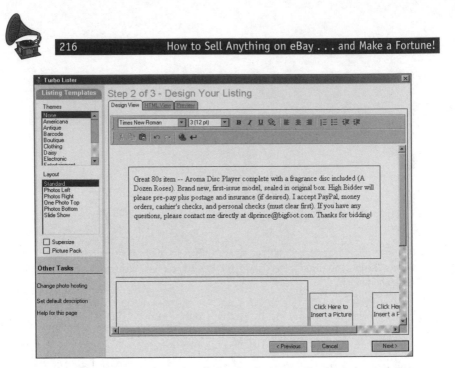

Figure 23-4   Enter an item description in the appropriately designated text box.

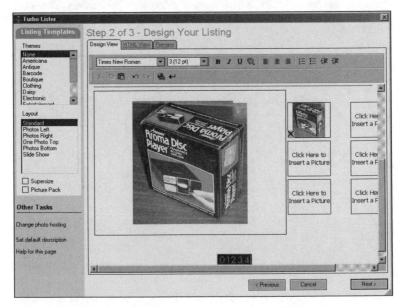

Figure 23-5   Select item images to accompany your bulk-listed items.

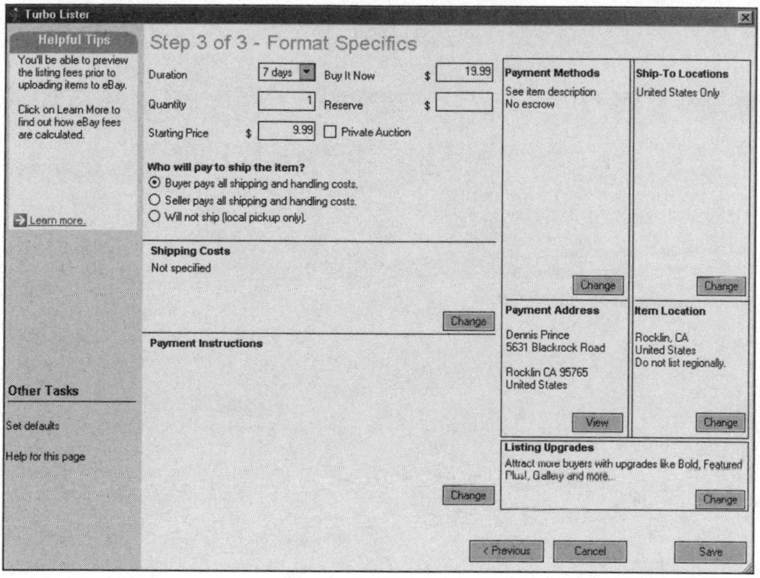

Figure 23-6 Step 3 of the Turbo Lister process includes designating auction specifics.

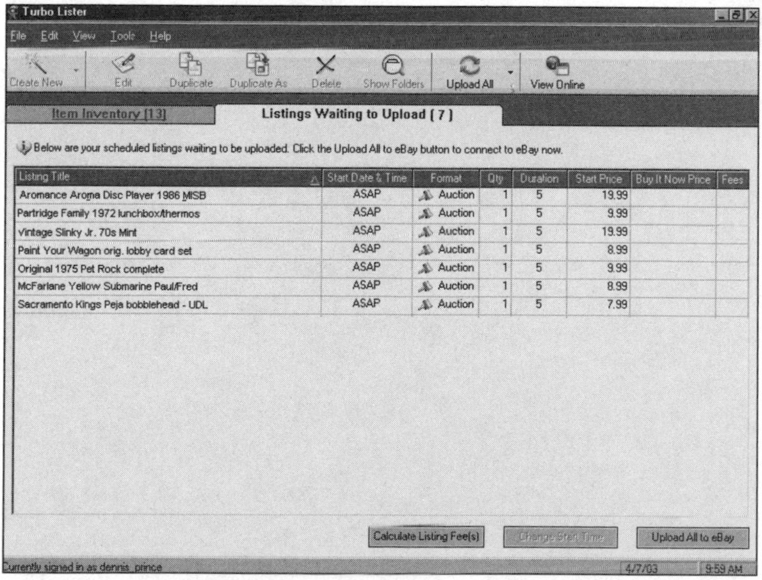

Figure 23-7 With many items now ready to launch, it's time to upload to eBay.

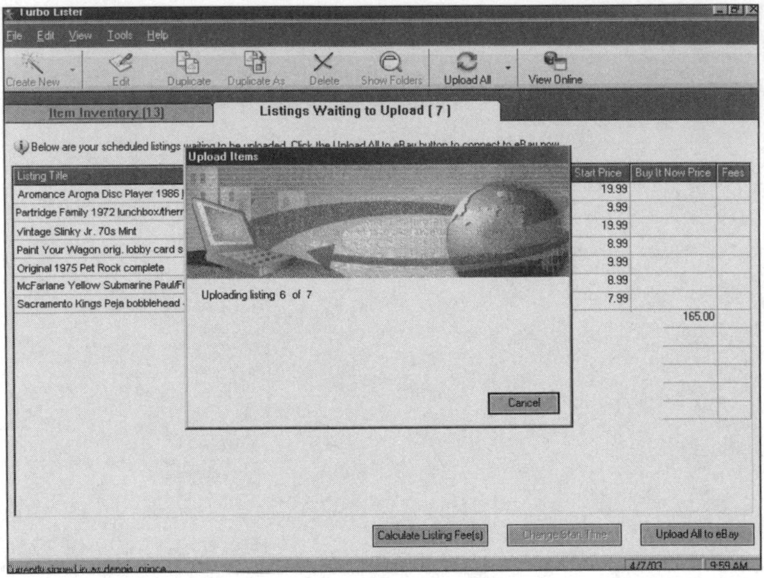

Figure 23-8 Upon choosing to upload items, Turbo Lister will connect directly to eBay to begin the data transfer process.

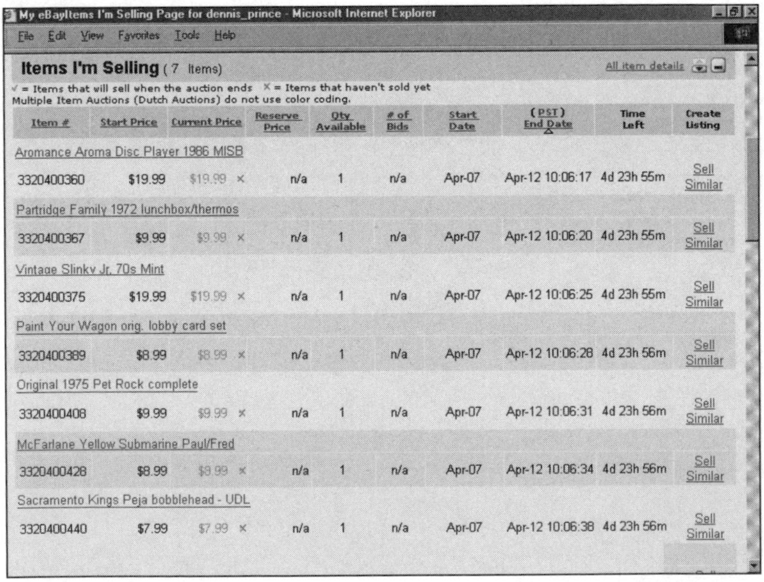

Figure 23-9 Immediately, you can visit eBay to verify the launch status of your bulk-listed auctions.

As you move forward on attaining your fortune in auctioning, you'll see that efficiency will play a key role in helping you earn the most for your efforts. Bulk listing will, in effect, exponentially reduce the amount of time it would otherwise take to list high volumes of goods using the single-item listing method. By taking advantage of Turbo Lister's offline operation, you'll be able to construct your batches of listings without being connected to the Internet, allowing you to plan your next wave of listings whenever and wherever you might be.

24

Establishing an Auction Workplace

Regardless of your volume of business, organization will be key to your success in any sustained level of auctioning. These days, efficiency seems to underscore everything, allowing for better opportunities, greater savings of time and money, and the ability to do more with less. So here is where you can effectively establish a rhythm and routine to your eBay activities. Although you needn't go overboard in organization, you will find that a little extra efficiency can significantly add to your eventual success (and profit).

ESTABLISH YOUR OWN AUCTION OFFICE

Many have dreamed of a workplace away from the "workplace." However, when it's time to get serious about keeping the online income flowing, it's time to set up an efficient workplace. A first step is to establish an "auction office," that dedicated place where you'll do your work, week in and week out. If you never considered where such an office might be located, here are a few ideas for auction spaces that could be right under your nose (or just down the hall and to the right):

- *The Extra Room.* If your home or apartment has an extra room used for storage, clean it out and use it as a virtual storefront instead. The extra room converted to a home office is typically the most desirable situation for managing auction activity: it's a self-contained work area that can go undisturbed and can be closed off from the rest of the living spaces when not in use. Remember, too, that a room used specifically for a business can usually be deducted from your taxes as a percentage of your rent or mortgage and your utilities.

- *Attic or Basement.* These are the other natural "extra spaces" that are prime choices for home office conversion. Sometimes special considerations need to be taken when using an attic or basement (consider adequate headroom, lighting, protection from excessive heat or moisture), and a preinhabitation bug bomb could be in order.
- *A Cozy Corner.* If you can't devote an entire room to eBay, is there a special area of a room where you can set up shop? Work spaces can be located in the corner of a living room, dining room, or family room (or any room, for that matter). Typically all it takes is about six to eight square feet of dedicated space and you're in business.
- *A Spare Closet.* Believe it or not, standard wardrobe closets make excellent work areas. A typical six-foot closet provides ample floor space for locating a desk, chair, and the other office tools you'll soon learn about. The bonus of a closet, much as with a spare room, is that it usually has doors that you can close to hide the workspace from view when it's not in use.

In this mobile-technology, laptop-laden culture, you might ask "why set up if you can be on the go?" Sure, that's an option, but typically not a good choice for a long-term auction business. Mobile computing and communication look great in advertisements, and are impressive at the cyber cafes, but here are some of the drawbacks of not having an established workplace:

- *Connectivity:* Connecting to the Internet (which is at the core of online auctions, right?) can be twitchy when it comes to mobile computing. Repeated tries at connecting to the Net with a cell-modem are definite time-wasters. Though connection isn't 100 percent guaranteed at all times in a permanent work area either, odds say you'll do better than if you're attempting to run your business while you're on the go.
- *Continuity:* If you look at someone's messy desk, you'll wonder how they get anything done. However, the occupant is typically quick to proclaim that he or she knows *exactly* where everything is and *exactly* where he or she last left off. A mobile environment doesn't support starting and stopping very well. After every use the work needs to be packed up and put away, usually disrupting a natural flow in progress. Plus, it's easier to lose important information (whether physical or virtual) in a transient environment.
- *Convenience:* Although mobile computing is much ballyhooed as convenience in the palm of your hand, there's not much convenience to *having* to work from the palm of your hand. Serious auction goers need to be able to spread out, to know that their office space is always ready and waiting for them, and, most important, to know that it's *their* space that can be cordoned off from other hands.

ALLOWING FOR NECESSARY OFFICE AMENITIES

As soon as you locate your prime office real estate, ensure that it will have the basic amenities you'll need to get into business and stay productive.

- *Online Access:*   There has to be a phone line or cable line available or there's no getting onto the Net. Be sure live access is nearby, preferably on the same wall as where you'll locate your work surface. Of course, wireless access is up-and-coming, but at this time it's still a bit too costly when compared to hard-wire connectivity (but maybe soon, huh?).
- *Proper Lighting.*   Mom was right about eyestrain: it'll mess you up. Though a PC monitor has a glow all its own, you'll need decent overhead lighting as well as desk lighting to keep your eyesight from suffering and to keep all your work materials within easy view.
- *Elbow Room.*   Though it's not necessary to have a 20 foot by 20 foot office to be effective, you do need a certain amount of space to work in. An overly cramped work area is not only difficult to keep in order, it can become physically uncomfortable. Be sure you have a work surface that offers at least a 4 foot by 3 foot work area (the more the better). Think about the PC monitor, the printer, the telephone, and many of the other office tools you'll need and want within easy reach.
- *Air Circulation.*   In most situations, this isn't much of a problem. However, if you're eyeballing the attic, the basement, or the garage, be sure you can maintain a comfortable room temperature and air flow. Avoid areas subject to extremes in temperature, static air, moisture, or dust.

AUCTION OFFICE TOOLS

You've got your space; now it's time to fill it with the tools you'll need (and some you'll want) to shift your business into higher gear. To start, consider these to be the bare essentials:

- *Computer.*   This was already discussed in Chapter 2, yet it's worth repeating here; be sure that your dedicated auction computer is located within your auction office.
- *Printer.*   Although it's an electronic age, there's still a need for printed matter (such as for printing invoices to include in shipments). These days, printers are being bundled with PC packages and can be had, PC and all, for around that $1000 price point. If you buy a

stand-alone PC, expect to pay between $150 and $300 (or more) for a printer, depending on your specific needs and wants. For your auction business, a simple color inkjet printer will meet your needs for years.

- *Telephone.* The phone in the kitchen may be just around the corner or down the stairs, but having a phone in your work area is a real convenience and time-saver. Keep a phone pad and pencil nearby, too.
- *Internet Access.* Again, this was discussed earlier in this book, but remember to be able to access the online world from within your auction office.
- *A Second Phone Line.* Time was when folks hooked up second lines to support a teen's talking habits. Today, second lines are almost indispensable for maintaining efficient access to the Internet while allowing for another line to be free for making phone calls.
- *Hands-Free Phone System.* Though you might not consider this as much more than a showy little upgrade, using a phone earpiece or headset really makes a difference. By keeping both hands free to type, maneuver a mouse, or whatever, you can stay productive while you're on hold or in the middle of a conversation. Speaker phones and PC phones achieve the same thing, but the sound is often of lesser quality for both you and the person on the other end
- *Postal Scale.* Consider purchasing a postal scale for your auction office; they're handy and ready on demand. These days there's a lot to choose from: some simply weigh items and indicate postage cost, while others have digital readouts and can print metered postage via a phone hookup.
- *Answering Machine/Voice-Mail Account:* Help buyers make voice contact with you even when you're away. An inexpensive answering machine or voice-mail account will help buyers leave those important messages without enduring the aggravation of "phone-tag."
- *A Comfy Chair.* Sounds silly until you wind up saddle-sore and back-weary from squirming in an unsuitable seat.

STAGING YOUR AUCTION ITEMS

Remember the earlier discussion about your auction office and your dedicated auction "work space?" Besides serving as a constant home to your auction tools (the PC, printer, and all the rest), your auction space also can serve as your auction "staging area." When you list your goods and treasures for sale in the virtual marketplace, your glowing descriptions aren't enough—you have to deal with the goods themselves in the physical world before, during, and after the auction. So why might you need a specific auction staging area? Here's why:

- A staging area provides space to examine, categorize, and catalog your auctionable merchandise.
- A staging area can serve as that mini photography studio discussed in Chapter 17, where you take digital pictures of your items.
- A staging area can also serve as a safe storage area to keep items clean and free from damage or loss (especially important if they're currently being bid on or ready for shipment).
- A staging area, if established properly, can provide further organization to your auction business, eliminating clutter and enabling you to deal with your merchandise faster and more efficiently.

A staging area doesn't necessarily need to be in the same place as your auction office (though that is preferable in terms of keeping all the auction activity in one central location). Many auctioneers use different rooms or storage areas for their staging and storing needs. Whichever approach you choose—concentrated or scattered—be sure your staging area meets these basic requirements:

- It should be clean, dry, and free from temperature extremes.
- It should be clearly identifiable as a devoted staging and storage area that will prevent others from moving or removing merchandise you intend to sell or are currently auctioning.
- It should be spacious enough to accommodate the goods you intend to auction without being crammed or overstuffed—the leading cause of postauction damage.
- It should be easily accessible to you, allowing you to get to your merchandise without needless climbing over stacks of boxes, crouching in crawlspaces, and creeping up shaky ladders.

Remember, the key to becoming organized and staying that way is to develop work areas that are easy to work in and to work with.

ESTABLISHING A SHIPPING STATION

Although shipping supplies and methods were discussed fully in Chapter 12, consider that effort and how it fits into the methodology behind establishing an auction office. Free yourself from rummaging for the last roll of tape or endlessly searching for the right box for an item. Beyond where you stage, list, and manage auction items, you likewise need a *supply room* that will be well-stocked with all the goods you need to make the easy transition from listing an item to packing an item.

eBay TIP: If your shipping area is organized, you'll always know when to order new packing supplies. Remember, you can order free packing materials from *shop.usps.com*.

Although you might be anticipating this by now, be sure your supply room has the following qualities:

- *It's a dedicated area.* No, you don't need a 10-bedroom home or condo to be an organized auctioneer. A single auction office located in a spare room can serve multiple auction uses (office, staging area, supply room). In fact, if you can find a large enough living space, the best auction environment is one where *all* of your auction activity can be contained within a single space. If not, find another corner where you can set up a supply shop.
- *It's a clean and well-lit area.* Cleanliness and good lighting will work in your favor as you pack up those items that customers have already paid for and are anxiously awaiting.
- *It's large enough to allow organization.* Again, a mansion isn't necessary, but you'll do better if all your supplies aren't stacked in a cramped corner or dumped into a carton that requires upending to get to what you need.
- *There's adequate work space to pack items.* It's where you'll keep your supplies and where you should expect to use them, too. Make sure you have enough room to work.

ORGANIZING YOUR SUPPLY ROOM

The key to organization is to have what you need when you need it, and within easy reach. As you establish your supply room, envision the actual flow of work: picture an assembly line process (moving from left to right) or a single-item packing station where all packing materials are within reach (boxes underneath, box fill above, tape to the left, labels to the right). Though it might sound a bit silly, the organization of your supply room is what will allow you to develop a repeatable and time-efficient packing process that will round out the establishment of your fully-functional auction office.

25

Record Keeping—
The Best Methods and Tools

A t this point, you're probably grinning at the premise that you are truly in charge of your *own business*. In seeking your online fortune, it's become clear that you can pull down a regular income selling almost anything at eBay. While you daydream about your newfound freedom—the satisfaction of finally being able to work as you please and manage your affairs as best suits your needs and desires—there is one thing you can't escape: the need to keep accurate records, analyze profit-and-loss statistics, and pay taxes. No, the dream hasn't come to a screeching halt, though some folks would rather endure a root canal than face the tedious task of sorting out their business affairs. But fear not—keeping records and keeping track of your auction exploits isn't such an arduous task, provided you establish good habits up front. This chapter explains how easy record-keeping can be and how facing Uncle Sam come April 15 can become a relatively painless process.

KEEPING UP WITH KEEPING RECORDS

Although it's been said a clean desk is a sign of a sick mind, the online seller who's well-organized will generally have an easier time in record keeping. Though much significance is given to proper pricing, impressive images, and compelling item descriptions, keeping track of your online sales, bidder and buyer information, and everything else that comes with selling at eBay is paramount if you want to maximize your potential for success.

No doubt about it, record keeping requires discipline, but if you consider this aspect of your business venture at the same time you plan what sorts of items you list and where you'll obtain your inventory, you'll stand the best opportunity of establishing an efficient operation. With a well-thought-out plan up front, you'll find it's easy to hit a stride in your offline duties, and you'll take the pain out of keeping track of your actions.

Why Keep Accurate Records?

Before getting into the principles of good record keeping, you may be wondering why it's important to keep accurate accounts of your work outside of the need to pay the government its due. Simply enough, if you don't keep accurate records, how will you ever know whether you're succeeding in making your fortune? If your business begins to suffer a financial downturn, will you be able to quickly recognize what is happening and make corrective adjustments based simply on your "feel" for how things are going? And how will you be certain that the financial decisions you make are well-founded and well-planned if you're never empirically certain of those decisions' impact? For any businessperson or any other person seeking a profitable enterprise, good records tell the story of how effectively their operation is running and how quickly they might be able to realize their financial goals.

IDENTIFYING THE KEY DATA

If you're convinced that good record keeping is vital to your efforts, you may wonder what sort of data you will want to keep. To help you get started, here is the sort of auction-related information that will be the foundation to your record-keeping objectives.

Inventory and Assets

- *Inventory Purchases.* Record all inventory you purchase or otherwise acquire that will be sold at auction. Record *when* you acquired the items, *where* you acquired them, and at *what cost.* Keep all related receipts in an organized filing system, and if you didn't receive a third-party receipt, write one up yourself on the spot to capture the date, place, and cost of the items (see Figure 25-1).
- *Capital Equipment Purchases.* If you're purchasing a dedicated PC, a printer, camera, office supplies, or other such items that will be used directly in your auction business, properly record each of these purchases by logging the item name, cost, date of purchase, place of purchase, and business reason for the purchase.
- *Inventory Sales.* Here's where your tax liability comes into play and where you need to be excruciatingly accurate in your record keeping. Whenever you sell an item, record sales price, sales tax (if applicable), and date of sale.

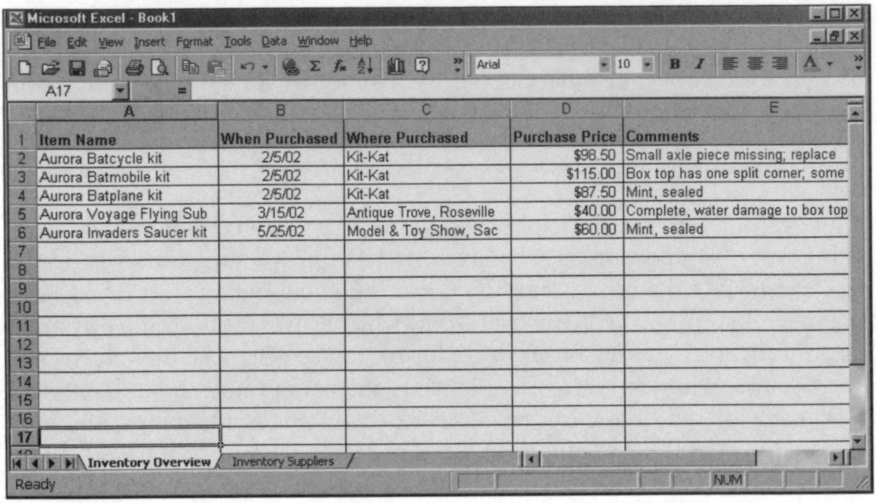

Item Name	When Purchased	Where Purchased	Purchase Price	Comments
Aurora Batcycle kit	2/5/02	Kit-Kat	$98.50	Small axle piece missing; replace
Aurora Batmobile kit	2/5/02	Kit-Kat	$115.00	Box top has one split corner; some
Aurora Batplane kit	2/5/02	Kit-Kat	$87.50	Mint, sealed
Aurora Voyage Flying Sub	3/15/02	Antique Trove, Roseville	$40.00	Complete, water damage to box top
Aurora Invaders Saucer kit	5/25/02	Model & Toy Show, Sac	$60.00	Mint, sealed

Figure 25-1 An inventory spreadsheet is easy to create and easy to maintain, as shown in this example using Microsoft Excel.

Hosting Venue Expenses

- *Standard Listing/Insertion Fees.* By now you're well acquainted with the insertion fees levied at eBay. This is part of your cost of doing business and is critical information to record to determine how profitable your business is operating.
- *Special Feature Fees.* Although you could lump these costs in with the standard insertion fees, recording and tracking these separately will help you recognize whether these additional costs are really paying dividends in your final price obtained.
- *Final Value Fees.* These comprise the final piece of the puzzle with regard to direct expenses incurred when listing items at eBay. Again, it's a good idea to separate out the costs of listing and ultimately selling an item at eBay so you can track and adjust (where possible) your direct cost of sales.

Transaction Fees

- *Shipping and Handling.* When you're buying for resale or buying equipment and supplies, be sure to capture any transit and delivery costs you paid.

- *Insurance and Tracking.* If you paid for these services when you made your purchase, be sure to record these fees as well.
- *Money Fees.* When you're using an online payment service, escrow, or purchasing money orders, be sure to record the cost of sending or receiving payments.
- *Travel.* If you're hunting for inventory or simply driving to a carrier's office to drop off or pick up packages, record the cost of travel be it by plane, train, or automobile.
- *Supplies.* When you purchase supplies specifically for managing your auction business, those are more costs you need to record.

General Expenses

- *Internet Fees.* If you're paying for online access, be it DSL, cable modem, or whatever, those are generally costs attributable to your business.
- *Storage and Insurance Fees.* If your inventory is stored offsite and/or you're paying specific fees to insure that inventory, these are costs you should also track.
- *Home Office Deductions:* The IRS permits you to claim a percentage of your costs of maintenance, mortgage interest or rent, utilities, and other direct and indirect expenses if your home office is used *regularly* and *exclusively* to operate your business.

Naturally, there may be additional costs and activities you'll want to track for your specific needs. Also, be sure to consult your tax advisor should there be items that could legally benefit you, and these should be recorded as well.

ESTABLISHING A RECORD-KEEPING PLAN

Everyone will have different ideas about the best way to organize records. Because of this, you'll find there is no "right way" to manage your sales data (although stuffing it all in a shoe box is definitely the "wrong way"). So, when devising a record-keeping strategy, review these key considerations to ensure your personal method is efficient and effective:

- Adopt a method that's easily repeatable and that can be useful for high-volume as well as low-volume selling.
- Be sure your method is efficient to the degree that *you* won't be tempted to abandon it in the near future. Record-keeping methods can be enhanced, but if you find yourself changing over to a new style every other month, you may have developed something too complex.

- Keep it as simple as possible. You don't have to keep every single bit of data. Decide on the most pertinent information that will serve you for one year's time and go with that.

Of course, there are many tools to help you manage your online sales records. From a paper-based system to a PC-based spreadsheet or database application to an onsite Inventory Management System or third-party software packages, there are many tools from which to choose. Whichever means you settle upon, be sure you're comfortable with it, have the proper storage facilities for such records (physical or electronic), and have some sort of backup or recovery method in case the unforeseen occurs.

ADDING EFFICIENCY TO THE TASK

Most less-than-organized sellers confess they spend more time digging for past sales information than they care to admit. That time is lost opportunity, plain and simple. Avoid this by establishing a filing plan, be it hard copy or electronic, and sticking to it faithfully. If you'll be dealing in the real world of paper, using clearly marked files will allow you to store and retrieve information in mere seconds. By logically ordering your various records and receipts in a simple cabinet of hanging file folders, you'll be able to keep all of your pertinent data easily within reach.

If you want to go electronic when filing data, there are a few simple applications and online destinations that will help you get organized and stay that way:

- *Spreadsheet Applications.* I've settled on Microsoft Excel for my spreadsheet needs, though MS-Access (a database utility) runs a close second. With Excel, I've been able to easily enter my pertinent sales and purchase data (refer back to Figure 25-1) easily and without any complications. All of the data is easy to view and even simpler to sort and analyze.
- *Online Service Sites.* Over the years, two sites in particular have continued to be valuable to me in my business exploits: *www.quicken. com/small_business* (see Figure 25-2) and *www.irs.gov/businesses/ small.* Both of these sites have been indispensable to me in the information they've provided and the downloadable tools I've been able to sample (though I admit that I have found that Excel meets most of my record-keeping needs in the single package). Quicken, the well-known electronic budgeting and bill-paying tool, has a Web site that caters directly to the small business or otherwise self-employed businessperson. I guarantee that you can spend hours poring over all the information and advice it has to offer—all time very well-spent. Like-

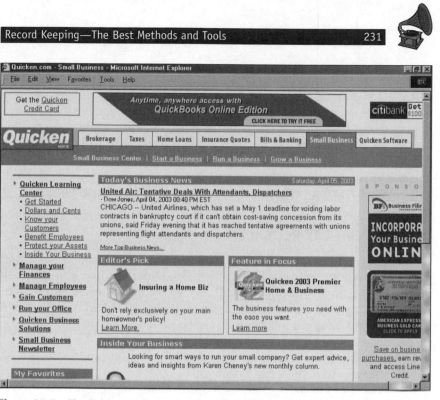

Figure 25-2 The Quicken Web site dedicated to small businesses offers answers to almost every question you might conjure up.

wise, the Internal Revenue Service provides numerous tips, forms, and even self-paced online training sessions to help entrepreneurs like you get your business running well and properly managed.

- *E-mail Tool.*   As much as I've encouraged you to excel in all your communications, you now need to be equally adept in filing and storing records of customer interactions. Practically all of the e-mail tools available today feature an embedded filing system. Create sensible file folders (e.g., "Items Listed," "Items Sold," "Payment Pending," and so on) and keep your messages stored appropriately.

eBay TIP: The programs and Web destinations on these pages are the ones that have been of greatest help to me in my activities. They may or may not suit your needs or desires. Choose whichever electronic tools work best for you, but try to refrain from utilizing *too many* tools. While there are so many business helpers and organizers available today, your business will be best served if you can focus in on one, two, or three (at the most) to manage your activity. Any more than this and you could end up spending more time servicing the tool than servicing your business.

AN IMPORTANT NOTE ABOUT SECURITY

Just a quick note about controlling your records: be sure you have *exclusive* access to your business records—meaning there isn't someone else in the household who might unwittingly reorganize or otherwise disrupt your organization system. It's a safe and practical measure that you're able to lock your physical files and be sure to utilize password protection for your electronic tools, too. If you work with a partner, be sure you both agree to the organization methods and communicate fully whenever a change or enhancement might be useful.

RECORDS THAT PAY REWARDS

As any good businessperson knows, a base of customers can be your best asset for long-term success. To an online seller, understanding who your best customers are and occasionally notifying them of the availability of the things they desire can leave the two of you standing quite happy and successful. To this end, keep the following customer-related information:

- The customer's name and contact information (address provided, e-mail, etc.)
- The dates of your auctions and other supporting transaction dates with the buyer
- Method of payment you received
- Method and cost of shipping used, plus any tracking numbers

Beyond providing you with the ability to keep in touch with your past customers, good auction records can also be critical to sorting out a potential snag in an auction transaction. A buyer could contact you weeks or months after you believe the deal was closed. Although this is not necessarily a reason to suspect a scam, your ability to quickly present detailed records and accounts of an auction transaction (via your spreadsheet of information (see Figure 25-3) or stored e-mail messages) will be your best tool to proving you held up your end of the bargain.

Though you wouldn't use their information irresponsibly or inappropriately, keeping track of the folks you've sold to in the past and their contact information will ultimately pay dividends as it helps you recognize a good returning customer, a potential deadbeat, or anyone who has expressed interest in the sorts of items you offer.

DECLARING INCOME AND PAYING TAXES

Every year around January 31, you should have collected your W-2 forms as you prepare to report your annual taxable income. But, there's likely one

	A	B	C	D	E	F	G	H	I
1	eBay Item #	Item Name	Start Date	End Date	Final Price	High Bidder	Payment Type	Shipping Method	Ship Date
2	3320400494	PS Allosaurus	2/9/03	2/16/03	$345.09	xxxxxxxx	PayPal	USPS Priority	2/19/03
3	3320400502	PS Flying Rep.	2/9/03	2/16/03	$140.25	xxxxxxxx	PayPal	USPS Priority	2/18/03
4	3320400512	PS Spiked Dino	2/9/03	2/16/03	$136.27	xxxxxxxx	Money Order	USPS Priority	2/25/03
5	2921800977	PS Giant Bird	3/16/03	3/23/03	$145.00	xxxxxxxx	PayPal	USPS Priority	2/18/03
6	2170187223	PS Cro-Magnon	3/16/03	3/23/03	$122.77	xxxxxxxx	Money Order	USPS Priority	2/24/03
7	2170673835	PS Neanderthal	3/16/03	3/23/03	$147.29	xxxxxxxx	Per. Check	USPS Priority	3/3/03

Figure 25-3 Sales information as shown in this spreadsheet excerpt can be vital to sorting out a complication or misunderstanding with a customer.

income form you haven't collected—your *auction income* statement. While the IRS continues to eyeball the auction venues, you'll be best served to keep your nose clean in reporting your auction income. To that effect, here are some tips on how and when you should report income and what sorts of expenses you might legally deduct.

Always Consult a Professional

At the outset, understand the information provided here is intended to guide you toward a better understanding of legally reporting income. Taxation rules can differ from state to state and even town to town, so always consult a licensed tax preparation expert to be sure you fully understand the tax liabilities, allowances, and limitations as they might pertain to your particular situation.

Gains and Losses

The rules are simple: wherever you make a profit, taxes are to be paid. Even if you decide to infrequently sell off prior investment pieces such as fine art, vintage automobiles, or antiques, if any sale earns you a profit over and above your original purchase price, the IRS deems the profit as taxable income. Conversely, if such a sale fails to recoup the original investment, you'll be faced with a loss which could be deemed a "declarable loss" (again, consult a tax professional in these matters).

Naturally, you'd prefer to see your gains exceed your losses, as would your government.

Making Estimated Payments

If your approach is to regularly buy and sell items at online auctions, you're unquestionably operating as a business that is in the business of making a profit.

If you're this sort of happily self-employed businessperson, recognize that you're responsible to make quarterly estimated tax payments based on the income realized for the tax period. Required payment dates are April 15, June 15, September 15, and January 15 of the following year. These payments are filed using Form 1040-ES (OCR). But, there's a catch to paying these taxes on your business: besides paying a regular tax on any profit, you're also responsible to pay an additional 15.3 percent to cover Social Security and Medicare contributions.

When it comes time to file your annual tax return in April, you should consider reporting your business' activity using Schedule C, *Profit (or Loss) from a Business or Profession,* with your Form 1040.

Declaring Business Expenses

More good news is that whenever your business incurs expenses while striving for a profit, those are probably deductible costs that can offset a portion of your net gain. Though some folks try to claim questionable expenses (e.g. vehicles, vacations, etc.), here are some of the expenditures that are generally acceptable deductions:

- Listing fees
- Business-related postage costs
- Phone and Internet connection fees
- Supplies
- Computer programs
- Office furniture and equipment
- Business-related training and educational expenses
- Tax preparation fees
- Legal fees
- A percentage of rent or mortgage if you have a separate office of a specific size

These are just some of the common deductions you can legally claim as you operate your business. Be sure to consider other expenses that you incur as part of keeping your business alive and thriving, and consult your tax adviser to see what additional deductions you may be letting slip through your fingers (and into Uncle Sam's hands).

26

Cutting Costs, Controlling Expenses, and Improving Your Profitability

Here's an adage you may not have heard before: in order to make a fortune, you first have to save a fortune. Similar to the venerable "penny saved, penny earned" vernacular, a large factor in truly becoming rich is your ability to retain that which you acquire. By controlling selling fees and other expenses, you'll be in better control of your overall business performance and bottom line profit than if you racked up costs indiscriminately and unmonitored. No, you don't need to become an absolute "tightwad," and you needn't relegate the special features in your auction listings to the bare-bones minimums (that would be poor selling strategy). This chapter will help ensure you remain aware of the fees and costs associated with online selling and how you can apply effective strategy to keeping those costs down while fortifying your fortune.

CONTROLLING eBAY FEES

When making your first listings, you may have been surprised and maybe even concerned about the number of various fees eBay levies. While it's true that almost every little enhancement seems to have some sort of associated cost, it should be comforting to know that many of these auction-related costs can be reduced and managed with a bit of foresight and careful planning. You won't be able to escape every fee but you can reduce and avoid many which really don't add that much to your profit potential and exist largely to chew into your bottom line.

The Fees You Can't Avoid

Be realistic—you *will* pay some sort of listing fee when you sell at eBay. The days of free online auctioning are long gone (those sites dried up back in the late '90s due to low traffic and sparse listing volume). Still, some cantankerously contend that eBay is getting rich because of its tariffs. Nevertheless, it's important to understand that the fees you pay provide the needed capital to fund useful new features, costly infrastructure (hardware and software maintenance), and user services and tools. Much like your own business, as eBay continues to grow, it needs to reinvest to ensure it can satisfy the needs and wants of the more sophisticated online seller. The listing and usage fees wind up being a small price to pay for the ability to list, sell, and collect at so large a site, and the advanced methods and tools (such as Turbo Lister) become worth the cost when you consider the time, effort, and, yes, money *you'll* save in the long run. Internet and online auction history have already proven that free sites simply cannot compete and perform to these levels.

The Little Things That Can Cost Big

While it's reasonable and affordable to manage basic eBay insertion fees, there *is* a lot of fluff in there and you *can* cut costs by carefully selecting which features and services you'll use in your listings. In fact, after doing some research and investigating, you might find that although some adornments and extras add plenty of eye candy, they also might offer little true return on the investment.

Cast a frugal eye on these questionable, and often costly, eBay listing enhancements:

- *Title Enhancements.* Be it bold, highlighted, or whatever, few bidders really pay much attention to the visual style of your item's title. Save a buck and make conservative use of capital lettering (not exclusively, though) to highlight the key element of your title. Make sure you use plenty of good "hit words," since most items are found via keyword searches.
- *Special Icons.* Whether it's a birthday cake, a Christmas tree, or a firecracker, when it comes to added title icons . . . who cares? When did you last leap at an item because of the cutesy little picture that accompanied it? Again, save the buck.
- *Home Page Featured Placement.* This is one of the most expensive listing options at eBay and, unless you've got an item that will gain you thousands of dollars in high bids or if you're continually selling a product with a tremendously high profit volume, it's best to bypass this one if you're trying to cut costs. Again, it's typically the keywords that get noticed, not the site real estate where your item is listed.
- *Cross-Category Listing.* This ability to have a single listing appear in two categories simultaneously will almost double the fee you

pay, yet may not truly pay off in the end (the additional category can be selected during Step 1 of the listing process). Revisit your research methods to determine the *best* category to list under and be willing to use a different category if your research indicates a better home for your goods. Besides, if you double-categorize, how will you know which category was ultimately responsible for your success?

- *Gallery Listings.*   For an extra cost, eBay allows you to have your item featured in a picture gallery for those shoppers who prefer to view images rather than titles. The jury's still out, though, regarding whether the Gallery is bringing in more bidders and higher bids. Without definitive proof of greater success, save the extra cost of the Gallery listing.

Learning to Choose Fees Wisely

Of course, this isn't to say that *all* fees are inherently evil and detrimental to your eventual profit. Just as it makes perfect sense to pay reasonable fees for site and service usage, it's also prudent to occasionally make use of features and enhancements when the situation calls for it. For example:

- *Reserve Prices.*   You may hate to pay the reserve surcharge, but do the math between putting a $200 reserve price on your item versus listing it with an opening bid of $200. At eBay, you'll find listing an item with a $9.99 opening bid and a reserve of $200 costs $1.30. If you opt for the opening bid of $200, sans reserve, the same listing will cost you $3.30. But don't be penny-wise and pound-foolish: If you need the reserve to protect you from losing on your investment, by all means use it.
- *Opening Bids.*   Of course, if current demand for your item easily will gain you your target price without the use of a reserve, then list in the lowest fee bracket and let the bidders work their magic.
- *Relisting.*   Well, it's typically free (at eBay, you're refunded listing fees if you get a sale), and the benefit is that you can make changes to the item title, description, and category to find your buyer on the site's dime. Take advantage of that.
- *Online Payment:*   Some sellers might not be happy that fees are levied by online payment sites, but remember that buyers who can pay with credit cards (via services like PayPal and Billpoint) will invariably spend more than if they must surrender their cash on hand. If your items sell at good prices, make it easier for your buyers to pay by offering the online payment opportunity, then collect their higher bids at the relatively low cost to you. (Some sellers even go so

far as to insist that if a buyer wants to pay through an online pay-ment service, then he or she—and not the seller—will have to fork over the necessary fees. Obviously, such a practice will cause some bidders to say thanks but no thanks. It's also against eBay's rules.)

Is It Cheaper to Have a "No Sale"?

Just when you thought sniping was the reigning king of online auction contro-versy, along comes "fee avoidance," the frowned-upon act of manipulating auc-tions and luring bidders off the venue to make a sale without paying site fees and commissions. But just as eBay is in the business of making money, well, so are you. Read the site's terms of service carefully on this issue; however, to date there's still no penalty assessed if you're contacted by a buyer who inquires about an item that fails to meet the reserve or possibly asks if you have more of the same to sell. It's a fine line, though: If the *seller* initiates offline transactions or additional sales, a swift site warning could be forthcoming, as well as possi-ble suspension since such actions are considered acts of fee avoidance.

eBay TIP: eBay openly counsels registered users to report incidents in which sellers make unsolicited contact with a buyer for the purpose of selling items outside of the auction site. Long-time eBay sellers and buyers know there is nothing wrong with this practice, from a person-to-person perspective, provided the contact isn't coercive or contin-uous (aka "spam"). Some buyers and sellers manage mutually agreeable deals in this manner, are able to review one another's eBay feedback ratings, and often develop long-lasting business relationships (even friendships) as a result. Since eBay receives no commission for such sales, it's certainly not pro-moting such ad hoc transactions.

In the interest of your sales and overall profit-to-cost ratio, be sure buyers can easily contact you (provide an e-mail address or Web site link in your item description) to assist them with any inquiries they may have, infor-mational or otherwise, during an auction or otherwise offsite. If a potential buyer initiates a potential transaction, then that's just simply good for busi-ness and could (not unfairly) save you some operating costs in the process.

eBay TIP: Amid the various fees you'll be hoping to reduce or dodge altogether, don't forget to load up on the freebies such as carriers' gratis shipping supplies, eBay tools like Turbo Lister, and even free advice from the eBay Discussion Forums (see the site map under "Community"). There are many services and supplies that are yours for the taking, provided you know where to look.

SAVINGS THROUGH SIMPLICITY

Sometimes the simplest things can pay off in ways you might not expect. When it comes to auctioning, simplicity and consistency in managing your sales can help boost your savings potential in the following ways:

- Simple listings are usually cheaper in regards to insertion fees, and with limited enhancements, the simpler listing is immediately less costly.
- If you'll be using HTML to add a bit of dazzle to your listings, using an effective style and then committing that to a repeatable template will save time in creating new listings while the HTML itself will add splashy features free of charge (as opposed to enlisting use of eBay's fee-based eye candy).
- While you want to offer options within your sales policy, adhering to shipping methods that are relatively simple to you (such as choosing carriers that are geographically nearby or selecting a carrier that offers all of the shipping options you'll support) makes it easy for your to anticipate your postauction activities without having you "reinvent" your methods at every turn.
- A simple, straightforward, and streamlined postauction process like-wise makes it easy to anticipate your upcoming activities and, when operating to a proven routine, you stand to gain time and efficiency through your repeatable methods.

eBay TIP: While not all materials necessary to your business are free, don't forget to search eBay itself for additional goods and equipment you might need such as office supplies, furniture, equipment, and even décor. There are plenty of bargains to be found at eBay so don't forget to search for good deals for these often mundane goods when *you're* in the buyer's seat.

TIMESAVING STRATEGIES THAT WILL SAVE YOU MONEY, TOO

From the equipment they use to the methods they manage, many eBay sellers are surprised to learn how much time they've lost in their *inefficient* endeavors. While you're focused on saving money, consider some of these simple yet effective efforts that will help you reclaim your most precious, nonrenewable resource.

Time Is Money

For starters, begin your profit refining by closely examining your use of time. Take two to four weeks to carefully log your time (be diligent here) to see how much you're really getting accomplished each day. You might learn you're surfing the Net too much or chatting the day away with friends. And if you're sitting around waiting for that ancient PC to chug its way through the Internet, it might be time to upgrade. The overall goal here is to ensure you can reduce the time it takes to complete your auction tasks. Set firm working hours, utilize listing and e-mail templates, carefully schedule trips into town, and whatever else you do as you tend to your auction business. Develop an efficient work plan that keeps the profits rolling in and makes the best use of your working day.

Intangibles That Inject More Savings

Your "approach" to your auctioning can save you countless hours every year. Turn your attention to tuning up your business behavior, often the element that can bring the greatest returns in the long run.

- *Establish working hours:* Whether you choose to work hours on end or segmented times of the day, put a schedule in place when work is to be done—and do it. So many home business enterprises fail due to lack of discipline in setting regular working hours.
- *Stay in your office:* With so many products and resources now available online, you can eliminate time wasted on "running errands." Today, you can order packing supplies online, you can buy postage online, and you can research your customer market online, all conveniently located at your fingertips.
- *Limit interruptions:* If your friends keep calling to chat, switch over to the answering machine. If incoming e-mail throws you off-track, close your e-mail window. Take control of whatever might be distracting you from completing your tasks, so it won't eat away at your productivity.
- *Develop a weekly work schedule:* Monday is record-keeping day. Tuesday is listing day. Wednesday is packing day. Whatever schedule works best for you, establish a routine so you can anticipate the next day's duties and avoid wasting time pondering, "Hmm. What should I do today?"
- *Focus on the task at hand:* While you're working the auctions, it's all to easy to become distracted and surf off to read, play, or shop. Stick to your task until it's done, *then* play.
- *Take a break:* Take regular breaks not only for your physical well-being (get out of that desk chair once in awhile) but also for your mental well-being. It's been proven that regular (but not excessive) breaks serve as a proven mental reenergizer, allowing you to return to work with a refreshed perspective and renewed motivation.

27

Creating Your Own Online Storefront and Presenting Your Business as a Brand

---

While the auction experience is invigorating for bidders and largely profitable for sellers, the real fortune to be had is found when you diversify your assets. In online selling terms, this means going beyond auctions themselves and incorporating a more permanent commercial presence at eBay and elsewhere. These days, creating an online "store" is easier than ever, while the financial results you stand to reap will definitely elevate your business into the big leagues.

CREATING AN eBAY STORE

Your commercial Web experience begins within eBay itself when you create an eBay store. From eBay's home page, click on the "eBay Stores" link under the Specialty Sites header, then, on the eBay Stores main page, click on the "Open your store now" text link to begin the store-building process. The first step in building a store is to establish who you are and what your store will be from the "Store Content" page (see Figure 27-1).

Enter the basic content for your store by entering information in the various screen fields, much as when you created your About Me page. When these items are complete, click the "Continue" button at the bottom of the page. The next step is to choose your store colors and graphics (see Figure 27-2).

> **eBay TIP:** When choosing your color scheme, think about matters of readability and easiness on the eye. A green color scheme with bright red text (or something similar) can be garish to behold.

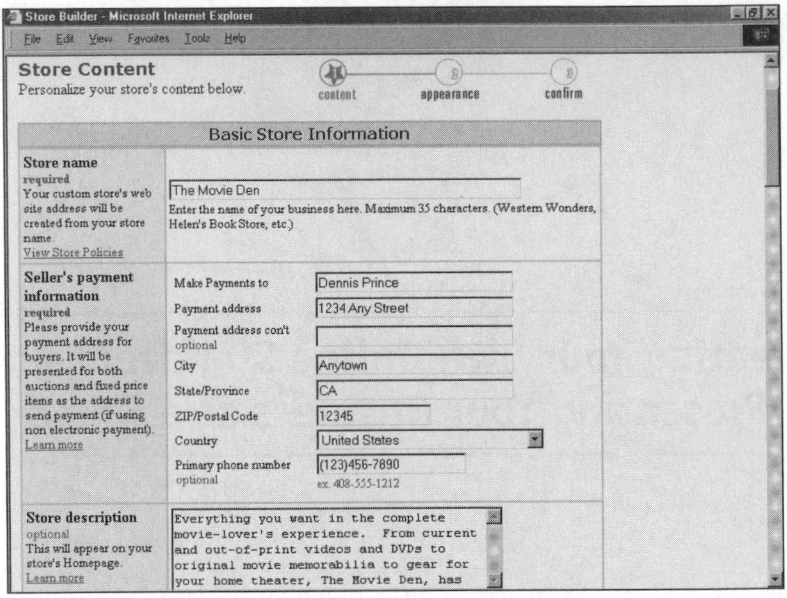

Figure 27-1 Begin building your eBay store by specifying your Store Content information.

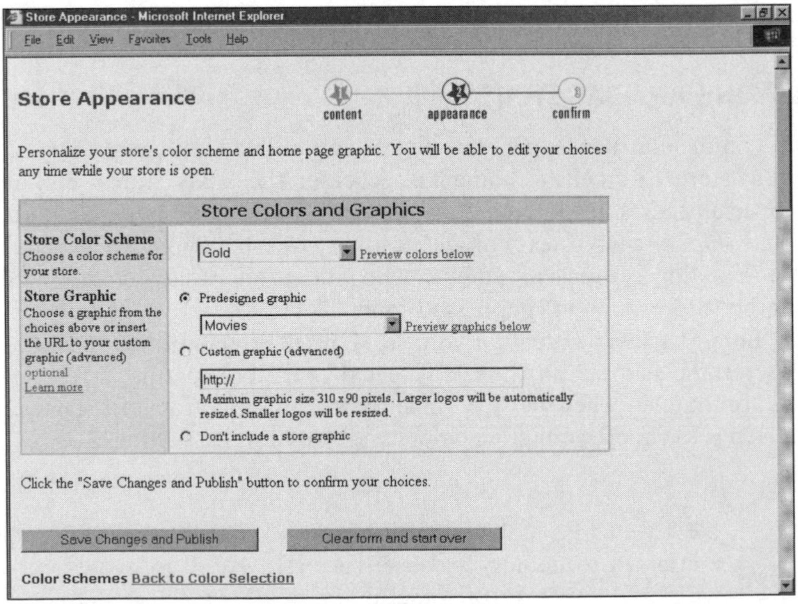

Figure 27-2 Choose the color and graphic scheme for your store.

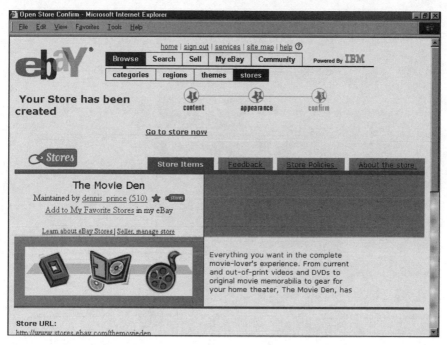

Figure 27-3 This image shows how quickly and easily you can establish an eBay Store.

When done, click the "Save changes and publish" button at the bottom of the screen. Immediately your eBay Store will be open and ready for business. The screen you see will reflect your initial store design (see Figure 27-3).

If you're not satisfied with your store and want to make changes, click on the "Seller Manage Store" text link from within your store page and make whichever changes you'd like, whenever you like.

eBay TIP: From this point forward, all items you list in your store and within the auction format will be easy to see when bidders search for your seller ID.

With your store now created, you can easily stock your virtual shelves in identical fashion to when you list auction items. Now that you're a store manager, eBay's listing page will display the additional selling format of "Sell in Your eBay Store." In addition to being able to easily host auction items and fixed-price (store) items, here are more benefits you'll find when you operate your eBay store:

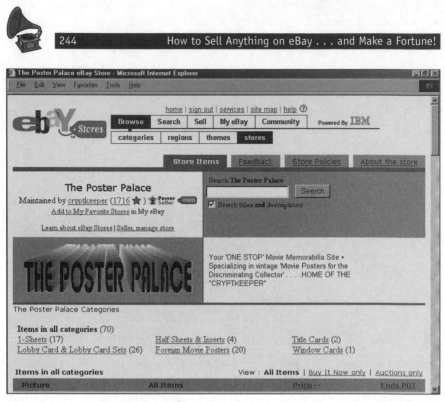

Figure 27-4   Deke Richards' Poster Palace eBay Store helps boost his sales by catering to buyers who wish to buy now.

- The ability to showcase auction and fixed-price items all in one place.
- Your own eBay store Web site address (e.g., *www.stores.ebay.com/ themovieden*)
- Your store's name and link highlighted in all of your eBay listings.
- Your store name featured in eBay's store directory, where buyers can browse or search for your store.
- A built-in store search engine for your customers' use.
- A store icon next to your eBay user ID so buyers can easily visit your store.
- The ability to create custom item categories within your own store.

But do eBay Stores really make a difference? According to Deke Richards, a purveyor in fine movie memorabilia and other collectibles, his eBay Store, The Poster Palace, has proven to be a boon to furthering his online commercial presence and feeding his business fortune (see Figure 27-4).

CREATING A STORE OUTSIDE OF eBAY

When venturing into the creation of an online store, don't just settle for an eBay shop. Broaden your horizons and increase your potential sales reach by creating a bona fide Web site all your own, open and ready for business in the wide expanse of the Internet. Although this chapter can't provide all the details of setting up such an operation (that's a topic for another entire book), consider investing the time in establishing your own Web site. Many eBay sellers have done this with great success over the years and have further increased their money-making potential by maintaining an active presence both inside and outside of eBay. Pay a visit to Deke Richards' commercial Web venue, *www.posterpalace.com* (see Figure 27-5) to see how he's effectively extended his reach beyond the confines of eBay and into the prosperous expanse of the entire Internet.

DEVELOPING YOUR BRAND, BOOSTING YOUR BUSINESS

Perhaps you now have presence in the auction realm as well as the online store space and, though business is brimming with terrific products, it seems to

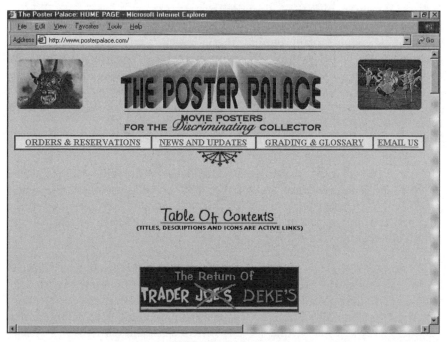

Figure 27-5   Deke Richards' Poster Palace business is active and in front of prospective customers' eyes every day on the World Wide Web.

struggle in developing a repeat customer base. Before you wonder if your diversification efforts have been to no avail, recognize that you might be in need of a brand—a name, a look, and a style that shoppers will remember and will associate with your high-quality goods and superb service. Don't leave it up to chance to have customers find you out there in the marketplace. Instead, consider developing an effective brand and positioning your business' name in the forefront of customers' minds, wherever they may find you.

Developing a Name that Sells

Choosing an effective business name is no simple task (just ask the large corporations that spend millions on such efforts). It's not necessary, though, to seek out an advertising firm to develop a winning name. According to some of the greatest marketing minds, an effective business (or product) name should have the following characteristics:

- It defines the benefit of your product or service
- It's easy to remember
- It's not too similar to any other established business name or brand
- It differentiates your business from your competitors
- It's multinational

Of course, the online realm requires that a few extra considerations be taken into account when developing a cyber-moniker. First, keep the name as short as possible, yet try to ensure it is mentally and verbally "pronounceable." Try to eliminate use of special characters (such as hyphens, ampersands, and the like) as well as numbers; these are the sorts of characters customers tend to forget easily.

eBay TIP: Notice how Deke Richards was careful to name both his eBay store and his Web site "The Poster Palace." Since he's grown active customer bases in both realms, his buyers can easily find him and his products inside and outside of eBay by remembering just one simple store name. *That's* effective.

Above all, select a name that's appropriate to your business or product. If you're in the business of selling books, choose a fitting name like "Book-World" or "RareBooks." More colorful names work well (consider "ReflectionsPast" for an antique mirror business) though you'll need to be careful the name isn't so esoteric that it's difficult to associate with your products. Expect that securing a desired online name could take some work—many choice domain names have been duly snatched up in previous years' .com frenzy. At the least, acquire an e-mail address with your business name (e.g., *RareBooks@aol.com*).

Adding Visual Recognition

Once you have a great business name, consider creating a uniquely recognizable business logo (after all, where would eBay be without that highly-recognizable upsy-downsy emblem?). Be it an evocative artistic representation of the name, an identifiable color scheme, or some sort of clever character, logos can be as big as the name in perpetuating a business' brand. If you develop a logo design, be sure to make it plainly visible (but not obnoxiously so) whenever and wherever you have items for sale.

Delivering on Your Business' Name

It's one thing to have a brand name that easily rolls off your customers' tongues or a business logo they recognize at first glance, but it's another thing to ensure that brand unequivocally delivers the sorts of goods it implies. While you shouldn't relegate yourself to only selling one specific product (such as antique stoves, mirrors, or carnival glass), be sure you're well stocked on what the name promises. Once you assure you can deliver what you advertise, it's easy to include additional items of interest that might likewise tempt your visitors' shopping and collecting tastes.

Developing Market Mindshare

Effective branding ultimately leads to firmly establishing a spot in your customers' minds. To make sure your brand can be working for you at all times, be sure to use it in all of your customer correspondence. If possible, overlay your business name in the corner of every item image you post (many photo editors allow the addition of the semitransparent "water-mark"). Include invoices or "thank-you" notes which bear your brand in all of your shipments.

Better Business for a Better Brand

Recognize that your *style* of business will make or break your brand. Keep your online destination tidy, well-organized, and informative. Be sure you've developed considerable "expert knowledge" about your featured commodity so that you can easily and reliably assist customers in their quest for information as well as merchandise. Establish operating policies that meet your customers' needs, taking into account the unique needs they might have as related to your product offerings. And keep your inventory fresh and enticing by actively rotating the goods for sale. Having done all this, your business name will likely mean more to your customers and they'll be eager to return time and time again. And every time they specifically seek out your business (whether online or elsewhere), your business' name will become further ingrained into your customers' consciousness. *That's* a successful brand.

Using Counters to Track Your Brand's Success

As mentioned in Chapter 18, counters provide you the opportunity to determine how many visitors are shopping at your Web site. Whereas the counters you used in your eBay auctions only provided data on the number of page display visits (that is, the number of times anyone—even the same person during multiple visits—viewed your listing), a successful business Web site will profit from a more sophisticated form of counting and even monitoring customer visits.

Begin by understanding the sort of specific data that should be collected and analyzed. Most successful Web enterprises track the following:

- Which areas of your Web site are visited most?
- On what days of the week do the majority of visits occur?
- How long do visitors spend at your Web site (and in which areas of the site do they linger)?
- How many errors occur at your site (pages that don't display properly or other such programmatic-type problems)?

To help Webmasters and business persons like you gain a better understanding of who's visiting your site and what happens while they're strolling your virtual aisles, programs known as *Web traffic analyzers* have been developed. Here are a few you might like to learn more about:

- WebLog Manager: Created by Monocle Solutions, this "traffic analyzer" is available for a free 30-day trial at *www.monocle-solutions.com/ weblog.*
- Surfstats: Another Web analyzer that's also available for a free trial download, at *www.surfstats.com.*

AUCTIONS VERSUS STORES—A NEW PRICE WAR?

Online sellers, you'll find, all operate under their own preferences and pronouncements of the best ways to do business. When it comes to listing formats and selling strategies at eBay and beyond, the lines are often drawn within the community between the fixed-price (store and Buy-It-Now offerings) and dynamic-price (ascending price auctioning) approaches. It's unlikely that you'll attempt to start up your own auction venue at a commercial Web site, yet it's highly important that you take this opportunity to further explore the differences between the pricing methods. Although purported by some as being opposing formats, some of the most successful offsite sellers have pursued the opportunities of both pricing formats ultimately to determine whether both methods can successfully coexist within any seller's business plan.

Understanding Fixed Pricing

To begin, online selling in and of itself has proven to be one of the most promising opportunities for traditional offline (brick-and-mortar) sellers, though many have yet to venture into the online realm. With all the buzz about eBay and auctioning, some traditional sellers often become confused regarding their options and opportunities in fixed versus dynamic pricing selling. In a nutshell, fixed-price selling is exactly how sellers do business in their offline (real world) sales establishments—they present an item, put a selling price on it, and, for all intents and purposes, have established the equivalent of an online fixed-price listing. The method here is the same; only the venue (virtual that it is) is different.

Dynamic Pricing Defined

The "dynamic" format, then, is characterized by the back-and-forth bidding that ensues when an item is placed up for bid in an auction environment. It's no secret that the gamesmanship of this competitive bidding is what's made eBay the multibillion-dollar success it is today. Of course, different auction formats, including Dutch auctions, reserve auctions, and so on, can sometimes cloud the definition. Generally, the dynamic format suggests ascending price bidding where the final price equals the highest bid at the auction's close.

When Fixed Becomes Dynamic and Vice Versa

What some sellers tend to overlook is how the fixed format can *become* dynamic, and vice versa. For example, if an item at an eBay store or other commercial site does not sell, the seller can reduce its price or have a limited-time sale, therefore dynamically altering the price at which it will be offered. Sellers can modify prices as they see fit, either in response to present market demand, to generate additional activity at their online Web store, or for any other reason that will suit their customers' wants and needs.

Similarly, the dynamic format has evolved into a sort of hybrid fixed format thanks to the addition of the "Buy It Now" sales feature at eBay auctions. A seller can offer an item to the bidders in dynamic format yet also dangle a fixed selling price, should anyone care to offer that price and close the auction immediately. In effect, this serves as an "auction stopper," but it also works as an effective method for a seller to tempt bidders with a reasonable price—perhaps the same price they'd use in a fixed format—and instills a sense of urgency to take it at that price before the opportunity is gone or the bidding possibly surpasses that price.

Dynamic Pricing Risk

A generally held misgiving over the dynamic format is the perceived lack of control over the price. In a fixed format, the price is the price, plain and simple, not subject to a whimsical or mercurial market. Really, the only risk is whether the item will or will not sell at that fixed-format price. Fixed-price sellers can safely venture into the dynamic format by utilizing either high opening bids, reserve prices, or those Buy-It-Now prices, all which could equal the original fixed-format price.

The concern that usually arises is whether an item up for bid (in dynamic format) without price protections makes for risky business, the seller being uncertain whether the bidders will ensure that fair market value is realized in the final high bid. No doubt that's a definite risk, but one that can be mitigated to a reasonable extent provided the seller has researched the current market value and would be satisfied to receive such a price. Nonetheless, the dynamic format doesn't *assure* what the final price will be.

eBay TIP: While I've fallen victim to the downside of a bidding war on occasion, more often than not I've gained much better prices than I had originally expected, thanks to the impassioned battling of bidders who were each determined to win—the "win" sometimes being more important than the final price.

The Value of Fixed-Price Sales History

There's a key intangible at work that has yet to be touched upon: in a fixed-format Web store, sellers are able to maintain and make public their history of past sales. Just as leading high-end auction houses Sotheby's and Christie's do, Web store sellers can provide a record of their past sales, allowing their customers to see the sort of goods sold in the past. This is viewed as a definite plus in the fixed-format environment since it works to visibly demonstrate the expertise and knowledge of the seller based on the goods and prices he or she has managed. eBay's short-duration dynamic listings, archived for only 30 days after an auction, can't quite offer that sort of "resume" of previous business. To some discerning buyers, this is important background information that will drive their decision to purchase or not. Realistically, for the reasons just stated, if yours is to be a Web store devoted to high-end goods, you likely wouldn't want to rely solely upon the dynamic (auction) environment. However, if you have less significant items to offer, trendy items that can provide healthy profits for a limited period, or temporarily seek to move some inventory that is otherwise languishing in a Web store, take advantage of the high traffic within the dynamic environment of eBay. At the least, you should expect to sell the item at a reasonable price, and in the best scenario, your low- to mid-range items might spark a bidders' battle. Whatever the outcome, the dynamic venue can then lead your ultimate buyer and possibly some of the under-bidders back to your fixed-format Web store, where you stand to gain additional sales and hopefully some repeat business as well.

To wrap up this brief discussion, a recommended approach is for Web sellers to offer at least one quality item within the dynamic environment— eBay, that is—at all times. The potential for attracting more viewers, which translates to increased clientele, is too valuable to pass up. This sentiment alone makes the case that a thorough understanding and strategic use of both formats simultaneously makes good business sense to the seller who will host auctions as well as a Web store.

TEN TIPS FOR IMPROVING YOUR FIXED-PRICE SALES

While eBay has the tools available to help you build your store, that help runs short when you want some advice on *how to run* your online shop, at eBay or elsewhere. To conclude this chapter's discussion of store building and brand boosting, here are 10 timely tips to help you gain better visibility, greater customer satisfaction, and maximum return on your fixed-price sales efforts:

1. *Be seen in everything you do.*   Whenever and wherever you auction or otherwise sell items, be sure to conspicuously advertise your online store or your auction goods, providing a link to either whenever you list goods for sale.
2. *Make your store inventory easy to browse.*   Categorize your fixed-price goods in meaningful ways that will help customers zero in on exactly what they're looking for. For example, if you sell clothing, you could organize your wares by men's, women's, and children's, and break shirts, pants, skirts, etc. into subcategories. Don't just dump an unsorted inventory in a heap and hope that visitors will have patience to comb through it all (many won't).
3. *Be accessible.*   Don't make it difficult for your customers—especially new customers—to get in touch with you. Be sure your contact information is clearly visible wherever and whenever you have items listed. If your e-mail address or other contact information can't easily be found, you've likely lost another customer.

4. *Keep a customer list.* Once you've satisfied a customer, keep the relationship alive by adding his or her name to your customer list. Use the list to inform your buyers of upcoming sales (and auctions) of items that might be of particular appeal. Of course, *always* allow customers to opt out of such notification if they choose.

5. *Make your terms known.* Be clear, concise, and complete when posting your business terms and policies. Shipping options, insurance, return policies, and guarantees all need to be clearly spelled out and easy to find.

6. *Diversify your listings.* Whether or not you specialize in a particular type of item, be sure to list items in multiple venues (there are other sites besides eBay) and use multiple selling formats (fixed and dynamic). The more you can diversify your location and sales methods, the better chance you will have of attracting an equally diversified clientele.

7. *Exhibit your expertise.* Don't be bashful. Make liberal use of "About Me" pages wherever possible and showcase your sales history, your related experience, your business credentials—everything that tells your customers why you're the seller with whom they can feel confident. And don't forget to post a picture of your most valuable asset—*you!* Customers like to see who they're dealing with.

8. *Give 'em more than just goods.* Most successful sellers offer generous amounts of additional information to their patrons. Post additional articles, images, and interesting information that will help your shoppers learn more about the goods they seek, the goods you're selling.

9. *Maintain customer "want" lists.* As you develop your customer base, get to know what else they're looking for. By keeping their wants in mind, you'll improve you ability to sell more goods faster (essentially, a *presale*) and you'll further enhance your customer relationships.

10. *Post customer testimonies.* With their permission, visibly post the comments of your satisfied customers. Not only will they feel special about seeing their name for others to see; you'll also help new customers get a better sense about your commitment to total customer satisfaction.

Unlike auction listings, an online store should advertise more than just the items you're selling—it reveals the details of how you run your business, how you manage your sales, and how you serve your customers. Make sure your online store incorporates these top 10 keys to success, thereby helping your customers find an easier and more satisfying experience when visiting your nonauction offerings.

28

Keeping Up with Changes
at Online Auctions

Within a relatively short span of time, eBay has logged an active and eventful history of its own. With regard to events, developments, shakeouts, and shake-ups, online auctions in general have seen so much activity that it might appear they've been around for decades (though it's been just under one decade at this writing). If you've been around the Internet and auctioning for at least five years, you've seen many would-be auction sites try and fail in their efforts to compete with eBay. Within eBay itself, you can expect to see ongoing changes in the form of new features and perhaps modified site policies or fee structures. While it's never been a problem to adapt to such changes, it's a good idea for you to keep up-to-date on the "latest and greatest" eBay has to offer so as to keep your business running smoothly and your fortune flowing. So how will you keep up with what's going on and what's coming up at eBay and elsewhere online? The purpose of this final chapter is to direct you to the sources of information where you can monitor upcoming changes to your online oasis. The good news here is that, thanks to the Internet itself, you can find a wide variety of information sources right at your fingertips.

MINING THE eBAY COMMUNITY BOARDS

Many sites host forums where members can meet and chat about the site, its members, and its direction. Good sites will have moderators who respond to member questions and comments while also posting notices of upcoming services, upgrades, or special events.

Be sure to click on the "Chat" link within the Community Talk area, then visit the "Discuss eBay's Newest Features" forum to see what's upcoming at eBay.

KEEPING CURRENT WITH OTHER ONLINE SOURCES

Of course, the Internet offers a virtual sea of information, much of which provides numerous perspectives of online buying and selling. Be sure to visit sites like these, which come from both amateur and professional reporting forums:

Vendio.com

Formerly AuctionWatch.com, Vendio has established a reputation as a leader in online business support, useful buying and selling tools, and general auction and e-commerce advocacy. With current events in mind, be sure to visit Vendio's Community pages (see Figure 28-1) where you'll find the most active and insightful discussions regarding eBay and other forms of e-commerce.

Internet.com

A division of industry leading analysis firm Jupiter Media, Internet.com offers plenty of information regarding tech trends and online business activities.

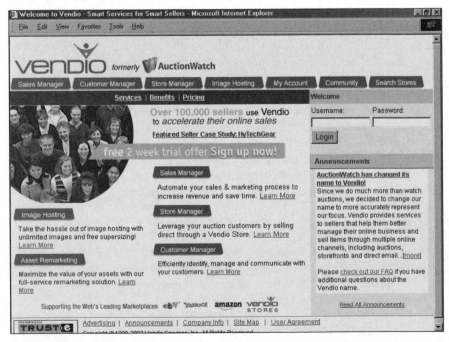

Figure 28-1 Vendio.com offers numerous buyer and seller tools and features the most active and informative community discussion boards next to eBay itself.

Nasdaq.com

When you're serious about maintaining a profit margin and buoying a business, you'll want to remain aware of the overall market for your industry. Yes, online auctioning is an industry, and it's tracked closely on the stock market. Nasdaq.com tracks all the publicly traded e-commerce venues (such as eBay; symbol EBAY) and provides extremely useful analyses and press releases that keep you informed of how well the site is doing in addition to the entire e-commerce industry.

CNET.com

If you're looking for more news and information about technology and the online world, C/NET offers generous helpings of insight and analysis. C/NET's "Top Tech News" features and special reports keep you up to date on the latest happenings at eBay and elsewhere.

Wired.com

More tech news you can use, with a bit more attitude thrown in. This site is great to get the down and dirty perspective of online business and other technology developments.

Portal Searches

With so much having been written about eBay and online auctions, don't forget to log on to your favorite Web portal site (such as Yahoo!, Google, or AltaVista) and search for auction-related keywords like "eBay," "online auctions," "e-commerce," and so on. There are plenty more sites out there who have reported on and are continuing to follow eBay and auction trends and developments; a search from a portal can help you uncover additional information you might otherwise miss.

THE POWER OF PRINT

Lastly, don't forget to visit your favorite magazine stand or bookseller to find additional information about eBay and auctions. Remember to review the trade papers, which, besides reporting on collectible and commodity trends, also keep close watch on developments in online selling and auctioning. Also look to publications like *BusinessWeek, Industry Standard,* and *Entrepreneur Magazine* for regular stories and features that pertain to the online marketplace.

Hopefully this book you're finishing now has brought you up-to-date with all that is eBay and all that is good for your online business. Your fortune is waiting for you, and by staying informed of new trends and established traditions of dealing in goods on the Internet, you'll be in the best position to sustain a profitable enterprise for years to come.

Glossary

A

Agreement   An expression of mutual assent by two or more parties on a given proposition. Refer to *Terms of Service.*

Appraisal   The act or process of estimating an item's value via expert *Authentication* and comparative pricing in the open market. Appraised values can change as the marketplace valuation of an item increases or decreases.

As Is   Selling an item without warranties in regard to its condition and fitness for a particular use. The buyer is responsible for judging the item's durability and lifetime. Also known as "as is, where is," and "in its present condition." Typically, this is a sign that no return privileges will be granted.

Auction   n (1) A method of selling a property in a public forum through open, competitive bidding. v (2) The act of putting an item up for sale in a competitive public auction.

Auction Block   The podium or platform from which an auctioneer conducts a physical auction. Online, refers to a "live listing" to be found in a listing *Category.* To place an item on the auction block means to make it available for competitive bidding.

Auction Listing Agreement   A contract executed by the auctioneer and seller, authorizing the auctioneer to conduct the sale. It also delineates the conditions of sale and the rights and responsibilities of each party. Also known as a *Listing Agreement.* Not to be confused with an online auction *Terms of Service.*

Auction Plan   The itinerary for preauction, auction day, and postauction activities, set by the auctioneer and seller.

Auction Value   The current price of a property during a competitive public auction. Also referred to as "Current Bid."

Auction with Reserve   An auction in which the seller has set a minimum price for the item and reserves the right to accept or decline any and all bids that fail to meet that price condition. Also known as *Reserve Auction.*

Auction without Reserve   An auction in which the property is sold to the highest qualified bidder with no limiting conditions or minimum price. Also known as a *Straight Auction.*

Authentication   (1) The act or process of determining whether an auction item is genuine and accurately represented by the seller. (2) A mark on an article to indicate its origin and authenticity.

B

Bid An indication and offer on an item up for sale at a competitive public auction. Bids are typically made in predetermined *Bid Increments*.

Bid Cancellation The cancellation of a bid from a buyer by a seller. During online auctions, sellers can cancel any bid if they feel uncomfortable about completing a transaction with a particular bidder.

Bid History A historical list of bidding activity for a particular auction, viewable during or after the auction.

Bid Increment The amount by which a bid will be raised each time the current bid is outdone. It is predetermined by eBay based on the current high bid.

Bid Retraction The legitimate cancellation of a bid on an item by a buyer during an online auction. At eBay, bid retractions cannot be made within five minutes of an auction close.

Bid Rigging An unlawful practice in which two or more people agree not to bid against one another in order to deflate the potential value of an item. See *Collusion.*

Bid Shielding Posting extremely high bids (which are withdrawn at the last moment) to protect the lower bid of an earlier bidder, usually in cahoots with the bidder who placed the shielding bid.

Bid Siphoning The practice of contacting bidders during an active auction and offering to sell them the same item they are currently bidding on, thus drawing bidders away from the legitimate seller's auction.

Bidder Search An online search that will generate a list of items a user has bid on at an online auction service. Availability of this tool can vary from site to site.

Bidding Offering to pay a specified amount of money for an item that is up for public auction.

Big-Ticket Item An item with a bid of $5000 or more.

Bulk Listing Listing a group of different items in separate *Lots* all at once using an eBay's bulk listing tool, Turbo Lister, or a specially designed third-party bulk listing tool.

Buying Up the Lot The practice of buying everything on offer in a Dutch auction, rather than bidding on some smaller number of the items. This is typically done for resale.

Buy-It-Now Auction Auctions with immediate-sell prices that, when agreed to, will halt an auction and prevent any additional bidding. Also referred to as *Fixed-Price Auction* or *Quick-Sell Auction.*

C

Category A logical item listing classification where similar or related items can be found. Many categories are further broken down into more granular subcategories.

Category Listings The categories in which an online auction site organizes its auctions.

Caveat Emptor The Latin phrase for "let the buyer beware." It is a legal maxim, meaning that liability is transferred from the seller to the buyer in regard to the quality or condition of the item or property up for sale.

Collusion An unlawful practice in which two or more people agree willfully and unfairly to manipulate the final price of an auction item.

Commission   A fee paid by the seller to the auction site (i.e., eBay) at the completion of an auction, calculated as a percentage of the final sale price. Also known as the *Final Value Fee (FVF)*.

Contact Information   The user information—generally name, street address, e-mail address, and phone number—provided when registering at eBay.

Contract   A binding legal agreement between two or more persons or entities.

Cookie   A piece of information sent from a Web server to a Web browser that the browser software saves and then sends back to the server whenever the browser makes additional requests from the server.

D

Deadbeat Bidding (Bidder)   The failure to deliver payment on an item after securing the high bid in an online auction. Repeat deadbeat bidding will result in the indefinite suspension of a user from an online auction site.

Due Diligence   The process of gathering information about the condition and legal status of items to be sold.

Dutch Auction   An auction format in which a seller lists multiple identical items for sale. Varying price determination methods exist: "authentic" Dutch Auctions determine price by lowering the price of the item until all units have been claimed (bid on); contemporary and online auctions use a format where all winning bidders pay the same price, which is the lowest successful bid. Often confused with the *Yankee Auction* format.

E

Emoticons   In-text icons created using common letters and punctuation marks to denote mood or attitude, for example:

:-)   smiling face
:-(frowning face
:-P   silly face with tongue sticking out

Escrow   Money held in trust by a third party until the seller makes delivery of merchandise to the buyer.

Estate Sale   The sale of personal property or real estate left by a person at the time of his or her death or incarceration.

F

Featured Auctions   eBay's most prominent auctions of the day. Featured Auction status typically incurs a significant additional insertion fee.

Feedback   One user's public comments about another user in regard to their auction dealings. Feedback comments cannot be removed or changed once submitted to an online auction site.

Final Value Fee (FVF)   A fee owed by the seller to eBay at the completion of an auction, calculated as a percentage of the final sale price. Also known as a *Commission*.

Fixed-Price Auction   See *Buy-It-Now Auction*.

FVF Refund Request   A request to eBay for the crediting of a levied *Final Value Fee*. Usually granted in situations where an auction transaction is not completed (for example, because of a *Deadbeat Bidder*).

G

Grading   Documenting the physical condition of an item with a specific set of labels, such as "Mint" condition or "Poor" quality. Different items have different grading terms. For instance, trading cards are graded from "A1" to "F1," while coins are graded from "poor" to "perfect uncirculated."

H

High Bidder   The present or final bidder in an auction, who has bid a higher price than any other bidder.

I

Insertion Fee   A fee paid by the seller to eBay in order to list an item for auction, calculated as a percentage of the opening bid or reserve price.

Item   The thing being auctioned. May be a single unit or a set of similar or even mixed objects, as long as the whole group is being sold as a unit to one buyer. Also called a *Lot.*

J

Jump Bid   A bid placed that significantly increases a current bid price over the established next *Bid Increment.* Used to scare off other bidders who might not be able to contend at higher price levels.

K

Keyword Spamming   Deliberately placing a popular word in listing titles even though it is completely unrelated or irrelevant to the actual item being offered. Used to have items show up in the results of item searches.

Knock-Off   Slang term for an unlicensed reproduction, or copy of an item that is made to appear as the real thing (such as brand-name watches, sunglasses, handbags, and so on).

L

Listing Agreement   A contract executed by the auctioneer and seller, authorizing the auctioneer to conduct the sale. It also delineates the conditions of sale and the rights and responsibilities of each party.

Lot   The single item or group of items offered in a given auction listing.

M

Market Value   The highest price a property will bring in the competitive, open market.

Maximum Bid   The highest price a buyer will pay for an item, submitted in confidence to eBay's automated bidding system to facilitate *Proxy Bidding.* The system's electronic "proxy" will automatically increase the buyer's bid to maintain the high bid. The proxy bidding system will stop when it has won the auction or reached the *Maximum Bid.*

Minimum Opening Bid   The mandatory *Starting Price* for a given auction, set by the seller at the time of listing.

N

NARU'd   An auction site term to describe eBay users whose memberships have been discontinued. NARU is the acronym for "not a registered user."

Neg   Short for "negative user feedback."

Net Cops   Auction users who actively seek out instances of fraud, such as shilling or bid shielding, to report to eBay.

Newsgroups   Public discussion forums that number in the thousands and are dedicated to specific topics of interest and conversation. See *Usenet.*

NR   Short for "no reserve." This indicates in the item description line that the auction has no reserve price specified.

O

Opening Bid   The lowest bid amount accepted for a particular item. Also known as the *Starting Price.*

Outbid   To submit a *Maximum Bid* that is higher than the one offered by another bidder. To "be outbid" indicates the reverse—someone who was the recognized high bidder has lost that status to someone else.

Outbid Notification   Communication sent by eBay via e-mail or wireless modes notifying a bidder of being outbid.

P

Private Auction   An auction in which the bidders' identities are hidden to preserve anonymity.

Proxy Bidding   To submit a hidden *Maximum Bid* to eBay's automated bidding system. The system's electronic proxy will automatically increase the buyer's bid to maintain the high bid. The proxy bidding system will stop when it has secured the high-bidder status or reached the maximum bid.

Q

Quick-Sell Auction   See *Buy-It Price Auction.*

R

Registered User   A person who has registered as a member of eBay.

Relisting   The relisting of an item occurs when it has not sold within its allotted auction time. An insertion fee is levied at the time of relisting but is refunded to the seller if the item sells.

Reserve Auction   An auction in which the seller has set a minimum selling price for the item and reserves the right to accept or decline any and all bids that have not met the established reserve.

Reserve Price   The minimum price a seller will accept for an item to be sold at a reserve auction.

Retaliatory   The user term for retaliatory negative *Feedback,* posted by one user in response to another user's negative *Feedback.*

S

S&H Charges   Shipping and handling charges.

Secure Server   A server that uses Secure Sockets Layer (SSL) encryption technology to protect the users' credit card and other confidential information.

Seller List   A list of items a seller has put up for sale at eBay.

Seller Search   An automated search that retrieves a list of all the items a seller has put up for sale at eBay, active and completed.

Shilling   Fraudulent bidding by the seller (using an alternate registration) or an associate of the seller in order to inflate the price of an item. Also known as *Bid Rigging* and *Collusion.*

Sniping   Bidding in the closing minutes or seconds of an auction to outbid other buyers.

Starting Price   The mandatory starting bid for a given auction, set by the seller at the time of listing.

Straight Auction   An auction in which there is no reserve and where only one item is up for sale. This is the most common type of auction. The seller sets the opening bid and must respect the final price at the end of the auction.

T

Terms of Service (TOS)   A legally binding agreement that outlines eBay's operations and policies. All registered users must agree to the site's terms before being allowed to participate.

Tie Bids   Bids for exactly the same amount, submitted by two or more buyers at the same time. At eBay, the first bidder to have bid the amount will be declared the prevailing high bidder.

Troll   A slang and somewhat derogatory term for someone who posts messages to public forums for the sake of stirring up tension, division, or confusion.

U

Usenet   An online hub of *Newsgroups* where visitors are invited to read public postings as well as post comments and observations of their own.

User ID   A moniker that identifies a user while on an online auction site.

User Information   Personal data provided by a user when registering at eBay, including name, postal address, e-mail address, and phone number.

V

Verification   Confirming the identity and evaluating the condition of an item.

W

Winner's Curse   An oxymoron that indicates an overzealous bidder-*cum*-winner will be faced with paying his or her high bid—a bid perhaps placed during a moment of passion or excitement yet financially difficult for the bidder to honor.

Y

Yankee Auction   An auction in which a seller lists multiples of an identical item. Unlike a *Dutch Auction* (in which all winning bidders pay only the lowest successful winning bid amount), in a Yankee auction each winning bidder pays the exact amount of their winning bid.

Index

About Me page, 39–41, 137
Account registration:
  eBay account, 22, 28–33
  seller's account, 34–38
Advanced Search function, 46–47
Agreement, 257
Antsy buyers, 120
Appraisal, 257
ARPANET, 3
Ascending-price auctions, 5, 248
As Is, 257
Auction block, 257
Auction formats:
  ascending-price auctions, 5, 248
  auction without reserve, 257
  auction with reserve, 257
  Buy-It-Now listings, 6, 168–169, 248–250, 258
  Dutch auction, 5, 58–59, 259
  fixed-price selling, 6, 169, 248–252
  private auctions, 6, 261
  reserve price auctions, 5–6, 167–168, 237, 262
  restricted-access auctions, 6
  straight auction, 262
  Yankee auction, 5, 58–59, 263
Auction income, 232–234
Auction insurance, 67–68
Auction Listing Agreement, 257
Auctions, 257
  auction details, 76–83, 162–164
  auction plan, 257
  day to start and end, 163–164
  end-of-auction (EOA) notification, 104–106
  history of, 2–3
  hour to start and end, 164
  length of, 162–164
  postauction sales, 169–170
Auction scams, 60–67
Auction staging area, 223–224
Auction: The Social Construction of Value
  (Smith), 7
Auction value, 257
Auction vigilantes, 203–205
AuctionWeb, 3–5

Authentication, 257
Authenticity of item scams, 64

Bad debt, 110
Basic Search box, 16, 44–45
Bidder search, 49, 258
Bidding on an item, 51–52, 258
  bid, 258
  bid cancellation, 258
  bid history, 258
  bid increment, 258
  bid retraction, 258
  item evaluation tips, 52–53, 200
  maximum bid amount, 53–55, 261
  minimum opening bid, 261
  placing a bid, 53, 54
  proxy bidding system, 55, 261
  tie bids, 262
Bidding scams:
  bid rigging, 258
  bid shielding, 61
  bid shilling, 60–61, 258
  bid siphoning, 66–67, 258
Bidding strategies:
  Dutch auction, 58–59
  incremental bidding, 53, 55
  jump bid, 260
  not bidding, 59
  penny principle, 55
  snipe bidding, 55–58
  Yankee auction, 58–59
BidPay, 87, 89
Big-ticket item, 258
Book recommendations, 7–8
Browse button, 18
Bulk listing tool, 212–219, 258
*Business Guide to Mail or Telephone Order
  Merchandise Rule* (FTC), 196
Business operations:
  auction staging area, 223–224
  business name, 245–248
  full-time approach to selling, 210–212
  hobby approach to selling, 209

Business operations (*Cont.*):
  logo use, 247
  office equipment, 222–223
  office space, 220–222
  part-time approach to selling, 209–210
  telephones and services, 223
  time management, 239–240
  (*See also* Taxes)
Buying on eBay:
  item evaluation tips, 52–53, 200
  newbie buyers, 33–34, 120, 124–126
  not bidding strategy, 59
  reasons to buy before you sell, 43
Buying up the lot, 258
Buy-It-Now listings, 6, 168–169, 248–250, 258

Cameras, 154
Categories, 16–17, 258
  browsing, 42–43
  category listings, 259
  organization of, 18–21
  selection when listing, 74, 75
Caveat emptor, 259
Character commands, 47–48
CNET.com, 255
Collectible Microcomputers (Nadeau), 7
Collusion, 259
Commission, 259
Community button, 24–25
Community discussion area, 238, 253
Computers:
  computer ownership, 9–10
  cost of, 11
  hardware specification recommendations,
    10–11
  internet connection types, 12
  older computers, 10
  software recommendations, 11–12, 156–158,
    230–231
  upgrade interval recommendations, 9
Condition of item:
  customer satisfaction and, 171–172
  online reputation and, 138–139
  scams about, 64–65
Contact information, 259
Contract, 259
Cookie, 259
Copyright infringement, 200–203
Counters, 164–166, 189–190, 248
Credit card payments, 64
Cross-category listing, 78, 236–237
Customer relationships:
  business records for, 232
  challenging customers, 119–122, 125
  communication with buyers, 128
  condition of item and, 171–172
  customer satisfying techniques, 129–132,
    247–248
  damage claims, 128–129
  end-of-auction (EOA) notification, 126–127
  importance of, 132

Customer relationships (*Cont.*):
  newbie buyers, 120, 124–126
  preselling and returns, 196

Damage claims, 65–66, 128–129
Deadbeat bidders, 121, 259
Deadbeat sellers, 63–64
Delivery policies, 94
Description of item, 76, 95, 137–138, 145–146
Description scams, 61–62
Digital cameras, 152–153
Discussion Forums, 238, 253
Due diligence, 259
Dutch auction, 5, 58–59, 259
Dynamic inventory management, 193–196
Dynamic price format:
  versus fixed price selling, 169, 248–250
  problems with, 250

eBay:
  changes to, 253
  fraud rate, 60
  growth of, 6–7, 98–99
  history of, 3–5
  logo, 15
  user statistics, 14
eBay stores, 241–244
Emoticons, 259
End-of-auction (EOA) notification, 104–106,
    126–127
Escrow, 259
Escrow Services, 89
eSnipe, 57–58
Estate sale, 259
Estimated payments (taxes), 233–234

Failed auctions, 169–170, 172–173, 237
Fake item scams, 64
Fake photo scams, 61–62
F'd Companies: Spectacular Dot-Com Flameouts
    (Kaplan), 8
Featured Auctions, 260
Federal Trade Commission, 196
Feedback Forum, 133–134, 139–140
  establishing positive reputation, 137
  feedback, 260
  feedback blocking, 135
  feedback ratings, 122–123, 134–135
  how to post, 135–136
  neg, 261
  retaliatory feedback, 262
Feedback Plus, Inc., 129
Fees:
  avoidance of, 238
  calculation with Turbo Lister, 213
  cross-category listing, 78, 236–237
  final-value fees, 6, 37, 68, 77, 260
  galley listings, 237
  handling fees, 93
  insertion fees, 77, 237, 260
  listing feature fees, 78, 151, 236–237

Fees (*Cont.*):
  management of, 235–238, 239
  for online payments, 237–238
  payment tip, 38
  record keeping, 228–229
  reserve price fees, 77, 237
  review of, 81
  shipping and handling, 62–63, 93–94, 117–118
Final price manipulation scam, 62
Final-value fees, 6, 37, 68, 77, 260
Financial account information, 35–37
Fire in the Valley: The Making of Personal Computers (Freiberger & Swaine), 7
Fixed-price selling, 6, 260
  Buy-It-Now listings, 6, 168–169, 248–250, 258
  versus dynamic price format, 169, 248–250
  tips for improving sales, 251–252
  value of, 250–251
Forbidden sale items, 197–200
Fraud:
  protection, 37, 67–68, 69
  resolution, 68–69
  scams, 60–67
Fraud Alert, 68
Full-time approach to selling, 210–212

Galley listings, 237
Grading techniques, 64–65, 138–139, 260

Haggling skills, 120–121, 184
Half.com, 29, 73
Handling fees, 93
Hardware specification recommendations, 10–11
Help button, 23–24
High bidder, 260
Hobby approach to selling, 209
Home office deductions, 229
Home page of eBay, 14–17
Home page search, 44
HTML in listings, 74, 146–151

Images (*see* Photos)
Insertion fees, 77, 237, 260
Internet.com, 254
Internet connection types, 12
Internet Fraud Complaint Center, 68
Inventory, 174–175
  acquiring for resale, 180–181, 183–185
  care and storage of, 176–177
  dynamic inventory management, 193–196
  investment return, 181, 184
  just-in-time inventory, 193–196
  organization of, 177–178
  record keeping, 227–228
  sources of, 175–176, 179
  turnover principle, 185–186
  wholesale outlets, 181–183
iPIX image tool, 78, 80, 213
Item, 260
Item description, 76, 95, 137–138, 145–146
Item evaluation tips, 52–53, 200

Item grading, 64–65, 138–139, 260
Item titles, 74, 76, 142–144

Jump bid, 260
Just-in-time inventory, 193–196

Keywords, 47, 142–144
Keyword spamming, 260
Knock-off, 260
Knock-off scams, 64

Lighting for photos, 154–155
Listing Agreement, 257, 261
Listing feature fees, 78, 151, 236–237
Listing process:
  auction details, 76–83, 162–164
  auction formats, 73–74
  category selection, 74, 75
  description of item, 76, 95, 137–138, 145–146
  HTML in listings, 74, 146–151
  listing features, 78, 80, 151, 236–237
  online counters, 164–166
  page update rate, 83
  payment methods, 80–81, 82
  photos, 78–80
  title of item, 74, 76, 142–144
  Turbo Lister, 212–219
  (*See also* Fees)
Listings page search, 44
Loss and damage claim scams, 65–66
Lot, 261

Mail fraud, 63–64, 65–66
Market trends:
  market research, 191–192
  personal biases, 192
  sales history data, 187–190
  supply and demand, 192–193
  what to sell, 190–191
Market value, 261
Maximum bid amount, 53–55, 261
Minimum opening bid, 261
My eBay link, 25–26

NARU'd, 261
Nasdaq.com, 255
National Consumer League, 60
National Fraud Information Center, 68
Neg, 261
Net Cops, 203–205, 261
Newbie buyers, 33–34, 120, 124–126
Newsgroups, 261
Nonpaying Bidder Alert, 68
NR, 261

Office (*see* Business operations)
Offline transactions, 238
Omidyar, Pierre, 3–5, 24, 133
Online counters, 164–166, 189–190, 248
Online information sources, 254–255

Online payments:
  benefits of, 90
  BidPay, 87, 89
  Escrow Services, 89
  fees for, 237–238
  online merchant accounts, 89–90
  payment methods, 80–81, 82, 91–92
  PayPal, 82, 87, 88
  process, 86–87
  security of, 85–86
  Yahoo PayDirect, 87, 88
Online reputation:
  condition of item and, 138–139
  description of item and, 137–138
  establishing positive reputation, 137
  expert status, 139
Online stores:
  eBay stores, 241–244
  pricing methods, 248–251
  tips for improving sales, 251–252
  web site development, 245–248
Opening bid, 261
Outbid, 261
Outbid notification, 261

Packing for shipment:
  how to pack, 113–117
  ship shop, 111–112
  supplies for, 112–113, 224–225
  unpacking instructions, 117
Paranoid buyers, 120
Part-time approach to selling, 209–210
Payment collection, 106–110
Payment methods, 80–81, 82, 91–92
Payment remittance policies, 92
PayPal, 82, 87, 88
PC Magazine, 9–10
Penny principle, 55
The Perfect Store: Inside eBay (Cohen), 7
Photos:
  cameras, 154
  digital cameras, 152–153
  editing and touch ups, 156–159
  fake photo scams, 61–62
  image quality, 159–161
  iPIX image tool, 78, 80, 213
  lighting for, 154–155
  in listing, 78–80
  scanners, 153
  setting up a studio, 154–155, 223–224
Portal searches, 255
Postauction sales, 120–121, 169–170, 238
Preselling items, 193–196
Price manipulation scam, 62
Pricing items, 100–103, 138–139, 166–167
Pricing methods:
  dynamic price format, 169, 248–250
  fixed-price selling, 6, 168–169, 248–251
  (*See also* Auction formats)
Printers, 222–223

Privacy policy, 28, 31–32
Privacy protection, 30–31, 35, 37
Private auctions, 6, 261
Profit (or Loss) from a Business or Profession (IRS), 234
Prohibited sale items, 197–200
Protection Claim, 68
Proxy bidding system, 55, 261

Questionable sale items, 199–200
Quicken software, 230–231
Quick search box, 15–16
Quick-sell auction, 262

Record keeping:
  business assets, 227
  expenses and fees, 228–229
  importance of, 226–227
  inventory, 227–228
  organization of records, 229–231
Reference recommendations, 7–8, 254–255
Refined Search function, 45–46
Registered user, 262
Register now button, 28
Registration for eBay account, 28–33
Relisting items, 172–173, 237, 262
Reproduction scams, 64
Reserve price auctions, 5–6, 167–168, 262
Reserve price fees, 77, 237
Restricted-access auctions, 6
Retaliatory feedback, 262
Return policies, 66, 94, 95, 128–129, 196

S&H charges, 262
SafeHarbor, 22
Sales history data, 187–190
Sales policy (*see* Selling on eBay)
Scams:
  authenticity of item, 64
  bid shielding, 61
  bid shilling, 60–61, 258
  bid siphoning, 66–67, 258
  condition of item, 64–65
  failure to ship merchandise, 63–64
  fake photos, 61–62
  final price manipulation, 62
  loss and damage claims, 65–66
  misleading descriptions, 61–62
  shipping and handling costs, 62–63
  switch and return, 66
Scanners, 153
Search strategies:
  auction status lists, 51
  completed auctions, 51
  misspelled terms, 50–51
  save search criteria, 51, 52
Search tools, 43–44
  Advanced Search function, 46–47
  Basic Search box, 16, 44–45
  character commands, 47–48

Search tools (*Cont.*):
  home page search, 44
  keywords, 47
  listings page search, 44
  Refined Search function, 45–46
  Search button, 23
  searching by bidder, 49
  searching by seller, 48–49
  searching eBay stores, 50
Security issues:
  business records, 232
  financial information, 35–37
  online payments, 85–86
  registration information, 28
  secure server, 262
  SSL (Secure Socket Layer) protocol, 35, 262
Sell button, 21–22
Seller list, 262
Sellers:
  deadbeat sellers, 63–64
  searching by seller, 48–49, 262
  seller's account, 34–38
Selling on eBay:
  copyright infringement, 200–203
  delivery policies, 94
  end-of-auction (EOA) notification, 104–106
  offline transactions, 238
  payment collection, 106–110
  payment methods, 91–92
  payment remittance policies, 92
  preselling items, 193–196
  prohibited items, 197–200
  questionable sale items, 199–200
  return policies, 94, 95, 128–129, 196
  sales policies, 96–97, 125
  taking a loss, 69–70
  tips for improving sales, 251–252
  what to sell, 72–73, 99–100, 190–191
  (*See also* Listing process; Shipment of
    merchandise)
Services button, 22–23
Shilling, 262
Shipment of merchandise:
  condition of item, 171–172
  damage claims, 128–129
  failure to ship, 63–64
  fees for, 62–63, 93–94, 117–118
  loss and damage claim scams, 65–66
Sign out link, 25
Site map link, 26–27
Slow payment, 108–109
Snipe bidding, 55–58, 262
Software recommendations, 11–12, 156–158,
  230–231
SquareTrade, 68
SSL (Secure Socket Layer) protocol, 35, 262
Starting price, 262
Straight auction, 262
Switch and return scams, 66

Taking a loss, 69–70
Taxes:
  auction income, 232–234
  business expenses, 153, 209, 234
  estimated payments, 233–234
  home office deductions, 229
  IRS information, 230–231
  Profit (or Loss) from a Business or Profession
    (IRS), 234
  record keeping, 227–228
Telephones and services, 223
Terms of Service (TOS), 262
Tie bids, 262
Time management, 239–240
Title of item, 74, 76, 142–144
Toolbars, 15–16
  Browse button, 18
  Community button, 24–25
  Help button, 23–24
  My eBay link, 25–26
  Search button, 23
  Sell button, 21–22
  Services button, 22–23
  sign out link, 25
  site map link, 26–27
Troll, 263
Turbo Lister, 212–219
Turnover principle, 185–186

Unhappy Harvey buyers, 121
United States Internal Revenue Service, 209,
  230–231
  (*See also* Taxes)
Unix User Network, 3
Unpacking instructions, 117
Usenet, 3, 263
User Agreement, 31–32
User ID, 30–31, 263
User information, 263
U. S. Postal Inspection Service, 68

Value determination, 100–103
  and item grading, 101, 138–139
  pricing strategies, 166–167
Vendio.com, 254
Verification, 263
Vigilantes, 203–205
Visible counters, 166

Web site development, 245–248
What to sell, 72–73, 99–100, 190–191
Whitman, Meg, 6
Wholesale outlets, 181–183
Winner's Curse, 263
Wired.com, 255

Yahoo PayDirect, 87, 88
Yankee auction, 5, 58–59, 263

About the Author

Dennis L. Prince is a business professional with a background in technical (computer) applications and corporate procurement principles. As a longtime online auction enthusiast, analyst, and advocate, he has studied the growth and potential of Internet auctioning as well as other forms of e-commerce since 1995. He has authored many successful books including *Online Auctions @ eBay* (1999) and *Starting Your Online Auction Business* (2000), both published by Prima-Tech/Premier Press Books, and was recognized by Vendio (formerly AuctionWatch) as one of the "Top 10 Online Auction Movers and Shakers."

Acclaimed for his commitment to promoting better understanding and execution in online selling, Prince has regularly contributed to a variety of noted Internet and auction service sites as Vendio, Auctiva, Krause, Collector Online, and ZDNet. He has been featured in the nationally distributed *Access* and *Entrepreneur* magazines and has been a guest of highly rated television and radio programs such as TechTV and C/Net Radio with Alex Bennett.